AF805938

Perspectives in Law, Business and Innovation

Series Editor

Toshiyuki Kono, Faculty of Law, Kyushu University, Fukuoka, Japan

Editorial Board

Hans-Wolfgang Micklitz, Robert Schuman Centre for Advanced Studies, European University Institute, Florence, Italy

Ryu Kojima, Faculty of Law, Kyushu University, Fukuoka, Japan

Erik P.M. Vermeulen, Law School, Tilburg University, Tilburg, The Netherlands

Urs Gasser, TUM School of Social Sciences and Technology, Technical University of Munich, Munich, Germany

Jane C. Ginsburg, Law School, Columbia University, New York, USA

Over the last three decades, interconnected processes of globalization and rapid technological change—particularly, the emergence of networked technologies—have profoundly disrupted traditional models of business organization. This economic transformation has created multiple new opportunities for the emergence of alternate business forms, and disruptive innovation has become one of the major driving forces in the contemporary economy. Moreover, in the context of globalization, the innovation space increasingly takes on a global character. The main stakeholders—innovators, entrepreneurs and investors—now have an unprecedented degree of mobility in pursuing economic opportunities wherever they arise. As such, frictionless movement of goods, workers, services, and capital is becoming the "new normal".

This new economic and social reality has created multiple regulatory challenges for policymakers as they struggle to come to terms with the rapid pace of these social and economic changes. Moreover, these challenges impact across multiple fields of both public and private law. Nevertheless, existing approaches within legal science often struggle to deal with innovation and its effects.

Paralleling this shift in the economy, we can, therefore, see a similar process of disruption occurring within contemporary academia, as traditional approaches and disciplinary boundaries—both within and between disciplines—are being re-configured. Conventional notions of legal science are becoming increasingly obsolete or, at least, there is a need to develop alternative perspectives on the various regulatory challenges that are currently being created by the new innovation-driven global economy.

The aim of this series is to provide a forum for the publication of cutting-edge research in the fields of innovation and the law from a Japanese and Asian perspective. The series will cut across the traditional sub-disciplines of legal studies but will be tied together by a focus on contemporary developments in an innovation-driven economy and will deepen our understanding of the various regulatory responses to these economic and social changes.

The series editor and editorial board carefully assess each book proposal and sample chapters in terms of their relevance to law, business, and innovative technological change. Each proposal is evaluated on the basis of its academic value and distinctive contribution to the fast-moving debate in these fields.

All books and chapters in the Perspectives in Law, Business and Innovation book series are indexed in Scopus.

Marcelo Corrales Compagnucci · Helena Haapio ·
Mark Fenwick
Editors

Generative AI, Contracts, Law and Design

Springer

Editors
Marcelo Corrales Compagnucci
Faculty of Law, CeBIL
University of Copenhagen
Copenhagen, Denmark

Mark Fenwick
Faculty of Law
Kyushu University
Fukuoka, Japan

Helena Haapio
School of Accounting and Finance,
Business Law
University of Vaasa
Vaasa, Finland

ISSN 2520-1875 ISSN 2520-1883 (electronic)
Perspectives in Law, Business and Innovation
ISBN 978-981-95-2057-2 ISBN 978-981-95-2058-9 (eBook)
https://doi.org/10.1007/978-981-95-2058-9

© The Editor(s) (if applicable) and The Author(s), under exclusive license to Springer Nature Singapore Pte Ltd. 2025

This work is subject to copyright. All rights are solely and exclusively licensed by the Publisher, whether the whole or part of the material is concerned, specifically the rights of translation, reprinting, reuse of illustrations, recitation, broadcasting, reproduction on microfilms or in any other physical way, and transmission or information storage and retrieval, electronic adaptation, computer software, or by similar or dissimilar methodology now known or hereafter developed.
The use of general descriptive names, registered names, trademarks, service marks, etc. in this publication does not imply, even in the absence of a specific statement, that such names are exempt from the relevant protective laws and regulations and therefore free for general use.
The publisher, the authors and the editors are safe to assume that the advice and information in this book are believed to be true and accurate at the date of publication. Neither the publisher nor the authors or the editors give a warranty, expressed or implied, with respect to the material contained herein or for any errors or omissions that may have been made. The publisher remains neutral with regard to jurisdictional claims in published maps and institutional affiliations.

This Springer imprint is published by the registered company Springer Nature Singapore Pte Ltd.
The registered company address is: 152 Beach Road, #21-01/04 Gateway East, Singapore 189721, Singapore

If disposing of this product, please recycle the paper.

Preface

The convergence of generative AI, contracts, law, and design represents a critical moment in history, offering unprecedented opportunities to reimagine the foundations and practice of economic and legal systems. *Generative AI, Contracts, Law and Design* explores this transformative intersection, providing an expansive perspective on the future of business and society.

At the core of this discussion lies the transformative impact and potential of generative AI. This book collection examines the challenges it poses for the legal community and highlights its capacity to prevent problems and drive positive business and societal outcomes. It demonstrates how AI is revolutionizing business and law through real-world applications—from automating routine tasks to developing predictive tools that anticipate and resolve legal risks across multiple sectors, such as technology, justice, and health care.

This volume goes beyond the technical aspects of algorithms and code. Instead, it places *design* at the forefront of the discussion, emphasizing its critical role in shaping the future of AI, legal systems, and our world. Design "thinking" and "doing" are essential to developing sustainable AI solutions that are human-centric, legally sound, and operationally effective.

How can we design AI systems that prioritize ethical outcomes and align with societal values? How can we integrate AI into commercial and legal information, services, and systems to achieve accessibility, usability, and understanding? What does responsible AI use look like, and how can design principles guide its implementation and outputs? These are among the core questions this book seeks to answer.

Through a rich blend of case studies, expert insights, and practical guidance, *Generative AI, Contracts, Law and Design* provides a roadmap for navigating these issues. It underscores the importance of design as a bridge between technology and humanity, ensuring that AI solutions are innovative, equitable, inclusive, and aligned with the needs of individuals and organizations.

This book is designed to serve both as an introduction for those new to the intersection of these fields and as a comprehensive resource for experts. It equips readers with the knowledge and tools to navigate the rapidly evolving landscape of AI, contracts, and law, offering targeted insights to leverage AI-assisted design effectively and ethically. By blending theoretical depth with practical real-world insights, it empowers professionals and enthusiasts to harness the potential of AI while upholding the principles of justice, fairness, and human-centric design.

This publication was made possible in part by the generous support of a Novo Nordisk Foundation (NNF) grant for a scientifically independent Collaborative Research Program in Bioscience Innovation Law (Inter-CeBIL program—grant no. NNF23SA0087056). We extend our deepest gratitude to the contributing authors and the dedicated Springer editorial team, and especially to Leila Hamhoum, for her invaluable assistance throughout the editing process. Their expertise and commitment have been instrumental in bringing this project to fruition.

In a world increasingly shaped by AI, this book stands as a call to action: to design systems that not only advance technology but also serve humanity, ensuring that innovation is guided by empathy, ethics, and excellence.

Copenhagen, Denmark — Marcelo Corrales Compagnucci
Helsinki, Finland — Helena Haapio
Fukuoka, Japan — Mark Fenwick

Contents

Editors and Contributors

About the Editors

Marcelo Corrales Compagnucci is Associate Professor and Associate Director at the Center for Advanced Studies in Bioscience Innovation Law (CeBIL), Faculty of Law, University of Copenhagen in Denmark. He is also Inter-CeBIL Research Affiliate at the Petrie-Flom Center for Health Law Policy, Biotechnology, and Bioethics at Harvard Law School. He specializes in information technology, privacy and data protection law. His research interests are the legal issues involved in disruptive innovation technologies and biomedicine. His past activities have included working as Consultant and Lawyer for law firms and IT companies. He was also Research Associate with the Institute for Legal Informatics (IRI) at Leibniz Universität Hannover in Germany and Visiting Research Fellow in various research centers around the world, including Harvard Law School, Cambridge University, the Max Planck Institute, University of Edinburgh, Turin University, and the Academia Sinica in Taiwan. He has a Doctor of Laws (LL.D.) degree from Kyushu University in Japan. He also holds a Master of Laws (LL.M.) in international economics and business law from Kyushu University, and an LL.M. in law and information technology and an LL.M. in European intellectual property law, both from the University of Stockholm in Sweden. He has several publications in the field of IT Law. His most recent book collections co-edited with various authors include *AI in eHealth: Human Autonomy, Data Governance and Privacy in Healthcare* (Cambridge University Press, 2022), *Smart Contracts: Technological, Business and Legal Perspectives* (Hart Publishing, 2021), and *Legal Design: Integrating Business, Design and Legal Thinking with Technology* (Edward Elgar Publishing, 2021).

Helena Haapio is Professor of Practice in Strategic Business Law at the University of Vaasa, Finland, Senior Researcher in the JARGONFREE Contract Language Research Group at Tampere University, and Docent of Proactive Law and Contract Design at the University of Lapland and Contract Strategist at Lexpert Ltd. As Pioneer of Proactive Law and Legal Design, she has been promoting the use of simplification and visualization of legal information for many years. Her research and practice focus on operationalizing legal information design and using AI and design tools to transform contracts into strategic business tools that take into account the needs of different user groups, prevent misunderstandings, ease implementation, and drive better outcomes. Together with Stefania Passera, she created the WorldCC Contract Design Pattern Library. After studying law at the University of Turku, Finland, and Cambridge University, England, she worked for several years as an in-house Legal Counsel in Europe and the United States, before returning to academia and earning a Doctor of Science (Econ) from the University of Vaasa. Her co-edited publications include *Research Handbook on Contract Design* (Edward Elgar Publishing, 2022), *Legal Design: Integrating Business, Design and Legal Thinking with Technology* (Edward Elgar Publishing, 2021), and *Legal Tech, Smart Contracts and Blockchain* (Springer, 2019). She has co-authored two books for Gower with George Siedel, *A Short Guide to Contract Risk* (2013) and *Proactive Law for Managers* (2011).

Mark Fenwick is Professor of International Business Law at the Faculty of Law, Kyushu University, Fukuoka, Japan. His primary research interests are in the fields of business regulation in a networked age and white-collar and corporate crime. Recent publications include *New Technology, Big Data and the Law* (Springer, 2017: co-edited with M. Corrales Compagnucci and N. Forgó), *Robotics, AI and the Future of Law* (Springer, 2018: co-edited with M. Corrales Compagnucci and N. Forgó), *Smart Contracts: Business, Legal and Technological Perspectives* (Hart, 2021: co-edited with M. Corrales Compagnucci and S. Wrbka), *Organizing-for-Innovation: Corporate Governance in a Digital Age* (Springer, 2023: co-authored with E. P. M. Vermeulen and T. Kono), and *The Law and Ethics of Data-Sharing* (Springer, 2024; co-edited with M. Corrales Compagnucci, T. Minssen, M. Aboy, and K. Liddell). He has a master's and Ph.D. from the Faculty of Law, University of Cambridge (Queens' College). He has been Visiting Professor at Cambridge University, Chulalongkorn University, Duke University, the University of Hong Kong, Shanghai University of Finance and Economics, the National University of Singapore, Tilburg University and Vietnam National University. He has also conducted research for the EU, OECD, and the World Bank and is Contributor to the *International Corporate Governance Network Yearbook*.

Contributors

Hilja Autto Faculty of Law, University of Lapland, Rovaniemi, Finland

Marietjie Botes School of Law, University of KwaZulu Natal, Durban, South Africa

Marcelo Corrales Compagnucci Center for Advanced Studies in Bioscience Innovation Law (CeBIL), University of Copenhagen, Copenhagen, Denmark;

Petrie-Flom Center for Health Law Policy, Biotechnology, and Bioethics, Harvard Law School, Cambridge, MA, USA

Tim Cummins Commerce and Contract Management Institute, World Commerce and Contracting, Virginia, USA;
School of Law, University of Leeds, Leeds, United Kingdom

Sarah de Heer Faculty of Law, Lund University, Lund, Sweden

Mark Fenwick Faculty of Law, Kyushu University, Fukuoka, Japan

Sally Guyer World Commerce and Contracting, WorldCC Foundation, Washington DC, USA;
Durham University Business School, Durham, Australia

Helena Haapio School of Accounting and Finance, Business Law, University of Vaasa, Vaasa, Finland;
JARGONFREE Contract Language Research Group, Tampere University, Tampere, Finland;
Lexpert Ltd, Helsinki, Finland

Petra Hietanen-Kunwald School of Business, Department of Accounting and Business Law, Aalto University, Espoo, Finland

Anna Hurmerinta-Haanpää School of Business, Department of Accounting and Business Law, Aalto University, Espoo, Finland

Perttu Isohanni School of Business, Department of Accounting and Business Law, Aalto University, Espoo, Finland

Tanel Kerikmäe Department of Business Administration and Department of Law, School of Business and Governance, Tallinn University of Technology, Tallinn, Estonia

Jaana Kovalainen Faculty of Law, University of Lapland, Rovaniemi, Finland

Ebru Metin Department of Business Administration and Department of Law, School of Business and Governance, Tallinn University of Technology, Tallinn, Estonia

Jouko Nuottila Faculty of Law, University of Lapland, Rovaniemi, Finland

Mikko Ranta School of Accounting and Finance, Accounting, University of Vaasa, Vaasa, Finland

Marika Salo-Lahti School of Accounting and Finance, Business Law, University of Vaasa, Vaasa, Finland

Patrick Shone OpenDialog AI Ltd, London, UK

Nina Toivonen Faculty of Law, University of Helsinki, Helsinki, Finland

Robert Waller School of Design, University of Leeds, Leeds, UK

Yueh-Hsuan Weng Inamori Frontier Program, Institute for Advanced Study, Kyushu University, and FRIS, Tohoku University, Fukuoka, Sendai, Japan

Generative AI and the Future of Contracts, Law and Design

Marcelo Corrales Compagnucci, Helena Haapio, and Mark Fenwick

Abstract This chapter serves as an introduction to this collection by exploring the transformative intersection of Generative AI (GenAI), contracts, law, and design. It highlights how advanced machine learning models are reshaping legal practice, contracts, and contracting. GenAI—a subset of artificial intelligence—uses large datasets to create original content and provide new opportunities for automating legal tasks, enhancing contract accessibility, and promoting proactive legal strategies. The chapter delves into the technological underpinnings of GenAI, including examples such as OpenAI's ChatGPT and DALL·E, Anthropic's Claude, GitHub Copilot, Google's Bard and Gemini, and DeepSeek. It also examines the ethical and regulatory implications of AI adoption, focusing on the principles of "Responsible AI," and discusses the importance of human-centric design in preparing legal tools and solutions intended to drive policy and strategic objectives. Additionally, it provides a brief overview of the book's content, outlining key topics such as proactive law, contract design, intellectual property, privacy communication, and health data governance. By providing case studies and practical insights, the chapter offers a comprehensive overview of GenAI's impact on contracting and the legal domain and sets the stage for further discussions on its applications, challenges, and future directions.

M. Corrales Compagnucci (✉)
Center for Advanced Studies in Bioscience Innovation Law (CeBIL), University of Copenhagen, Copenhagen, Denmark
e-mail: marcelo.c.compagnucci@jur.ku.dk

Petrie-Flom Center for Health Law Policy, Biotechnology, and Bioethics, Harvard Law School, Cambridge, MA, USA

H. Haapio
School of Accounting and Finance, Business Law, University of Vaasa, Vaasa, Finland
e-mail: helena.haapio@lexpert.com

JARGONFREE Contract Language Research Group, Tampere University, Tampere, Finland

Lexpert Ltd, Helsinki, Finland

M. Fenwick
Faculty of Law, Kyushu University, Fukuoka, Japan

© The Author(s), under exclusive license to Springer Nature Singapore Pte Ltd. 2025
M. Corrales Compagnucci et al. (eds.), *Generative AI, Contracts, Law and Design*, Perspectives in Law, Business and Innovation,
https://doi.org/10.1007/978-981-95-2058-9_1

Keywords Generative AI · Legal design · Proactive law · Responsible AI · Ethics · Privacy

1 Introduction

The intersection of Generative Artificial Intelligence (GenAI), contracts, law, and design presents an unprecedented opportunity to reshape the foundations of our business and legal systems. This volume, *Generative AI, Contracts, Law and Design* takes a deep dive into this convergence, offering a fresh perspective on these developments and their intersection with the future of business, law, and society at large.

GenAI refers to advanced machine learning models capable of producing new content that mimics human creativity, including text, images, code, and music.[1] Unlike traditional AI, which relies on predefined rules and data for task execution, GenAI learns from vast datasets to generate original and contextually relevant outputs.[2] Popular examples of GenAI include OpenAI's ChatGPT,[3] which can draft and design documents, and DALL·E,[4] which generates digital art; Anthropic's Claude,[5] which can create content and code; GitHub Copilot,[6] which assists developers with coding; Google's Gemini,[7] which enhances search engine experiences with generative capabilities; and DeepSeek,[8] known for its capacity to analyze and generate data-driven insights.

This collection highlights GenAI's transformative potential, not only in terms of new challenges for the legal community but also in terms of preventing problems and promoting desirable business and societal outcomes. It presents real-world applications of AI in business and law, ranging from task automation to the development of predictive tools that anticipate and address potential legal challenges in various sectors, in particular, technology, justice, healthcare, and commercial contracting across diverse sectors.

Beyond algorithms and code, this work underscores the importance of design "thinking" and "doing."[9] Key questions include: How can we design sustainable AI solutions that produce outcomes that are human-centered and legally and operationally functional? How can AI assistance be seamlessly integrated into legal information, services, and systems to improve accessibility and understanding? Can GenAI help us bridge the implementation gap in contracting? What constitutes the

1 Tasabat and Özçay (2025), p. 53.

2 Marr (2023).

3 See https://openai.com/chatgpt/.

4 See https://openai.com/index/dall-e-2/.

5 See https://www.anthropic.com/claude.

6 See https://github.com/features/copilot.

7 See https://gemini.google.com/.

8 See https://www.deepseek.com/.

9 See, e.g., Corrales Compagnucci et al. (2021), Doherty et al. (2021).

responsible use of AI, and how can we make it happen? Through a mix of case studies, expert insights, and practical guidance, this book provides answers to these questions and more.

Generative AI, Contracts, Law and Design serves as both a primer for those new to the convergence of these fields, as well as a comprehensive guide for experts, illuminating the path forward in the ever-evolving field of technology, design, and law. This focus ensures that our audience is not only informed about the evolving GenAI landscape but is also equipped with targeted insights to navigate and leverage AI in contracting and legal design effectively and ethically. As such, this anthology promises a blend of theoretical insights and practical applications tailored to professionals and enthusiasts at the intersection of AI, contracting, law, and design.

2 Key Themes and Issues

The following themes and issues are recurrent throughout and are worth emphasizing.

2.1 AI as a Catalyst for Change in Law and Contracting

Traditionally, contracts and legal systems have relied on human cognition, interpretation, and decision-making. The emergence of GenAI challenges this paradigm by introducing automation, predictive analytics, and self-executing legal instruments. These technologies offer game-changing solutions for optimizing legal workflows, reducing transactional costs,[10] and enhancing access to justice.

AI-driven contracting tools now have the capacity to draft, design, review, summarize, and negotiate agreements with unprecedented efficiency. Additionally, AI is making contracts and legal information more comprehensible through natural language processing (NLP) and automation, thereby bridging the gap between complex legal jargon and practical business applications.

For instance, platforms like LawGeex[11] use AI to review contracts in seconds, detecting errors and inconsistencies that might take human lawyers hours to identify. Similarly, companies like IBM have developed AI tools that assist with regulatory compliance by continuously analyzing changing legal frameworks.[12]

[10] For more on emerging technologies, contracts and transaction costs, see, e.g., Corrales Compagnucci (2020), pp. 8, 82–88, 90–92.

[11] See https://www.lawgeex.com/.

[12] Olivera (2024).

2.2 *Beyond Automation: AI as a Proactive Legal and Strategic Tool*

Beyond streamlining existing processes, GenAI opens new avenues for proactive legal strategies,[13] contract design, and beyond.[14] By integrating AI into legal design thinking and doing, we can move from reactive to proactive law—a shift that activates both the preventive and promotive power of the law and contracts. On the preventive side, AI-assisted design helps anticipate potential disputes, regulatory challenges, and compliance risks before they arise, and offers ways to prevent them. On the promotive side, it can help turn contracts into drivers of strategic objectives, both business objectives and societal objectives such as sustainability. AI-powered simulations, predictive analytics, and intelligent contract design patterns allow for the identification of vulnerabilities and the implementation of preventive measures.

AI-assisted legal information design plays a central role in ensuring that legal documents are accessible, understandable, and human-centered. Using AI as a design assistant can help transform contracts and legal documents into proactive legal and strategic tools. This book explores the intersection of AI and legal information design, highlighting how structured information, simplification, visualization, and interactive legal interfaces can improve comprehension, usability and actionability.

2.3 *Balancing Innovation with Ethical and Legal Constraints*

While the benefits of AI in law and contracts are immense, they are not without ethical and regulatory concerns. The deployment of AI in legal processes raises important questions about privacy, data protection, fairness, transparency, and accountability. Additionally, the increasing reliance on AI-generated content challenges traditional notions of authorship, intellectual property rights (IPRs), and the rule of law.

The concept of "Responsible AI" emphasizes the development and deployment of AI systems that are safe, transparent, and aligned with societal values.[15] This involves adhering to legal requirements and addressing ethical concerns such as bias, discrimination, and the potential for misuse. Regulatory frameworks like the EU AI Act,[16] along with principles like fairness, accountability, and transparency, play a crucial role in guiding the ethical use of AI. As AI becomes integral to our legal infrastructure, policymakers, businesses, and legal professionals must collaborate to

---

[13] See, e.g., Haapio (2013), Berger-Walliser et al. (2016), Corrales Compagnucci et al. (2022), Autto et al. (2024).

[14] See, e.g., Corrales Compagnucci et al. (2022).

[15] Raji (2024).

[16] Regulation (EU) 2024/1689 of the European Parliament and of the Council of 13 June 2024 laying down harmonized rules on artificial intelligence and amending Regulations (EC) No 300/2008, (EU) No 167/2013, (EU) No 168/2013, (EU) 2018/858, (EU) 2018/1139 and (EU) 2019/2144 and Directives 2014/90/EU, (EU) 2016/797 and (EU) 2020/1828 (Artificial Intelligence Act).

establish robust governance models that prevent misuse and enhance trust in AI-driven legal solutions.

2.4 Ensuring Human-Centricity in Both the Tools We Design and Their Outputs

GenAI should not simply replicate existing legal and business practices—it should be used to reimagine and improve them. AI-assisted writing and design tools can help create contracts and legal documents prioritizing clarity, human-centricity, and accessibility. Visual contracts, interactive tools, and user-centered design patterns can bridge communication gaps—not only between legal professionals and their clients, but also between the contracting parties and among the different stakeholders—to promote better understanding and collaboration.

In addition to improving communication, design thinking and doing provide methods for addressing the ethical implications of AI deployment. By placing human needs and societal values at the center of AI development, we can ensure that technological advances contribute to the social good rather than exacerbate existing inequalities.

Crucially, AI tools should be designed to be human-centred—not just in their interfaces but also in their outputs. In addition to creating intuitive and responsible tools, their designers should ensure that their outputs, recommendations, and decisions are consistent with human needs, values, and understanding. If a tool's output is not clear, or if it is difficult to act on, its value is diminished. Genuine human-centered AI design goes beyond interface and usability considerations to focus on how the tool's output empowers users, facilitates informed decision-making, and builds trust and transparency.

2.5 GenAI as a Driving Force Behind Transformation

GenAI, powered by large language models and advanced machine learning techniques, is fundamentally altering how we create, process, and utilize information. Tools like OpenAI's ChatGPT, Anthropic's Claude, Google Bard, and DeepSeek have demonstrated remarkable capabilities in generating text, images, and code that closely mimic human creativity.

The legal field, historically cautious when confronted by technological disruption, is now experiencing a paradigm shift due to these advancements. AI-powered legal research tools can analyze vast amounts of case law and regulatory texts within seconds, enabling lawyers to focus on strategic decision-making rather than mundane tasks. Smart contract platforms built on blockchain technology facilitate self-executing agreements that automatically execute contractual obligations, reducing the need for dispute resolution.

However, with this newfound power comes significant responsibility. GenAI must be developed and deployed with a keen awareness of potential risks, including biases in training data, privacy infringements, and regulatory non-compliance. The concept of "Responsible AI" underscores the importance of aligning AI applications with ethical principles, legal norms, and societal values.

3 Structure of the Book

This book is structured to provide a comprehensive exploration of the relationship between GenAI, law, contracts and design. Each chapter delves into specific aspects of this intersection, offering theoretical insights, practical examples, and actionable recommendations.

Helena Haapio discusses how the business world and the legal profession are undergoing a historical transformation as a result of GenAI. Traditional approaches to contracting and lawyering are being challenged, accelerated by the simultaneous rise of AI technologies and the spread of design-led thinking. These changes are reshaping the very nature—and legitimacy—of legal writing, particularly in the context of contracts. For decades, contracts have been treated as formal legal documents written by lawyers for other lawyers. Their structure, tone and language have remained remarkably consistent over time, often reflecting inherited drafting conventions rather than the needs of the people who use them. If the purpose of contracts is to set and reach common goals, why does their language so often feel mysterious, like a kind of magic spell? The chapter explores how traditional legal writing has functioned as a form of inherited linguistic power. Yet that spell has started to unravel with the rise of visual and redesigned contracts, plain language, and the increasing integration of GenAI into the contracting process. These developments do more than make contracts easier to read; they challenge long-standing assumptions about what and who contracts are for, and how they can work. If we can move beyond legal writing "as usual," we can begin to see contracts not as formal legal documents, but as tools for understanding and action. "No more legal writing in contracts!" is more than a slogan. It is a call to reimagine how contracts are communicated, how legal professionals work and how legal knowledge is shared and applied. It is also a call for lawyers to rethink their role—not only as firefighters or interpreters and guardians of rules, but as proactive solution providers and strategic enablers: partners in designing and building a better future.

Tim Cummins and Sally Guyer examine the evolving role of GenAI in the contracting process, questioning whether it is making a difference. While AI has long been embedded in Contract Lifecycle Management systems, it largely remained an internal tool within organizations. The advent of cloud computing introduced new efficiencies, but it wasn't until 2022, with the rise of GenAI, that a fundamental shift occurred. No longer confined to enterprise software, AI became widely accessible through personal devices, sparking excitement, skepticism, and a wave of speculation. While GenAI is poised to reshape contracting in significant ways, its actual impact remains a work in progress. This chapter explores the tangible changes GenAI has introduced so far and anticipates how its role in contracting will continue to evolve.

Marika Salo-Lahti, Mikko Ranta, Nina Toivonen, and Helena Haapio discuss how generative AI tools designed with a human-centered approach can help companies with financial management and contribute to sustainable finance. EU regulation related to sustainable finance aims to help achieve the objectives of the Green Deal. According to the Triple Bottom Line theory, the three parts of sustainability—environmental, social, and economic—are strongly interlinked. However, economic efficiency and sustainability are often perceived as conflicting goals. The authors look at practical ways to reconcile the two perspectives with the help of *AI crew*, a group of AI agents each specialized in their field. The authors test and review how this crew can be used to create solutions for some of the key challenges in sustainable financial management, using the perspective of an example company, a European textile firm.

Rob Waller, Helena Haapio, and Patrick Shone address the persistent "implementation gap" in contracting caused by traditional contracts that are crafted for legal purposes rather than for the practical purposes of contract performance. Bridging this gap, they argue, requires an understanding of what information is most relevant to each type of business user. GenAI's ability to simplify the language of contracts is well established, but the authors explore what else it can do to bridge the gap and how well it can anticipate the needs of particular audiences—including people responsible for implementation in the field, without a strong background in law. They compare GenAI's skills in producing a contract guide with those of an experienced information designer and challenge AI systems by asking them to explain their own limitations and the level of human oversight required. Finally, they provide a primer on how users can get the most out of GenAI.

Ebru Metin and Tanel Kerikmäe examine the intersection of GenAI and responsible AI in the legal sector, questioning whether the rule of law is being compromised for the sake of efficiency. Discussions on AI's role in modernizing the justice system often focus on capacity, theoretical potential, and resistance from traditional legal practitioners. However, deeper concerns—such as deepfake risks, algorithmic bias, and human oversight—must be assessed within frameworks like the European Ethical Charter on AI in judicial systems and the AI Act. While legal tech innovations promise progress, this chapter highlights a critical oversight: the lack of user-centered processes that prioritize transparency, accountability, and access to justice. Without thoughtful implementation, AI-driven legal systems risk benefiting service providers more than the clients they are meant to serve.

Hilja Autto, Jouko Nuottila, Anna Hurmerinta-Haanpää, and Yueh-Hsuan Weng discuss proactive privacy communication for emotional robots, which are increasingly becoming part of human–machine interaction. These AI-driven robots recognize and respond to human emotions, raising both opportunities and concerns, particularly regarding personal data privacy. While regulatory initiatives exist, this chapter argues that proactive privacy communication—through clear, multi-channel messaging, visual design, and tailored interactions—is essential for informed user consent. By integrating speech, gestures, and screen-based communication, emotional robots can provide more transparent data policies, ensuring that even less motivated users understand their privacy choices. The chapter underscores the importance of using plain language, appropriate tone, and personalized communication strategies to foster user trust and engagement in human–robot interactions.

Nina Toivonen, Marika Salo-Lahti, Mikko Ranta, and Helena Haapio explore how GenAI can function as a financial coach, promoting sustainable financial management and supporting individuals in overcoming debt. Applying the behavioral COM-B model, they examine how AI can enhance people's capabilities, opportunities, and motivation to achieve financial stability. Taking inspiration from fitness apps, they developed "Finance Friend," a prototype financial adviser powered by OpenAI's GPT Builder, to assess its effectiveness as a personalized financial coach. While the tool offers promising solutions, the chapter underscores the need for responsible AI design, regulatory oversight, and trust-building measures to ensure that financial AI applications genuinely serve users in an ethical and effective manner.

Petra Hietanen-Kunwald and Perttu Isohanni investigate the impact of artificial intelligence on both the legal and artistic domains, with a particular focus on copyright issues. AI-generated art presents unique challenges, as it blurs the lines between original and derivative works, often conflicting with existing copyright frameworks. Drawing on systems theory, this chapter analyzes the structural tensions between AI-driven creativity and legal protections for artists. The authors argue that while legislation plays a crucial role, a broader institutional approach—encompassing ethical, technological, and legal measures—is necessary to address emerging conflicts. By applying the Double Diamond framework and systemic design principles, the chapter proposes strategies for balancing innovation with the protection of artistic rights.

Perttu Isohanni and Petra Hietanen-Kunwald explore how GenAI is reshaping the creative economy, particularly in relation to intellectual property rights. While AI-generated works challenge traditional notions of authorship, a more pressing concern is the replication of distinctive artistic styles. Style, as both an economic asset and an expression of personal identity, is difficult to protect under copyright law, which historically grants rights to expressions rather than ideas. This chapter examines the complexities of regulating stylistic imitation and argues for reinforcing moral rights to prevent misattribution and reputational harm. Additionally, it proposes adapting intellectual property frameworks to compensate artists when their names and styles are used in AI-generated works, ensuring a fairer balance between technological innovation and artistic integrity.

Marietjie Botes examines the potential of AI-generated comics to facilitate public engagement in bioethical discussions, particularly in the realm of emerging biotechnologies such as human germline gene editing. Applying the concept of "Ethics by Design," the chapter examines how visual storytelling can make complex scientific and ethical dilemmas more accessible to a broader audience. By leveraging AI tools, bioethicists can create compelling narratives that foster dialogue and critical reflection. A case study, "The Artist," illustrates how interactive storytelling—such as a public "Dine-and-Draw" event—can encourage audiences to explore ethical scenarios in imaginative ways. While AI-generated comics offer efficiency and reach, challenges remain regarding quality control, creative agency, and ethical considerations. This chapter ultimately argues that AI-assisted storytelling can be crucial in shaping ethical discourse and democratizing bioethics.

Jaana Kovalainen and Sarah de Heer examine how GenAI can enhance the usability of health data, particularly in the context of debates around access to justice. The global challenge of making health data more accessible intersects with both UN Sustainable Development Goals and human rights concerns. In Europe, discussions center on secondary data use and patients' rights to access their own records, while other regions engage with broader issues of healthcare access. This chapter explores how large language models, such as GPT, can aid in improving the accessibility and clarity of health information, ultimately empowering individuals to make informed decisions. While the chapter primarily adopts a micro-level perspective, it also outlines how AI-driven legal design can facilitate broader systemic improvements in healthcare service delivery.

These chapters reflect a diverse array of perspectives, combining academic research, industry insights, and practical case studies to provide a holistic understanding of the subject matter.

4 Conclusion

As we move further into the digital age, the integration of AI into legal and business processes will become increasingly pervasive. GenAI's potential to enhance efficiency, accessibility, and innovation is undeniable. However, realizing this potential requires a concerted effort to address ethical, legal, and societal concerns.

This collection provides a foundation for understanding and engaging with these complex dynamics. By adopting principles of proactive law, human-centered design, and responsible AI, we can harness the power of GenAI to build legal systems that are more inclusive, efficient, and fair. But the impact goes beyond the legal system—when GenAI and design come together to reimagine contracts and the law, we don't just improve legal systems; we create better environments for collaboration, trust, and sustainable decision-making, ultimately transforming the way people and businesses interact, work and build the future.

The road ahead involves continuous learning, adaptation, and collaboration. With the right design, strategies, and ethical frameworks, GenAI can become a powerful ally in shaping a future where technology serves humanity's best interests rather than undermining them.

References

Autto H, Haapio H, Nuottila J (2024) Contracts rethought and redesigned: a new era with AI. Int J Commerce Contracting 8(1–2):7–34

Berger-Walliser G, Shrivastava P, Sulkowski A (2016) Using proactive legal strategies for corporate environmental sustainability. Michigan J Environ Adminis Law 6(1):1–35

Corrales Compagnucci M (2020) Big data, databases and "Ownership" rights in the cloud. Springer, Singapore

Corrales Compagnucci M, Haapio H, Fenwick M (eds) (2022) Research handbook on contract design. Edward Elgar Publishing, Cheltenham

Corrales Compagnucci M, Haapio H, Hagan M, Doherty M (eds) (2021) Legal design: integrating business, design and legal thinking with technology. Edward Elgar Publishing, Cheltenham

Doherty M, Corrales Compagnucci M, Haapio M, Hagan M (2021) A new attitude to law's empire: the potentialities of legal design. In: Corrales Compagnucci M, Haapio H, Hagan M, Doherty M (eds) Legal design: integrating business, design and legal thinking with technology. Edward Elgar Publishing, Cheltenham

Haapio H (2013) Next generation contracts: a paradigm shift. Lexpert Ltd, Helsinki

Helsinki Design Lab (n.d.) What is strategic design. https://www.helsinkidesignlab.org/pages/what-is-strategic-design. Accessed 4 March 2025

Marr B (2023) The difference between generative AI and traditional AI: an easy explanation for anyone. Forbes, 24 Jul. https://www.forbes.com/sites/bernardmarr/2023/07/24/the-difference-between-generative-ai-and-traditional-ai-an-easy-explanation-for-anyone/. Accessed 23 Feb 2025

Olivera J (2024) IBM watsonx platform: compliance obligations to controls mapping. IBM, 30 Oct. https://www.ibm.com/products/blog/ibm-watsonx-platform-compliance-obligations-to-controls-mapping. Accessed 23 Feb 2025

Raji A (2024) Responsible AI: from principle to practice: how to achieve maturity in responsible AI. Medium, 19 Feb. https://araji.medium.com/responsible-ai-from-principles-to-practice-6c28c4e52841. Accessed 23 Feb 2025

Tasabat SE, Özçay T (2025) Pushing the limits of creativity: a brief study of GenAI. In: Reddy CKK, Malhotra M, Ouaissa M (eds) Combating cyberbullying with generative AI. IGI Global, Hershey

No More Legal Writing in Contracts—Time to Break the Magic Spell!

Helena Haapio

Abstract The business world and the legal profession are undergoing a historic transformation. Traditional approaches to contracting and lawyering are being challenged, accelerated by the rise of generative AI (GenAI), and the spread of design-led thinking. These changes are reshaping the very nature—and legitimacy—of legal writing, particularly in the context of contracts. For decades, contracts have been treated as formal legal documents written by lawyers for other lawyers. Their structure, tone, and language have remained remarkably consistent over time, often reflecting inherited drafting conventions rather than the needs of the people who use them. If the purpose of contracts is to set and reach common goals, why does their language so often feel mysterious, like a kind of magic spell? This chapter begins by taking this question seriously. It explores how traditional legal writing has functioned as a form of inherited linguistic power, a dark legacy. Yet that spell and legacy have begun to break with the rise of visual and redesigned contracts, plain language, and the increasing integration of GenAI. These developments do more than make contracts easier to read; they challenge long-standing assumptions about what and who contracts are for, and how they can work. If we can move beyond legal writing as usual, we can begin to see contracts not as formal legal documents, but as tools for understanding and action. "No more legal writing in contracts" is more than a slogan. It is a call to reimagine how contracts are communicated, how legal professionals work, and how legal knowledge is shared and applied. It is also a call for lawyers to rethink their role—not only as firefighters or interpreters and guardians of rules, but as proactive solution providers and strategic enablers: partners in designing and building a better future.

Keywords Contract language · Dark legacy · Design · Generative AI · Magic spell · Visuals

H. Haapio (✉)
School of Accounting and Finance, Business Law, University of Vaasa, Vaasa, Finland
e-mail: helena.haapio@lexpert.com

JARGONFREE Contract Language Research Group, Tampere University, Tampere, Finland

Lexpert Ltd, Helsinki, Finland

© The Author(s), under exclusive license to Springer Nature Singapore Pte Ltd. 2025

M. Corrales Compagnucci et al. (eds.), *Generative AI, Contracts, Law and Design*,
Perspectives in Law, Business and Innovation,
https://doi.org/10.1007/978-981-95-2058-9_2

1 Introduction: The Magic Spell of Legal Writing

Contracts have a long history, evolving from simple oral agreements to complex written documents. For a long time—too long—contracts were written by lawyers for other lawyers,[1] with little regard for how others might read or use them. Contracts were written primarily to allocate risk and create legal effect, often at the expense of clarity and usability for the people responsible for implementing them.[2] Conventional legal writing prevailed, and contracts became *walls of text*,[3] often written in a language that to many is as impenetrable and mysterious as the mystical language used in *magic spells*.[4] Even the name of Spellbook—a Canadian legal tech startup—offering a tool for contract creation and review, is indicative.[5]

It is easy to draw parallels between legal documents and magic spells. Both rely on specialized, ritualistic language to exert control and produce specific outcomes. This magical, spell-like nature of the language can serve to distance the layperson from expert texts, creating a barrier that only those with specialized knowledge—in our case, lawyers, judges, and legal scholars—can cross. While this language is expected to ensure precision, it also conveys a sense of mystery and, by extension, power.[6]

The dominance of legal writing in contracts is odd, considering that, according to the International Association for Contract and Commercial Management (IACCM), nearly 80% of B2B contract terms concern business and financial matters.[7] In recent years, an increasing number of scholars and practitioners have called for a reimagining of contracts—not merely as legal instruments designed to mitigate risk and guard against worst-case outcomes, but as enablers of effective and collaborative business relationships.[8] Nevertheless, most commercial contracts today remain firmly rooted in the classical legal paradigm, shaped predominantly by the objectives and preferences of the legal function. This disjunction has resulted in a persistent mismatch between contracts and the business and managerial needs they are intended to serve. As Thomas D Barton observes, a recurring obstacle to successful contracting lies in the "exaggerated and largely unnecessary separation between the business

[1] See, e.g., Berger-Walliser et al. (2011).

[2] See, e.g., Passera (2017), Haapio (2013a), Haapio (2020).

[3] Passera (2017).

[4] See, e.g., Puiu (2024).—For the history of legal English, see e.g., Tiersma (1999), Williams (2022).

[5] Spellbook states on its website that it helps lawyers "do more of the work they love." See Spellbook (2025b). The name playfully acknowledges the traditional nature of legal writing. However, it also raises the question: does Spellbook merely generate more of the same, but faster?

[6] Haapio and Ketola (forthcoming a). See also Martínez et al. (2024).

[7] Cummins (2003), p. 4. IACCM is the predecessor of World Commerce and Contracting (WorldCC), which has over 75,000 members from 20,000 organizations across 180 countries worldwide.

[8] Haapio and Barton (2018). See also Section 2.1 below.

goals that clients seek to achieve, and the legal methods by which contractual relationships are created and managed."[9] Or, as simplification expert Irene Etzkorn puts it more pointedly, a common corporate misstep is "allowing the Legal department to tyrannize the rest of the company."[10]

1.1 From Roman Incantations to Modern Legal Spells

> [The lawyers] described contract terms as "magic incantations" and "talismans," [and] referred to contract drafting as a "ritual." – Mitu Gulati and Robert E Scott[11]

Those of us who studied legal history at law school may recall the *legis actio* procedure. In ancient Roman law, this early legal process required parties to recite specific verbal formulas to initiate a legal action. If the prescribed words were not said correctly, the claim was invalid. It was law as incantation: perform the spell correctly, and the gates of justice would open. Fail, and you were left outside.

This tradition of "magic words" is not just a thing from the past, it still persists in many countries' contract law or sales law. For example, in the United States, under the Uniform Commercial Code (UCC), to effectively disclaim the implied warranty of merchantability, a seller must explicitly mention the term "merchantability," and the disclaimer must be conspicuous.[12] Similarly, phrases like "as is," "time is of the essence," and "liquidated damages" commonly used in contracts carry particular legal effect that may not be clear for people without legal training.

Many practitioners and scholars—including legal scholars—have questioned the continued reliance on magic words in contract drafting. Lori D Johnson, in her article "Say the Magic Word: A Rhetorical Analysis of Contract Drafting Choices," argues that while some traditional terms serve as efficient shorthand for complex legal concepts, their overuse can obscure meaning and hinder clarity. However, she also presents empirical studies and theories that support the retention of certain magic words and concludes her article by stating that as advocates, drafters must always strive to use "correct magic" on their clients' behalf.[13]

As early as 1936, Yale Law Professor Fred Rodell observed: "There are two things wrong with almost all legal writing. One is its style. The other is its content."[14] His criticism still applies to much legal writing today. According to David Mellinkoff, legal writing has four outstanding characteristics: It is (1) wordy, (2) unclear,

---

[9] Barton (2012), p. 108.

[10] Etzkorn (n.d.).

[11] Gulati and Scott (2013), p. 109—cited in Johnson (2015), p. 455.

[12] Uniform Commercial Code Code Sect. 2-316, Subsect. 2.

[13] Johnson (2015), p. 490.

[14] Rodell (1936), p. 38. Fred Rodell revisited his critique on legal writing in Rodell (1962), noting that the problems he critiqued had not been corrected.

(3) pompous, and (4) dull[15]; it "is full of 'long sentences, awkward constructions, and fuzzy-wuzzy words.' The result is often nothing less than a failure of communication."[16]

If our goal is successful communication, why are we translating people's intentions, expectations, plans, goals, and commitments into legal writing—only to ask them (or computers) to translate that writing back into natural language in order to act on it? It makes no sense.

1.2 *The Spell-Like Language: A By-Product of Tradition or a Deliberate Choice?*

The comparison of legal writing with spells is not merely figurative. Research suggests that the language often found in legal texts indeed serves a purpose similar to that of a spell: to convey authority, invoke legitimacy, and maintain power hierarchies.[17] Such language is not just a by-product of tradition or of careless copying. It is, in many cases, a deliberate choice—one that reinforces the authority of the law.[18] Like spells in fiction,[19] legal language and recycled boilerplate are repeated and treated as sacred incantations—understanding is secondary.

Others before us have drawn inspiration from fiction, particularly JK Rowling's Harry Potter series,[20] where the word "Muggles" is used to refer to people without magical abilities: they cannot read, write, or cast spells. Legal writing can feel the same to non-lawyers. To them, lawyers may seem to belong to a closed world of trained wizards or spellcasters, an elite club with its own language and rules. The more complex the spell (or contract), the more powerful the wizard (or lawyer)

---

[15] Mellinkoff (1963), p. 24.

[16] Mellinkoff (1963), p. 27 citing Rodell's work.

[17] See, e.g., Puiu (2024) and Butler (2024), both referring to Martínez et al. (2024): "much like the mystical language used in magic spells, legalese signals a unique kind of authority. In other words, the complexity of legal writing is quite intentional" Puiu (2024); "just as 'magic spells' use special rhymes and archaic terms to signal their power, the convoluted language of legalese acts to convey a sense of authority" Butler (2024).

[18] Martínez et al. (2024). See also, Mitchell (2015), p. 7: "Traditional (if not necessarily optimal) forms persist because the form itself—as a social artefact—is symbolic of legitimacy and legality. The document just looks and feels legal."

[19] The metaphor of spells is inspired by the fictional world of Harry Potter, where spells are verbal or written incantations that produce effects: some protective, others harmful. In this chapter, the term dark spell is sometimes used to describe traditional legal language that often obscures meaning and excludes understanding. In contrast, we also introduce what we call "counter-spells," such as visuals and plain language, that are designed to clarify, invite, and empower. For spells in Harry Potter's world, see, e.g., Rowling (1997).

[20] See, e.g., Rowling (1997).

seems—and the harder it is for Muggles to participate, ask questions, or understand what is going on.[21]

This chapter asks whether the magic-spell-like language of legal writing is truly necessary—or whether it can be replaced. The call for "no more legal writing in contracts" in the title reflects the urgent need to rethink, rewrite, and redesign contracts to better serve the needs of all stakeholders—individuals, small businesses, and public organizations alike—and even societies as a whole.[22] Contracts are not made for the sake of making contracts, they are made to achieve the parties' goals, and these are rarely just legal goals. For example, in the context of sustainability, policymakers, and regulators are increasingly relying on private actors—businesses and their value chains—to achieve environmental and human rights goals.[23] Achieving these goals, both business and societal, requires someone to translate contractual requirements and commitments into action. This is easier said than done—but much easier now than before the advent of contract design and technology tools, such as GenAI.

1.3 Contractual Legacy

Very few contracts are started from scratch. Instead, contracts are produced using forms, templates, and earlier contracts as the basis. Inherited forms, templates, models, and drafting conventions get passed down through generations of contract writers. With their outdated language they create a self-reinforcing mechanism that is often strengthened with the support of technology. Old contract language is repeated in modern clause libraries and contract assembly and management systems. The language and writing style go unquestioned and are embedded into contracts, faster and faster, over and over again.

In this way, technology spreads and reinforces the spell-like nature of legal writing in contracts, easily leading to "an exercise in garbage in, garbage out."[24] When someone uses technology to reflect the deal terms, the user does not even think of

---

[21] The concept of Muggles has been applied metaphorically to the legal world for example by Mark Edwin Burge, in his chapter "Who Wants to Be a Muggle? The Diminished Legitimacy of Law as Magic," who draws parallels between the exclusivity of the wizarding world and the legal profession. He argues that legal language often functions like magic—accessible only to those trained in its use. See Burge (2010).—The metaphor of lawyers as wizards and non-lawyers as Muggles has also appeared informally in legal blogs and education, often to highlight how legal language and practice can exclude those without specialist training.

[22] See, e.g., Autto et al. (2024)—In some jurisdictions, drafting contracts for others without legal qualifications may be deemed unauthorized practice of law. In this way, contract writing can become the exclusive domain of lawyers, reinforcing the magic spell: it is not only what is written that matters, but also who is permitted to write it. Jurisdictional variations, however, lie beyond the scope of this chapter.

[23] Haapio and Ketola (forthcoming b).

[24] Adams (2009). For "dysfunctional drafting," see Adams (2008) and for "the illusion of quality in contract drafting," Adams and Allen (2012). See also Haapio and Linna (2020).

changing the template (nor does the user necessarily have the right to do so). The result is inertia[25] and path dependence.[26]

In its white paper, BearingPoint, a global consulting firm, defines *legacy* as the accumulation of cultural, operational, technical, and/or psychological realities shaped by past decisions and actions, influenced by the path taken to reach the present.[27] We add to the list what we call *contractual legacy*—the inherited structures, practices, and assumptions that are embedded in the continued use of old contract templates, clauses, and boilerplate. It is a dark legacy that easily leads to contracts that in the eyes of their users are a necessary evil, a nuisance that gets in the way of doing business. Echoing the title of a book chapter by Deepak Malhotra, even a *great deal* may end up with a *terrible contract*: "Great Deal, Terrible Contract."[28] Yet this does not need to happen.

2 Breaking the Magic Spell and the Dark Legacy

Having identified the role of the magic spell and the dark legacy in contracts, we now turn to solutions aimed at freeing contracts from them. No longer confined to being necessary evils—legal documents filed away and forgotten—contracts can then become strategic tools that actively guide relationships and help achieve the parties' goals.

But this transformation will not happen, unless the dark contractual legacy and current legal thinking and writing practices are fundamentally changed. In the following sections, we will explore a new mindset as well as tools and approaches that are about to break the magic spell—and to some extent, already have.

[25] See, e.g., Adams and Allen (2012). According to Ken Adams' blog post of January 29, 2013(a), "inertia has rendered most of corporate America either complacent about suboptimal contract templates or incapable of doing anything about them."

[26] See, e.g., DiMatteo et al. (2012), p. 61 and Triantis (2013), p. 194: "standard contract terms are often sticky or locked-in practices" and Triantis (2013), p. 181: "Departures from standard terms raise the reading costs of contracting partners as well as their suspicions." See also Adams (2013b): "For lawyers unwilling or unable to overhaul their traditional contract language, the excuse of choice is that traditional language has been 'tested'—if you meddle with it, you're exposing yourself to all sorts of risk."—For path dependence more generally and how history matters in organizations, see, e.g., Schreyögg et al. (2011).

[27] BearingPoint (2024).

[28] Malhotra (2012).

2.1 The Spell Starts Breaking: Questioning Legal Writing in Contracts

Contracts matter, and they are created to support real-world business objectives. They are expected to shape and guide business transactions and relationships: their planning, communication, coordination, and collaboration. In commercial contracting, they are management tools and not just legal ones,[29] and most of their readers are not judges or lawyers, but business people, project teams, and partners working toward common goals.

What, then, is the purpose of a contract? WorldCC defines the purpose[30]:

> To safeguard and promote the economic and financial interests of the parties by establishing a clear, mutual agreement on their rights, obligations, and expectations. While it includes the theoretical aspect of legal enforceability, its practical value lies in creating a moral and ethical responsibility that encourages parties to fulfil their commitments, fosters trust and cooperation, and provides a framework for resolving disputes. The contract thus serves as both a legal tool and a foundation for achieving mutually beneficial financial outcomes.

Current contracts still often focus on worst-case scenarios rather than on achieving mutually beneficial outcomes. The way they are framed is based on risks rather than opportunities. Contracts inherit their writing style, word choice, and look and feel from the existing *contractual legacy*. They are dense, formal, and full of ritualistic language, often copy-pasted from legislation; from there, this style has spread throughout supply chains and the contracting community.[31] Newcomers may have questioned the language and style at first, but have soon adopted it themselves. The pressure to appear "professional" and "legal" has reinforced the cycle.[32] As a result, contracts have become documents written to meet legal expectations rather than to guide human behavior.

Surveys by WorldCC reveal that there is a recognized misalignment between traditional contract drafting and the needs and expectations of business. One of the most consistent findings in WorldCC reports is the call for simpler contracts. The people surveyed constantly call for making contracts easier to read and understand by reducing legal jargon, focusing on the key terms, and structuring the overall agreement in a way that it is easier to find and use.[33]

How can this happen, if current legal writing in contracts is allowed to continue? In research and practice, the voices calling for a fresh approach to contract language and design are becoming louder. They are starting to be heard, and things are beginning to change: contracts are no longer seen solely as "documents written by lawyers for lawyers." WorldCC predicts that the role of contract managers and lawyers will

---

[29] See, e.g., Haapio (2013a), Haapio (2013b), Haapio and Siedel (2013), p. 11.

[30] WorldCC (2024b), p. 17.

[31] Haapio and Ketola (forthcoming b).

[32] Haapio (2013a), Haapio (2013c). See also Mitchell (2015), p. 7.

[33] WorldCC (2024a), p. 17.

become increasingly strategic, ensuring that contracts deliver on their intended business outcomes.[34] With this new perspective, a visual and design-led turn, and the arrival of GenAI, the magic spell embedded in contracts has begun to break. But much work still remains.

For computer scientists, contracts and legal texts might be written in what they call "natural language"—as opposed to formal programming languages. But in our context, the term "natural language" is misleading. Conventional contracts are written in a style and language that is dramatically different from the way people typically communicate. Some might say that contract language is lawyer-readable, and most would agree that it is often far from human-readable, truly natural language.

Breaking the spell is not just a matter of replacing difficult words with simpler ones. Once the spell is broken, we are free to imagine the next generation of contracts and new ways of writing and designing them: contracts that invite rather than exclude and empower rather than intimidate.

2.2 Plain Language and Plain Writing: The Foundation

Traditionally, loan forms and credit card agreements have been long, text-heavy documents filled with legal and financial jargon, often making them difficult—if not impossible—for ordinary users to understand. A change began in 1975 when Carl Felsenfeld, a lawyer, and Alan Siegel, a language and design expert, collaborated to create a more user-friendly loan form for Citibank. Their pioneering work laid the groundwork for a growing movement to write contracts in plain English—a movement that would later be reflected in the title of their 1981 book, Writing Contracts in Plain English.[35]

The Plain Writing Act, passed in the United States in 2010, requires government agencies to use clear communication. The purpose of the Act is "to improve the effectiveness and accountability of Federal agencies to the public by promoting clear Government communication that the public can understand and use."[36] Since then, many countries around the world have followed suit and passed laws to ensure that legal and government documents use plain, clear communication.[37]

Documents that technically comply with plain language laws can still overwhelm readers due to their length and complexity. In the United States, President Trump issued a new Executive Order on April 15, 2025, titled "Restoring Common Sense to Federal Procurement." Its goal is to streamline procurement and "create the most agile, effective, and efficient procurement system possible."[38] The title sounds

[34] WorldCC (2024b), p. 17.

[35] Felsenfeld and Siegel (1981).

[36] See Plain Writing Act of 2010, Sect. 2.

[37] See, eg., Blasie (2024).

[38] Executive Order 14,275 of 15 April 2025, *Restoring Common Sense to Federal Procurement*, 90 Federal Register 24,567.

promising—it remains to be seen whether this Executive Order will actually help cut through the complexity and break the spell of legal writing in federal procurement contracts.

In breaking the spell, the work of plain language advocates has been essential—and continues to be. Yet the change, while meaningful, often remains invisible. A contract written in plain language can still look like a wall of text. The first impression—the look and feel—often stays the same, and contracts remain complex. The contracting experience needs an overhaul.

2.3 *Contract Visualization as the First Visible Spellbreaker*

For decades, perhaps even centuries, contracts have been text-only documents. This legacy has long limited how contracts communicate. However, digitization and visualization have begun to break this spell.

The digital age opened a new era in which contracts were not only written documents: they could be stored, shared, and signed electronically. A major leap forward came with computable[39] and self-executing contracts called "smart" or even "wise" contracts.[40] A parallel development was the emergence of *contract visualization,*[41] which began to take shape in the late 1990s in the context of contract education and practice. After visuals *about* contracts came visuals *for*, *in,* and *as* contracts: a continuum.[42] The early publications built on the work of information designers and introduced the idea of *a visual turn in contracting.*[43] The real spellbreaker was the emergence of *visual contracts*—visuals embedded in contracts themselves[44] and *visual law.*[45]

Yet the journey was not without its challenges. Attempts to change conventional thinking met resistance. A telling example comes from a 2011 discussion on the *Adams on Contract Drafting* blog, where Ken Adams, a writer and speaker on contract drafting, reacted to using visuals in contracts.[46] His scepticism—echoed by many commenters—centered around fears of ambiguity, enforceability, and judicial acceptance. Many remained hesitant, anchoring their reasoning in precedent and legal conservatism. In 2011, visuals were still considered outsiders, and the idea of contracts as visual communication tools had not yet gained legitimacy. The spell, it seems, had not yet broken.

[39] See, e.g., Clack (2018), with references. The authors use the term "computable contracts" for "legal contracts that are understandable by both humans and computers."

[40] See, e.g., Clack et al. (2017), Hazard and Haapio (2017).

[41] See, e.g., Haapio (2011), Barton et al. (2011), Passera and Haapio (2011).

[42] Haapio et al. (2017). See also Haapio (2022).

[43] See, e.g., Haapio et al. (2012).

[44] See, e.g., Passera (2017), Mitchell (2018), Willey et al. (2025).

[45] Brunschwig (2014), Haapio and Passera (2013).

[46] See Adams (2011).

The scepticism surfaced again in 2013, when Ken Adams offered unsolicited advice to those organizing the Legal Design Jam at Stanford.[47] In a blog post, he urged participants to focus on improving traditional contract prose, recommending they consult his style manual, and cautioned against being "distracted by superficial stuff."[48] The implication was clear: design was still seen as peripheral. At that time, the belief was that contracts are and remain text-only documents, best improved by better wording and writing style. The possibility that design might fundamentally reshape contracts had yet to enter the mainstream legal imagination.

Perhaps the most significant shift happened in 2016, when attorney Robert de Rooy introduced Comic Contracts—visuals *as* contracts. These were not comics about contracts; the comic became the contract, originally designed to be understood by South African people with limited literacy. This idea disrupted the traditional, text-only format and proved that contracts could look and feel different and still be both legally binding and understandable.

While the pioneers of contract visualization had previously experimented with visual contract clauses in both research and practice, Robert de Rooy's Comic Contracts opened the door to contracts that did not just read differently—they looked different. This new approach gathered significant media attention in many parts of the world.[49]

Contract visualization became the first *visible* spellbreaker. It did not just *tell* us that different contracts were possible—it *showed* us. The spell was no longer just weakened; it was publicly and visibly disrupted.[50] Contracts became less a wall of text and more of user guides and business blueprints. Visualization had become the driver of contract innovation.[51] These developments led to new transdisciplinary fields of research and practice, now known as *legal design*[52] and *contract design*.[53]

---

[47] The author of this chapter was among the organizers of the Stanford Legal Design Jam, which, despite the dismissals, marked a turning point. Events like it began to challenge the dominance of text-only thinking and writing, and opened up space for experimentation.

[48] See Adams (2013c).

[49] See, e.g., Finnish Broadcasting Company (Yle) (2016). This Yle Areena clip featuring the author discussing the complexity of online service terms and highlighting Robert de Rooy's Comic Contracts as a solution. This appearance and Comic Contracts' media coverage in various parts of the world illustrates how contracts, typically overlooked by mainstream media, began to capture public attention.

[50] The innovation that had started in education and research publications quickly spread from research to practice. Even the business world recognized the emerging change. In 2019, the Financial Times published an article asking "Can contracts use pictures instead of words?," see Love (2019).

[51] For a visual showing the trajectory, see Visualisation as a driver of contract innovation, an image from 2023 by Annika Varjonen in celebration of the 25 years of Proactive Contracting, available at https://www.lexpert.com/wp-content/uploads/2025/04/Visualisation-as-a-driver-of-contract-innovation-Annika-Varjonen.jpg. See also Haapio (2016).

[52] See, e.g., Brunschwig (2021), Corrales Compagnucci et al. (2021).

[53] See, e.g., Corrales Compagnucci et al. (2022b).

2.4 *From One-Off Visualizations to Scalable Patterns: Early Automation Attempts*

The pioneers of contract visualization recognized early on that isolated visual prototypes, no matter how promising, were not enough. To transform the way contracts look and feel, they knew their innovations had to be scalable. This realization sparked attempts to automate contract visualization.

At the 2014 IRIS conference, Stefania Passera, Helena Haapio, and Michael Curtotti presented a paper titled "Making the Meaning of Contracts Visible—Automating Contract Visualization."[54] In the paper, they introduced three proof-of-concept tools that they had built to generate visual representations of three specific contract clauses: termination, payment terms, and liquidated damages.[55] These early prototypes were clause-specific. Achieving broader reusability remained challenging.

As the field progressed, the focus shifted from visualizing individual clauses to identifying broader design patterns and applying these innovations into portfolios of contracts. The concept of *contract design patterns* emerged, and pioneers began to identify, collect, document, share, and organize visual and other design patterns to address common communication challenges in contracts.[56] The patterns approach, originally developed in fields such as architecture and software engineering, led Stefania Passera and Helena Haapio to create the *WorldCC Contract Design Pattern Library*, available at https://contract-design.worldcc.com.[57] This open-access library is free and currently contains ten pattern families, one of which is visuals. The others focus on structure, language, navigation, layering, and more. Examples of contract designs in the library are shared by early adopters of contract innovation, such as Shell and Airbus.

However, despite having the pattern logic in place, scaling remained difficult. We and others experimented with editable templates, image libraries, and other ideas to transform patterns into repeatable, automatable building blocks. These experiments taught us valuable lessons, but they also highlighted a shared constraint: even with documented patterns, most implementations were resource-intensive and difficult to replicate at scale. A further obstacle became apparent when attempting to integrate these approaches into existing contract management and other systems. Visual formats—even simple tables—were not supported by the technology infrastructure. What worked best for human users turned out to be the hardest for machines to process.

Resistance and the dark contractual legacy remained strong, and those who wanted to use visuals lacked the necessary tools, resources, and technology support. The ideas and methods were there, but the means were missing. For years, scaling visual, plain

[54] Passera et al. (2014).

[55] The proof-of-concept tools for the automation of the creation of visual contract clauses are available at https://users.cecs.anu.edu.au/~Michael.Curtotti/visualcontracting/.

[56] See, e.g., Haapio and Hagan (2016).

[57] WorldCC Foundation et al. (n.d.).

language contracts, and contract design patterns remained challenging. Until GenAI appeared.

2.5 *Enter Generative AI: From Vision to Action*

In November 2022, OpenAI released ChatGPT 3.5, making advanced AI tools available to anyone with an internet connection. Since then, GenAI has evolved rapidly, moving beyond text to include image generation, multimodal capabilities, and increasingly intuitive interfaces for editing and iteration. What's more, GenAI could read and "understand" a contract not just as text, but also in visual form, even tables—formats that traditional contract management systems found difficult to process but which people found clear and helpful. This shift opened the door to entirely new ways of designing, presenting, and interacting with contracts. A new era had begun: one where contracts can become visual, intelligent,[58] chattable,[59] and beyond.

What once took hours—drafting plain language clauses, creating timelines, sketching skimmable headings, or formatting layered contract layouts—can now be accomplished in seconds with a well-crafted prompt.[60] More importantly, it is no longer a privilege reserved for teams with design expertise or high-end tools. Anyone can now create quick summaries, explain contract content, simplify complex language, personalize contract terms, and even tailor the style and tone to suit the needs of the audience—whether a business executive, a consumer, or a legal professional.[61] It is even possible to generate comic-style panels.[62]

GenAI did more than speed things up. It began to shift the very mindset of legal and contracting professionals. Rather than starting from a blank document or recycled template, we can now start with a prompt, a voice command, a visual sketch, a diagram, or a collaborative prompt. But are we ready to go there?

We still face one major barrier: mainstream mindsets and outdated systems. To bring about real-world impact at scale, we must break not only the magic spell of legal writing, but also the legacy ways of thinking and working. In many cases, this means a major challenge—and opportunity—to technology providers, especially in the field of Contract Lifecycle Management (CLM).

---

[58] Stathis et al. (2024).

[59] Ketola et al. (forthcoming).

[60] See, e.g., Autto et al. (2024).

[61] See, e.g., Autto et al. (2024), Toivonen et al. (2025).

[62] Botes (2025) in this Book.

Some CLM vendors have already begun incorporating AI,[63] design principles, visual aids, and modular thinking into their platforms.[64] But these are still early steps. True integration of spell-breaking plain language and design patterns into mainstream CLM ecosystems remains a work in progress. With the combined power of GenAI and forward-thinking CLM providers, we now have a historic opportunity: to rewire the corporate contracting world and create a new, better world.

Visuals broke the spell. Design patterns gave us ideas, examples, and tools for thought. GenAI opened the door for scaling, and CLM systems can help us scale. The result is not only a different way of generating, reviewing, and managing contracts—it is a different way of thinking about contracts: contracts can now truly act as *interfaces*[65] and *visible scripts for collaboration.*[66] They can reach their full potential and serve their intended purpose.

2.6 RIP Most Legal Work as Usual?—Welcome AI-Assisted Contract Designer!

A recent post on X (formerly Twitter) captured the frustration many feel with traditional legal services. In this case, a business professional sought advice on a corporate structure issue. After waiting three weeks for a convoluted memo, attending a required one-hour meeting and receiving a $5,000 bill, he turned to Claude, a GenAI tool from Anthropic, with the same question. Within seconds, Claude provided a clear and actionable answer—effectively the same advice, but delivered faster, cheaper, and in clearer language: "It basically said the same thing, except instantly and easy to understand."[67]

The comparison was stark, and the post's final comment, "RIP most legal work," resonated widely, sparking conversations about the future of lawyering in an AI-driven world. In the comments, even lawyers acknowledged that using GenAI to draft legal documents could significantly reduce costs for clients by providing a high-quality first draft. However, concerns were raised about the accuracy of AI-generated advice and the impact of potential errors. What if the advice is incorrect and results in loss: who can the person seeking the advice turn to and claim compensation from?

---

[63] Spellbook (see fn 5) was one of the first legal tech companies to deliver a GenAI-based contract creation and review tool to the market. For how their products have developed, see Spellbook (2025a), Stevenson (2024), Artificial Lawyer (2024).

[64] See, e.g., Juro (2024), Juro, https://juro.com/, Spellbook, https://www.spellbook.legal/, WordSmith, https://www.wordsmith.ai/, Icertis, https://www.icertis.com/, LawGeex, https://www.lawgeex.com/, Agiloft, https://www.agiloft.com/, Axdraft, https://axdraft.com/.

[65] Haapio and Passera (2021).

[66] Haapio and Haavisto (2005), Haavisto (2006), pp. 250–252, Rekola and Haapio (2009), pp. 36–37, Berger-Walliser et al. (2011), pp. 63–65.

[67] Andrew Wilkinson (2025), a successful co-founder and owner of many ventures, shared this story in a viral post, highlighting dissatisfaction with traditional legal services and the transformative potential of AI.

While AI may occasionally make mistakes, so do humans, even experienced professionals. This raises a key question: Should lawyers continue to focus primarily on identifying problems, mitigating risks, and preparing for the worst, or should they adopt a more proactive approach that emphasises seizing opportunities and achieving optimal outcomes?

This question lies at the heart of the distinction between reactive and proactive law, and between traditional and proactive contracting. Proactive law is a forward-looking approach that views law not merely as a set of constraints but as a tool to achieve goals, create value, foster successful relationships, and prevent problems and disputes.[68] Originating in the Nordic countries in the late 1990s, this approach first gained prominence in the context of contracting.[69] The integration of visualization and design methods into proactive contracting and proactive law was instrumental in this development.[70] More recently, the incorporation of AI into these practices has further enhanced their effectiveness and opened new avenues for research and practice.

Whatever happens to other legal work, the future looks bright for future-oriented design-minded proactive lawyers with AI as their teammate. They can work as members of transdisciplinary teams and focus on designing a better future, asking the right questions, simplifying complex communication, creating new opportunities, aligning expectations, and fostering collaboration—something in contexts where human traits such as creativity, enthusiasm, and intuition will thrive.

By harnessing GenAI and embracing a proactive approach, businesses and legal professionals can move beyond traditional, reactive methods, to create value and drive innovation. This view is supported by industry analysis that highlights the role of AI in streamlining business and legal processes. The Financial Times, for example, reports on various initiatives where AI is effectively removing legal barriers that traditionally slow down business operations.[71] Being proactive is crucial in a world where, as Mark Zuckerberg aptly puts it, "The biggest risk is not taking any risk. In a world that's changing really quickly, the only strategy that is guaranteed to fail is not taking risks."[72]

In our earlier work[73] we envisioned a future where the role of a "computable contract designer" would become pivotal. We drew parallels to the evolution of web design, where the integration of multidisciplinary tools transformed the creation process into a more efficient and user-friendly endeavor. We anticipated that, similarly, contract design would evolve through the use of no- or low-code software solutions, enabling the development of customized digital contracts tailored to specific situations and user needs.

---

[68] Haapio and Berger-Walliser (2025), p. 3.

[69] Haapio (1998), Haapio (2006).

[70] Berger-Walliser et al. (2017), Haapio (2022).

[71] Saunders (2024).

[72] Mark Zuckerberg in an interview at Y Combinator's Startup School held at Stanford University on 29 October 2011. See Tobak (2011).

[73] Corrales et al. (2019), Corrales Compagnucci et al. (2022a).

At that time, we observed early developments in sectors like insurance and reinsurance, where efforts were underway to design digital contracts based on modular approaches, ensure interoperability across platforms, and create repositories for contract components. We posited that such advancements would lead to the emergence of "automated computable contract builders," facilitating the automation of user-friendly contracts equipped with features like explanatory diagrams and layered layouts, catering to both human and machine readers.

Today, merely a few years later, these predictions are materializing before our eyes. The integration of GenAI into contract writing and design is revolutionizing the field, aligning with our earlier forecasts. After decades of arguing that contracts need to be designed, not just drafted,[74] the paradigm is finally shifting. The time has come for the AI-assisted contract designer.

3 Experimenting with GenAI Tools

3.1 ChatGPT, How Can You Break the Magic Spell in Contracts?

To test the ways in which GenAI can assist contract drafters to become contract designers and break the magic spell, we wrote a simple prompt: "I am writing a book chapter on No More Legal Writing in Contracts—Time to Break the Magic Spell! ChatGPT, how can you help break the magic spell in contracts?".[75]

ChatGPT did not need an explanation of what we meant. Off it went:

> If we think of "**the magic spell**" as the obscure, exclusionary, and overly legalistic language that has dominated contract drafting for centuries, ChatGPT can be a powerful spellbreaker in the following ways:
>
> 1. **Detecting the Spell: Spotting the Jargon and Legalese**
>
> ChatGPT can help identify the "magic words" and archaic structures that preserve legal mystique (e.g., notwithstanding the foregoing, hereinafter, best efforts, force majeure).
>
> **How?** You can feed a contract clause into ChatGPT and ask:
>
> "Highlight the terms that are difficult for a layperson to understand."
>
> "Which parts of this clause are written in legalese?"

[74] See, e.g., Corrales Compagnucci et al. (2022b).

[75] The conversation with ChatGPT is on file with the author and available upon request. AI tools like ChatGPT are designed to adapt to users' preferences and interaction styles. With the introduction of long-term memory features, ChatGPT can now recall user-specific information across sessions. It is possible that the suggestions provided during this experiment reflect the author's prior interactions with the interface, where similar topics were discussed.

2. **Rewriting the Spell: Translating to Plain Language**

ChatGPT can rewrite clauses in plain, accessible, and user-friendly language. **You can ask**:

"Rewrite this clause in plain English for a freelancer and a small business owner."

"Make this clause feel human, clear, and trustworthy."

3. **Designing Alternative Structures: Layering, Summaries, TL;DR**

ChatGPT can help structure contracts into **digestible layers**, by generating:

- TL;DR summaries for each clause
- Headings and visual-friendly bullet points
- Question-and-answer versions of terms

"Can you make a TL;DR summary of each clause in this contract?"

"Turn this contract into a FAQ-style format."

4. **Co-Writing the Script: Turning Contracts into Dialogues or Scenarios**

You can co-create **contract-as-script** formats, where obligations become actions and roles are explicit.

"Turn this collaboration agreement into a script with characters and scenes."

"Frame this clause as a step-by-step action sequence."

5. **Training the Spellbreakers: Empowering Non-Lawyers**

ChatGPT is a low-threshold tool for empowering users to edit, ask questions, and understand contract content – without needing legal training.

You might also use it in workshops with prompts like:

"What does this term actually mean?"

"Give me a friendlier version of this that still works legally."

6. **Breaking the Spell of Power: Rebalancing the Voice**

Many contracts still echo a **top-down voice** – protective of one party and excluding the other. ChatGPT can help **identify bias**, suggest **neutral language**, and reshape tone.

"Who is this contract written to benefit most?"

"Suggest edits to make this more balanced and mutual."

7. **Iterating and Prototyping Faster**

You can use ChatGPT to **quickly iterate** through versions, test readability, and prototype more engaging contract formats – even **visual, story-based, or modular** ones.

3.2 *ChatGPT Suggesting Sample Prompts*

We did not have to think how to proceed. ChatGPT suggested.

> Would you like sample prompts or examples you can include in your chapter?

It was sufficient to say "Yes, please!" and off it went again, by offering sample prompts organized by the seven spell-breaking powers it had mentioned in our earlier conversation, along with "a bonus"—here are some examples:

> **Spot the Spell (Detecting Legalese and Jargon)**
>
> "Highlight the outdated, confusing, or overly legalistic terms in the following clause. Suggest simpler alternatives."
>
> **Break the Spell (Rewrite in Plain Language)**
>
> "Rewrite this contract clause so that a high school student or a first-time freelancer can understand it, without losing its meaning."
>
> **Break It into Layers (Summaries and Structure)**
>
> "For each section of this contract, provide a one-sentence summary ('tl;dr') in plain English."
>
> "Can you turn this clause into a three-layer structure: 1) title, 2) plain-language summary, 3) full legal text?"
>
> **Democratize the Spellbook (Empowering non-lawyers)**
>
> "Explain this clause as if you're talking to someone who has never seen a contract before – what's the point, and what should they watch out for?"
>
> "What questions should I ask myself before signing this agreement?"
>
> **Neutralize the Spell of Power (Bias & Tone)**
>
> "Does this clause give more protection or power to one party than the other? Suggest a more balanced version."
>
> "Rewrite this clause to sound more mutual, respectful, and collaborative."
>
> **Prototype Fast (Iterate and Experiment)**
>
> "Give me three alternative versions of this clause: one formal, one friendly, and one visual or step-based."
>
> **Bonus: Combine Tools for Total Spellbreaking**
>
> "Turn this clause into a visual layout with title, summary, actions, and warnings. Add icons if helpful."

3.3 *ChatGPT Applying the Approach to a Model Contract Clause*

To test how AI can help dismantle the "magic spell" of legal writing in contracts, we ran a small experiment using a clause from a set of sustainability model clauses known as the European Model Clauses (EMCs)—specifically, EMC Zero Draft Clause 3.2(c).[76] The original reads:

> In the event of an actual Adverse Impact that Supplier individually or jointly caused that renders the Goods nonconforming goods that cannot be released or sold in the European market because of applicable European regulations, "Nonconforming Goods," Buyer shall have the right to reject such Nonconforming Goods and the costs associated with such rejection, including but not limited to the costs of disposing of the Goods and finding a replacement contract with another supplier, shall be borne by Supplier unless Supplier is an SME or unless both Buyer and Supplier jointly caused the actual Adverse Impact at issue by breaching their respective HREDD Obligations.

We asked ChatGPT to apply two of its suggested prompts to this Clause. ChatGPT immediately responded:

> Excellent choice. That clause is a classic example of a "magic spell" – dense, conditional, packed with jargon, and hard to parse in one reading.

It then applied two prompts from our earlier session to this clause. First came the "Spot the Spell" prompt. The output highlighted, one by one, "the outdated, confusing, or overly legalistic terms" embedded in the original wording and suggested alternatives and improvements: "In the event of" → consider "If"; "including but not limited to" → redundant; ChatGPT could rephrase with specific examples"; "breaching their respective HREDD Obligations" → legal insider language, should be explained in plain terms elsewhere". For space reasons, we do not reproduce the full list here, but it was thorough and persuasive.

Next, it moved on to the "Break the Spell" prompt. This time, the output proposed a rewritten version of the clause, offering a clearer, more accessible alternative:

> **Plain-Language Rewrite**:
>
> If the Supplier (alone or together with the Buyer) does something that causes the Goods to break European rules – so that the Goods can't be sold or used in Europe – then those Goods are called "Nonconforming Goods."
>
> In that case, the Buyer can reject the Goods. The Supplier must then pay the costs for rejecting them. This includes, for example, the cost of throwing the Goods away and the cost of finding another supplier.
>
> However, the Supplier doesn't have to pay these costs if:
>
> – the Supplier is a small or medium-sized business (SME), or
> – both the Buyer and the Supplier broke their responsibilities related to human rights or environmental due diligence (HREDD).

Our experiment did not stop there—ChatGPT suggested optional next steps, such as creating a layered version or a checklist. In another conversation, it even offered to build a Contract SpellChecker, offered, of course, with a smile.

---

[76] European Working Group for Responsible and Sustainable Supply Chains (2024), p. 9. The EMCs are a set of model clauses designed to align with the EU Corporate Sustainability Due Diligence Directive (Directive (EU) 2024/1760.

After applying ChatGPT's suggestions to a few more sample clauses, we were convinced: this was a compelling proof of concept. GenAI has the potential to become the ultimate Spellbreaker—not just a tool for simplifying contract language, but also a catalyst for transforming the world of contracting and shaping a better, spell-free future.

4 Conclusion

Traditionally, contracts have been complex documents written in legal language largely inaccessible to the layperson. Many people—including contract drafters and technology providers—assume this state of affairs is permanent: that contracts will always be dense, text-heavy documents from which even basic information is difficult, if not impossible, for non-lawyers to extract. This chapter challenges the notion that legal writing in contracts is a fixed constant. It argues that, for some, the time for business as usual may soon be over.

Contract writing conventions are not dictated by law. Rather, they are deliberate choices made by writers. Like any choice, these conventions can—and should—be reconsidered. A new era of human-AI collaboration is emerging, one that invites us to rethink not just how we write contracts, but what we want them to achieve.

Drawing on recent research and experimentation, this chapter approaches contract language and style as a kind of spell. We asked: do contracts really need to be written this way? Is traditional legal writing fit for today's world? Our answer is no. What matters is that the contract enables the parties to reach their goals and avoid unnecessary problems. It should also be clear for the people it impacts, not just the lawyers who draft it or the judges who interpret it in the event of a dispute.

Rather than focusing on the well-known risks of GenAI, this chapter has explored what becomes possible when it is used thoughtfully and responsibly. When combined with design-led thinking, GenAI can help dismantle the dark legacy of traditional legal writing. It can identify and flag spell-like clauses, suggest clearer alternatives, improve templates, tailor content to different users, and ultimately make contracts more useful, usable, and aligned with real-world action.

Our examples show that the spell has already begun to break, with the help of visuals, plain language, and emerging design patterns. GenAI can now help us merge and scale these approaches and make contracts easier to create, manage, and act upon. What once relied on inherited formulas can now be reimagined—and redesigned—with the help of AI.

Shifting the focus from legal writing to meaningful communication allows us to see contracts as tools that support collaboration and goal-reaching. With the help of GenAI and thoughtful design, we can begin to rewrite—not just the words, but the role of contracts in business and society.

The time for legal writing in contracts is over—it's time to break the spell!

References

Adams K (2008) Dysfunctional drafting. National Law J 8 Sep

Adams KA (2009) Retooling your contract process for the downturn. New York Law J 19 Feb. https://www.adamsdrafting.com/wp-content/uploads/2013/11/nylj-retooling.pdf. Accessed 4 Mar 2025

Adams K (2011) Using visualizations in contracts. Adams on Contract Drafting, 7 Nov. https://www.adamsdrafting.com/using-visualizations-in-contracts/. Accessed 22 Apr 2025

Adams K (2013a) At companies, who calls the shots about template contracts? Adams on contract drafting, 29 Jan. http://www.adamsdrafting.com/at-companies-who-calls-the-shots-about-template-contracts/. Accessed 4 Mar 2025

Adams K (2013b) Someone else takes on "tested" contract language. Adams on Contract Drafting, 8 Jun. http://www.adamsdrafting.com/someone-else-takes-on-tested-contract-language/. Accessed 4 Mar 2025

Adams K (2013c) A suggestion to those organizing the upcoming legal design jam. Adams on Contract Drafting, 23 Sep. https://www.adamsdrafting.com/a-suggestion-to-those-organizing-the-upcoming-legal-design-jam/. Accessed 22 Apr 2025

Adams KA, Allen T (2012) The illusion of quality in contract drafting. New York Law J 248(11). https://www.adamsdrafting.com/wp-content/uploads/2014/05/Illusion-of-Quality-NYLJ.pdf. Accessed 4 Mar 2025

Artificial Lawyer (2024) Spellbook launches associate: "first full-fledged" legal AI agent. 22 Aug. https://www.artificiallawyer.com/2024/08/22/spellbook-launches-associate-first-full-fledged-legal-ai-agent/. Accessed 23 Apr 2025

Autto H, Haapio H, Nuottila J (2024) Contracts rethought and redesigned: a new era with AI. Int J Commerce Contracting 8(1–2):7–34

Barton TD (2012) Collaborative contracting as preventive/proactive law. In: Berger-Walliser G, Østergaard K (eds) Proactive law in a business environment. DJOF Publishing, Copenhagen

Barton T, Berger-Walliser G, Haapio H (2011) Visualization: seeing contracts for what they are, and what they could become. In: Henschel RF (ed) Proceedings of the 2011 IACCM academic symposium for contract and commercial management. The International Association for Contract and Commercial Management, Ridgefield (CT)

BearingPoint (2024) Legacy—the situation you are in, because of the history you have. White paper. https://www.bearingpoint.com/files/BearingPoint-Legacy-Whitepaper.pdf. Accessed 20 Apr 2025

Berger-Walliser G, Barton TD, Haapio H (2017) From visualization to legal design: a collaborative and creative process. Am Bus Law J 54(2):347–392

Berger-Walliser G, Bird RC, Haapio H (2011) Promoting business success through contract visualization. The J Law Business Ethics 17:55–75

Blasie M (2024) Plain language surges among governments. The Clarity J 89:24–29

Botes M (2025) AI-generated comics: enhancing public engagement and ethical awareness in bioethics. In: Corrales Compagnucci M, Haapio H, Fenwick M (eds) Generative AI, contracts, law and design. Springer, Singapore

Brunschwig CR (2014) On visual law: visual legal communication practices and their scholarly exploration. In: Schweighofer E, Handstanger M, Hoffmann H, Kummer F, Primosch E, Schefbeck G, Withalm G (eds) Zeichen und Zauber des Rechts—Festschrift für Friedrich Lachmayer. Editions Weblaw, Bern. https://www.ius.uzh.ch/dam/jcr:00000000-0b7f-a3b8-ffff-ffffe92cd50/ColetteRBrunschwigOnVisualLaw2014.pdf. Accessed 23 Apr 2025

Brunschwig CR (2021) Visual law and legal design: questions and tentative answers. In: Schweighofer E, Kummer F, Saarenpää A, Eder S, Hanke P (eds) Cybergovernance. Proceedings of the 24th international legal informatics symposium IRIS 2021. Editions Weblaw, Bern

Burge ME (2010) Who wants to be a muggle? The diminished legitimacy of law as magic. In: Thomas JE, Snyder FG (eds) The law and Harry Potter. Carolina Academic Press, Durham (NC)

Butler M (2024) Researchers explore why legal documents use convoluted language. Courthouse News Service, 19 Aug. https://www.courthousenews.com/researchers-explore-why-legal-documents-use-convoluted-language/. Accessed 4 Mar 2025

Clack CD (2018) Smart contract templates: legal semantics and code validation. J Digital Banking 2(4):338–352

Clack CD, Bakshi VA, Braine L (2017) Smart contract templates: foundations, design landscape and research directions, vol 3. https://arxiv.org/abs/1608.00771. Accessed 22 Apr 2025

Corrales M, Fenwick M, Haapio H (2019) Digital technologies, legal design and the future of the legal profession. In: Corrales M, Fenwick M, Haapio H (eds) Legal tech, smart contracts and blockchain. Perspectives in law, business and innovation. Springer, Singapore

Corrales Compagnucci M, Fenwick M, Haapio H (2022a) Digital technology, future lawyers and the computable contract designer of tomorrow. In: Corrales Compagnucci M, Haapio H, Fenwick M (eds) Research handbook on contract design. Edward Elgar Publishing, Cheltenham

Corrales Compagnucci M, Haapio H, Fenwick M (eds) (2022b) Research handbook on contract design. Edward Elgar Publishing, Cheltenham

Corrales Compagnucci M, Haapio H, Hagan M, Doherty M (eds) (2021) Legal design. integrating business, design and legal thinking with technology. Edward Elgar Publishing, Cheltenham

Cummins T (2003) Contracting as a strategic competence. International Association for Contract and Commercial Management IACCM. https://www.worldcc.com/Portals/IACCM/resources/files/contracting.pdf. Accessed 13 May 2025

DiMatteo L, Siedel G, Haapio H (2012) Strategic contracting: examining the business-legal interface. In: Berger-Walliser G, Østergaard K (eds) Proactive law in a business environment. DJØF Publishing, Copenhagen

Etzkorn IA (n.d.) Ten commandments of simplification. Center for Plain Language. Archived on 13 Oct 2013 at: https://web.archive.org/web/20131013040154/centerforplainlanguage.org/about-plain-language/ten-commandments-of-simplification/. Accessed 13 May 2025

European Working Group for Responsible and Sustainable Supply Chains (2024) Zero draft for consultation: the European model clauses (EMCs) for responsible and sustainable supply chains. https://www.responsiblecontracting.org/_files/ugd/fcee10_538d4de3351d4b699cd1c47e81ba8f22.pdf. Accessed 13 May 2025

Felsenfeld C, Siegel AM (1981) Writing contracts in plain english. West Publishing, St Paul (MN)

Finnish Broadcasting Company (Yle) (2016) Ylen aamu-TV, Nettipalvelujen sekavat käyttöehdot. Yle Areena, 7 Nov. https://areena.yle.fi/1-3807740. Accessed 22 Apr 2025

Greenberg LJ (2025) I asked several AI tools to draft a contract from a partnership deck. LinkedIn, 9 Apr. https://www.linkedin.com/posts/laurajeffordsgreenberg_i-asked-several-ai-tools-to-draft-a-contract-activity-7315674849115320320-giVi. Accessed 22 Apr 2025

Gulati M, Scott R (2013) The three and a half minute transaction: boilerplate and the limits of contract design. University of Chicago Press, Chicago (IL)

Haapio H (1998) Quality improvement through proactive contracting: contracts are too important to be left to lawyers! In: ASQ's 52nd annual quality congress proceedings, American Society for Quality, 4–6 May, Philadelphia (PA)

Haapio H (2006) Business success and problem prevention through proactive contracting. In: Wahlgren P (ed) A proactive approach. Scandinavian studies in law, vol 49. Stockholm Institute for Scandinavian Law, Stockholm

Haapio H (2011) Contract clarity through visualization—preliminary observations and experiments. In: Banissi E, Bertschi S, Burkhard R, Cvek U, Eppler M, Forsell C, Grinstein G, Johansson J, Kenderdine S, Marchese FT, Maple C, Trutschl M, Sarfraz M, Stuart L, Ursyn A, Wyeld TG (eds) Information visualization: visualization, biomedical visualization, visualization on built and rural environments and geometric modelling and imaging. Proceedings of the 15th international conference on information visualisation, IV2011, 13–15 Jul, London. IEEE Computer Society, Los Alamitos (CA)

Haapio H (2013a) Next generation contracts: a paradigm shift. Lexpert, Helsinki

Haapio H (2013b) Designing readable contracts: goodbye to legal writing—welcome to information design and visualization. In: Schweighofer E, Kummer F, Hötzendorfer W (eds) Abstraction and application. Proceedings of 16th international legal informatics symposium IRIS 2013. Österreichische Computer Gesellschaft, Vienna

Haapio H (2013c) Visualising contracts for better business. In: Svantesson DJB, Greenstein S (eds) Internationalisation of law in the digital information society. Nordic yearbook of law and informatics 2010–2012. Ex Tuto Publishing, Copenhagen

Haapio H (2016) Contract visualization: the trajectory. Lexpert Ltd. https://www.lexpert.com/wp-content/uploads/2016/02/Contract-Visualization-Trajectory-2016.jpg. Accessed 23 Apr 2025

Haapio H (2020) Transforming contract creation: goodbye to legal writing—revisited. In: Schweighofer E, Hötzendorfer W, Kummer F, Saarenpää A (eds) Responsible digitalization. Proceedings of the 23rd international legal informatics symposium IRIS 2020. Editions Weblaw, Bern

Haapio H (2022) Visualisation in contract education and practice. The first 25 years. In: Allbon E, Perry-Kessaris A (eds) Design in legal education. Emerging legal education series. Routledge, New York (NY)

Haapio H, Siedel GJ (2013) A short guide to contract risk. Gower Publishing, Farnham

Haapio H, Barton TD (2018) Business-friendly contracting: how simplification and visualization can help bring it to practice. In: Jacob K, Schindler D, Strathausen R (eds) Liquid legal. Management for professionals. Springer, Cham

Haapio H, Berger-Walliser G (2025) From concept to practice: a snapshot of proactive law after 25 years. TalTech J Europ Stud 15(1):3–8

Haapio H, Berger-Walliser G, Walliser B, Rekola K (2012) Time for a visual turn in contracting? J Contract Managem 10:49–57

Haapio H, Haavisto V (2005) Sopimusosaaminen: tulevaisuuden kilpailutekijä ja strateginen voimavara. [Contracting Capabilities: Emerging Source of Competitive Advantage and a Strategic Resource]. Yritystalous—Leader's Magazine 2/2005:7–15

Haapio H, Hagan M (2016) Design patterns for contracts. In: Schweighofer E, Kummer F, Hötzendorfer, Borges G (eds) Networks. Proceedings of the 19th international legal informatics symposium IRIS 2016. Österreichische Computer Gesellschaft, Vienna

Haapio H, Ketola A (forthcoming a) From rhetoric to action: the transformative power of AI, proactive law and legal design. In: Dan S, Mäntylä N, Fountain JE (eds) Artificial intelligence and power in government. Palgrave Macmillan

Haapio H, Ketola A (forthcoming b) Sustainability: from aspirations and jargon to reality. In: Ducato R, Strowel A, Marique E (eds) LDR 2024 proceedings/commentary to the declaration of EU digital rights and principles

Haapio H, Linna DW Jr (2020) Contract quality and AI: garbage in, garbage out? Contracting Excellence J 31 Aug. https://www.worldcc.com/Resources/Content-Hub/View/ArticleID/10897. Accessed 22 Apr 2025

Haapio H, Passera S (2013) Visual law: what lawyers can learn from information designers. VoxPopuLII Blog, 15 May. Cornell University Law School. https://blog.law.cornell.edu/voxpop/2013/05/15/visual-law-what-lawyers-need-to-learn-from-information-designers/. Accessed 4 Mar 2025

Haapio H, Passera S (2021) Contracts as interfaces: visual representation patterns in contract design. In: Katz DM, Dolin R, Bommarito MJ (eds) Legal informatics. Cambridge University Press, Cambridge

Haapio H, Plewe DA, de Rooy R (2017) Contract continuum: from text to images, comics and code. In: Schweighofer E, Kummer F, Hötzendorfer W, Sorge C (eds) Trends and communities of legal informatics. Proceedings of the 20th international legal informatics symposium IRIS 2017. Österreichische Computer Gesellschaft, Vienna

Haavisto V (2006) Contracting in networks. In: Wahlgren P (ed) A proactive approach. Scandinavian studies in law, vol 49. Stockholm Institute for Scandinavian Law, Stockholm

Hazard J, Haapio H (2017) Wise contracts: smart contracts that work for people and machines. In: Schweighofer E, Kummer F, Hötzendorfer W, Sorge C (eds) Trends and communities of legal informatics. Proceedings of the 20th international legal informatics symposium IRIS 2017. Österreichische Computer Gesellschaft, Vienna

Johnson LD (2015) Say the magic word: a rhetorical analysis of contract drafting choices. Syracuse Law Rev 65:451–490

Juro (2024) Visual contracts: a modern approach to legal agreements. 29 Jan. https://juro.com/learn/visual-contracts. Accessed 23 Apr 2025

Ketola A, Haapio H, de Rooy R (forthcoming) Chattable contracts: AI-driven access to justice. In: Palmirani M (ed) Legal design: teoria, modelli, pratica. Aracne. Pre-publication version presented at the JURIX Workshop on AI and access to justice, 18 Dec 2023. https://drive.google.com/file/d/1k4tyhjYS80vuj2655run69DxgUL1OsCm. Accessed 26 Mar 2025

Love B (2019) Can contracts use pictures instead of words? Visuals and plain language make an adversarial process more constructive. Financial Times 23 Oct. http://www.ft.com/content/032ddcb0-e6b1-11e9-b8e0-026e07cbe5b4. Accessed 22 Apr 2025

Malhotra D (2012) Great deal, terrible contract: the case for negotiator involvement in the contracting phase. In: Goldman BM, Shapiro DL (eds) The psychology of negotiations in the 21st century workplace. New challenges and new solutions. Routledge, New York (NY)

Martínez E, Mollica F, Gibson E (2024) Even laypeople use legalese. Proc Nat Acad Sci (PNAS) 121(35):e2405564121. https://doi.org/10.1073/pnas.2405564121. Accessed 4 Mar 2025

Mellinkoff D (1963) The language of the law. Little, Brown & Co, Boston (MA)

Mitchell JA (2015) Putting some product into work-product: corporate lawyers learning from designers. Berkeley Business Law J 12:1–44

Mitchell JA (2018) Whiteboard and black-letter: visual communication in commercial contracts. Univer Pennsylvania J Business Law 20(4):815–862

Passera S (2017) Beyond the wall of contract text: visualizing contracts to foster understanding and collaboration within and across organizations. Aalto University, Helsinki

Passera S, Haapio H (2011) Facilitating collaboration through contract visualization and modularization. In: Dittmar A, Forbrig P (eds) Designing collaborative activities. ECCE 2011 European conference on cognitive ergonomics 2011—The 29th annual conference of the European association on cognitive ergonomics, Rostock, Germany, 24–26 August 2011. Universität Rostock, Rostock

Passera S, Haapio H, Curtotti M (2014) Making the meaning of contracts visible—automating contract visualization. In: Schweighofer E, Kummer F, Hötzendorfer W (eds) Transparency. Proceedings of the 17th international legal informatics symposium IRIS 2014. Österreichische Computer Gesellschaft, Vienna

Plain Writing Act of 2010, Public Law 111–274, 124 Stat. 2861, 13 Oct 2010

Puiu T (2024) Why legal documents sound like magic spells: power over clarity. ZME Science, 22 Aug. https://www.zmescience.com/science/news-science/why-legal-documents-sound-like-magic-spells-power-over-clarity/. Accessed 4 Mar 2025

Rekola K, Haapio H (2009) Industrial services and service contracts: a proactive approach. The Federation of Finnish Technology Industries, Helsinki

Rodell F (1936) Goodbye to law reviews. Virginia Law Rev 23:38–45

Rodell F (1962) Goodbye to law reviews—revisited. Virginia Law Rev 48:279–290

Rowling JK (1997) Harry Potter and the philosopher's stone. Bloomsbury, London

Salo-Lahti M, Haapio H (2024) Possibility-driven design and responsible use of AI for sustainability. In: Ducato R, Strowel A, Marique E (eds) Design(s) for law. Ledizioni, Milan

Saunders (2024) How AI is removing legal obstacles that slow down business. Financial Times, 17 Oct. https://www.ft.com/content/6c251704-a17b-43be-b65d-18f3b2f26fb5. Accessed 4 Mar 2025

Schreyögg G, Sydow J, Holtmann P (2011) How history matters in organisations: the case of path dependence. Managem Organizat History 6(1):81–100. http://www.wiwiss.fu-berlin.de/forschung/pfadkolleg/downloads/paper/history_matters.pdf. Accessed 4 Mar 2025

Spellbook (2025a) OpenAI's spellbook: optimize legal work with AI. 10 Apr. https://www.spellbook.legal/learn/optimize-legal-work-with-ai. Accessed 23 Apr 2025
Spellbook (2025b) We help lawyers do more of the work they love. https://www.spellbook.legal/about. Accessed 23 Apr 2025
Stathis G, Trantas A, Biagioni G, de Graaf KA, Adriaanse J, van den Herik J (2024) Designing an intelligent contract with communications and risk data. SN Comput Sci 5:709. https://doi.org/10.1007/s42979-024-03021-x. Accessed 13 May 2025
Stevenson S (2024) Introducing spellbook: AI legal assistant for lawyers. Spellbook. https://www.spellbook.legal/blog/spellbook-associate. Accessed 23 Apr 2025
Tiersma PM (1999) Legal language. University of Chicago Press, Chicago
Tobak S (2011) Facebook's Mark Zuckerberg—insights for entrepreneurs. CBS News MoneyWatch, 31 Oct. https://www.cbsnews.com/news/facebooks-mark-zuckerberg-insights-for-entrepreneurs/. Accessed 4 Mar 2025
Toivonen N, Ketola A, Haapio H (2025) Transforming norms: legal design, plain language and AI for personalized law. J Ethics Legal Technol 7(1):159–181, Special Issue "Through Norms, beyond Norms: The Construct Socio-digital World"
Triantis GG (2013) Improving contract quality: modularity, technology, and innovation in contract design. Stanford J Law Business Finan 18(2):177–214
Uniform Commercial Code, Section 2-316. Legal Information Institute, Cornell Law School. https://www.law.cornell.edu/ucc/2/2-316. Accessed 23 Apr 2025
Wilkinson A (2025) I recently hired a lawyer to give me an opinion on a personal corporate structure question, vol 10. https://x.com/awilkinson/status/1874865457469235287. Accessed 4 Mar 2025
Willey R, Tran T, Hinkle L, Matthews A (2025) Visual contracts in U.S. courts. Drake Law Rev 72(1):73–158
Williams C (2022) The impact of plain language on legal english in the United Kingdom. Routledge, New York and London
Wordsmith (2025) Wordsmith legal AI. https://www.wordsmith.ai/. Accessed 23 Apr 2025
WorldCC Foundation, Passera S, Haapio H (n.d.) Contract design pattern library. https://contract-design.worldcc.foundation/. Accessed 9 Apr 2025
WorldCC (2024a) Most negotiated terms 2024: including exploration of the distinctions between big businesses and SMEs. https://info.worldcc.com/mnt-2024. Accessed 22 Apr 2025
WorldCC (2024b) The purpose of a contract: how clarity of purpose is required to measure contract quality and effectiveness. https://info.worldcc.com/purpose-of-contracts. Accessed 22 Apr 2025

Contracting: Is Generative AI Really Making a Difference?

Tim Cummins and Sally Guyer

Abstract Artificial Intelligence is not new and has been evident in the contracting process for a decade or more. But this was largely an additional functionality embedded in Contract Lifecycle Management (CLM) systems, initially operating entirely within an organization's own systems. While Cloud computing introduced a new dimension, it did not take data into the public domain. When Generative AI (GenAI) burst onto the scene in 2022, it represented a revolutionary change. Suddenly, from being a hidden presence within enterprise software, it was freely available on laptops and mobile devices. This was accompanied by the typical reaction to technological innovationa mix of excitement, fear, skepticism and wild over-optimism. While there is no question that GenAI will have significant impact on contracting, this chapter explores the impact to date and anticipates the way that this will evolve.

Keywords Blockchain · Digital · Generative AI · Smart contracts

T. Cummins (✉)
Commerce and Contract Management Institute, World Commerce and Contracting, Virginia, USA
e-mail: tcummins@worldcc.com

School of Law, University of Leeds, Leeds, United Kingdom

S. Guyer
World Commerce and Contracting, WorldCC Foundation, Washington DC, USA
e-mail: sguyer@worldcc.com

Durham University Business School, Durham, Australia

© The Author(s), under exclusive license to Springer Nature Singapore Pte Ltd. 2025
M. Corrales Compagnucci et al. (eds.), *Generative AI, Contracts, Law and Design*,
Perspectives in Law, Business and Innovation,
https://doi.org/10.1007/978-981-95-2058-9_3

1 Introduction: The Situation (and the Problem) Today

"Modern economies are held together by innumerable contracts."[1] Yet in spite of their ubiquity and our dependence on them, it is universally recognized that contracts today consistently fall short in their underlying purpose, whether as effective instruments of control or in their delivery of economic value.[2] The primary reason for the shortfall is the innate complexity of their design, structure and content. This limits their use as practical business instruments, both at the level of each individual contract and especially in the context of a contracts' portfolio.

Efforts to overcome this complexity have been constrained by the enormity of the task.[3] It has in general proved impossible to achieve the scale of consensus needed to develop and adopt international and industry norms and standards. In consequence, business executives tend to accept the limitations of contracts, either ignoring the limits to their effectiveness, or investing in costly control mechanisms which include both headcount and technology. Like the contracts themselves, the true "cost of contracting" is obscure, but has on average been estimated to equate to more than 8% of an organization's annual revenue.[4]

It is this situation that AI has the potential to remedy, providing us with tools that operate beyond the boundaries and constraints of human capability.

2 The Business Opportunity

The incorporation of AI into contract and commercial management represents an opportunity to re-imagine the purpose and form of contracts and the value that can be delivered through an integrated contracting process. AI tools will centralize contract data, providing real-time intelligence, and enable the alignment of contract offerings and obligations with overall business objectives. Through this transformation, contract management becomes a source of dynamic assessments of business capability, resilience, and proactive decision-making that respond to market and operational risks and opportunities.

However, many of these benefits relate to AI capabilities embedded within internal applications, such as Contract Lifecycle Management (CLM) systems, rather than

---

[1] The Royal Swedish Academy of Sciences (2016).

[2] IACCM (2017), WorldCC (2024b).

[3] For example, projects such as "One NDA" have failed to deliver an accepted standard for even this most basic of agreements. Other efforts to create industry standards (for example, in Construction) have also met with rival approaches and examples such as the CISG (United Nations Convention on Contracts for the International Sale of Goods) are typically ignored or excluded by the corporate sector.

[4] IACCM (2015), WorldCC (2023b). This "cost" is not only the expense associated with the production and management of the contract, but also the value erosion that occurs from poor performance—for example, use of sub-optimal contract terms, failure to institute effective change management provisions, disagreements over scope.

deployment and use of Generative AI. It may be helpful to briefly summarize these use cases, since in some cases GenAI will build from them.

3 Examples of AI Use in Internal Systems

AI has proved effective in enhancing both contract creation and post-signature management. For example, AI tools within a CLM system automatically review contracts for compliance with internal policies and regulatory requirements, flagging potential risks or deviations. Similarly, AI helps generate standard contract clauses, drawing from pre-approved clause libraries, templates and historical data, ensuring consistency and reducing drafting errors. World Commerce and Contracting (WorldCC) research has identified that approximately 8% of large corporations are using it for this purpose.[5]

Looking at post-award, a key application of AI is in obligation extraction and contract performance tracking. AI-driven analytics monitor contract execution against key performance indicators (KPIs), automatically alerting stakeholders when a contract term is about to be breached or when a milestone or obligation is missed. This proactive approach enables timely interventions and reduces the risk of disputes or costly renegotiations.

While these AI features have streamlined processes and reduced inefficiencies, they remain primarily reactive and limited by the data available within the organization's own systems. GenAI has the potential to build on these developments and revolutionize contracting even further by providing far more dynamic and flexible tools.[6]

4 Generative AI and Contracting: Real-World Uses

The release of GenAI in 2022 brought the possibility of creating content, summarizing information, and even drafting contracts, using vast amounts of publicly available data. This is enabling thinking to evolve beyond simply improving contract management processes and allowing a fundamental rethink into how contracts are generated and understood.

However, these potential uses also rapidly revealed constraints. For example, an obvious question related to drafting would be to understand market norms. While there are large bodies of contracts available, they are not necessarily representative of negotiated norms and not reflective of all jurisdictions or industries. Hence, we are constrained by the quality of the data that is readily accessible.

---

[5] WorldCC (2023a).

[6] See WorldCC (2024a).

However, Generative AI is relatively good at producing first drafts of contracts that are tailored to the specific needs of a particular negotiation or business relationship. For instance, it can quickly generate complex contract structures, aligning terms to industry norms or specific regulatory requirements, drawing on a far wider pool of data than any single organization might hold internally.

A practical example is the use of GenAI to support creation of draft contracts for international trade agreements. By pulling from existing legal frameworks, regulations, and contract clauses used in similar agreements, GenAI can draft contract terms that are not only relevant but also optimized for cross-border compliance, which would otherwise require extensive manual research and drafting. Similarly, there are already use cases in banking and finance, such as the derivatives market.[7]

GenAI is assisting in reviewing contracts, and can provide feedback on risks, redundancies, or gaps that take human reviewers far longer to identify. For example, it can compare terms with industry benchmarks to advise whether a company is facing or requesting terms that sit outside market norms.

Negotiation support is another area where GenAI is demonstrating its capabilities. Early users found it helpful with developing negotiation strategies and various experiments have confirmed potential benefits in terms of speed and value achieved.[8] By analyzing previous negotiations and contract data, GenAI can suggest counteroffers or highlight clauses that are likely to cause friction. This helps organizations enter negotiations better prepared, focusing on the approaches and key terms that matter most to their business objectives.

However, the adoption of GenAI in these roles remains constrained due to concerns around security, data privacy, and the integrity of the information it generates.[9] As a result, many organizations are cautious about integrating these tools directly into contracting processes, particularly when it comes to sharing sensitive or proprietary information with public AI models.

5 Secure, Private Versions of Generative AI

In response to these concerns, organizations are increasingly developing private, secure versions of GenAI to leverage its benefits without exposing sensitive data to public AI models. These customized versions are designed to operate within a company's internal ecosystem, ensuring that all data remains secure and confidential.[10]

[7] International Swaps and Derivatives Association (2024).

[8] For example, Cummins and Jensen (2024).

[9] WorldCC (2024a).

[10] Greenstein et al. (2024).

One of the main benefits of these private GenAI systems is that they can be trained on proprietary contract data, ensuring that the outputs align with the organization's specific needs, policies, and legal standards. For example, a large corporation might develop an in-house GenAI tool that is fed with all historical contracts, negotiation outcomes, and performance data, enabling it to generate highly relevant contract drafts tailored to the company's existing practices and risk appetite. It might include selected external data or data feeds to augment this content—for example, industry-specific nuances and jurisdictional differences. By keeping the system internal, companies avoid the risk of their sensitive contract terms or business strategies being used to train public models, which could inadvertently expose valuable competitive information.

Private GenAI tools can incorporate security features, such as encryption and access controls, that meet the strict compliance requirements of regulated industries like finance, healthcare, and government contracting. They are also able to customize the AI's learning algorithms, so that it continuously evolves based on internal feedback loops and becomes increasingly adept at understanding the specific needs and preferences of the organization.

6 Future Potential: Generative AI and Smart Contracts

There are emerging interfaces between GenAI and smart contracts, and the convergence of these technologies opens up exciting possibilities for automating and enhancing contract creation, execution, and enforcement, creating opportunities to re-imagine contracts in a digital form.

Smart contracts are self-executing contracts with the terms of the agreement directly written into code. They reside on blockchain platforms, enabling decentralized, fully automated transactions when predefined conditions are met. They offer transparency, security, and efficiency. However, smart contracts have traditionally been limited in scope due to their reliance on explicit, predefined conditions, often written in simple logic that is difficult to adapt to more complex commercial agreements. This is where GenAI can play a role.

- GenAI can automatically generate the legal language or clauses needed for smart contracts, helping translate complex contractual terms into executable code. This can reduce the time and expertise needed to create smart contracts, expanding their use beyond simple financial transactions to more sophisticated commercial agreements.
- GenAI can analyze existing smart contracts and suggest improvements. For example, it could help ensure that terms are clear and enforceable, reducing the risk of disputes caused by ambiguities or gaps in the logic. This makes smart contracts more adaptable to complex business arrangements.
- GenAI could be used alongside traditional Contract Lifecycle Management (CLM) systems, enabling smart contracts to be integrated into broader business

processes. For example, GenAI could help create hybrid contracts that contain both coded elements (smart contract terms) and traditional language-based terms, supporting interoperability between digital and traditional contracting systems.

7 Links to Blockchain Technology

The combination of blockchain's immutable ledger and GenAI's ability to process vast amounts of contract data opens up possibilities that extend beyond smart contracts. For example, blockchain technology is a platform which ensures that all parties have access to the same version of a contract. GenAI could assist by monitoring contract performance and suggesting real-time updates or amendments as business conditions evolve. Let's say a delivery deadline is missed, GenAI could recommend new terms or renegotiate clauses automatically.

The integration of GenAI with blockchain could also streamline dispute resolution by automatically generating documentation based on a review of the entire blockchain ledger, identifying areas of non-compliance or ambiguity, and provide suggestions for resolving the issue. This could streamline what is traditionally a complex and costly legal process.

In principle, the decentralized and tamper-proof nature of blockchain should provide inherent trust in the execution of contracts and, paired with GenAI, create an intelligent, transparent contract system where terms are not only securely stored and executed but also dynamically generated and updated in line with evolving needs and conditions.[11]

8 Moving Toward Digital Contracts

As previously mentioned, the integration of GenAI and blockchain-based smart contracts is leading us toward a future where digital contracts could become the norm, replacing traditional paper-based or document-based agreements, along with their inherent limitations.

Traditional contracts are static documents which struggle to reflect or support the dynamic nature of modern business relationships. Once a contract is signed, it becomes challenging to adapt terms without renegotiation, even if forward-thinking organizations increasingly embed governance frameworks that reduce the likely extent of friction this often involves. GenAI, in combination with smart contracts, offers a solution to this problem by enabling contracts to be more flexible and adaptive, even generating or proposing new terms or modifying existing clauses based on real-time performance data, market conditions, or evolving business needs.

[11] See, e.g., Nguyen et al. (2024).

As is made clear in much of the referenced research undertaken by WorldCC, one of the biggest limitations of traditional contracts is their complexity, particularly when managing portfolios of contracts across multiple jurisdictions, regulatory environments, or business units. GenAI can manage and optimize this complexity by automatically adjusting clauses based on legal and regulatory changes, while smart contracts provide an automated framework to ensure these changes are implemented without the need for manual intervention.

This move to digital contracts brings greater efficiency in all aspects of contract execution and will have a dramatic impact on the quality of contract performance. WorldCC benchmarks show that, on average, 29% of an organization's workforce is in some way involved in contract management, yet finds it difficult to access or understand the right agreement. Furthermore, in large organizations, contract-related data is stored in an average of 24 different systems, with highly variable interfaces between them. This inevitably leads to errors and delays which digitization could eliminate or reduce. GenAI can support this by generating contracts that are more closely aligned with actual business processes, reducing the time spent on negotiation and ensuring smoother execution.

A significant amount of time is today spent on human oversight to ensure compliance with terms. However, digital contracts—especially when supported by GenAI—offer continuous monitoring and real-time risk mitigation. GenAI can identify areas where performance is slipping, suggest remedial actions, and in the case of smart contracts, enforce those actions automatically.

The ability of GenAI and smart contracts to handle and analyze large volumes of data and transactions means that digital contracting is not only scalable, but also provides insights that are beyond realistic human capabilities. For example, one unpublished study shows how a government agency was able to review 7,500 agreements and identify the frequency of contract amendments and their impact on risk and price, revealing potential savings equivalent to almost 6% of current spend. Traditional contract management systems often struggle to keep up with the speed and complexity of modern commerce. With GenAI's ability to analyze data at scale and blockchain's ability to handle decentralized transactions, digital contracts can scale to meet the needs of large multinational organizations.

9 Understanding and Overcoming the Barriers

Any change generates questions, objections and resistance. GenAI is certainly no exception, and this chapter has highlighted the issues around security, privacy and accuracy. Beyond this, as we explore the possible move towards digital contracts, there are questions around environmental impacts and, of course, the threat to current employment. We also have to recognize the dependency on human intelligence and the ways that this may impact adoption and use.

The convergence of AI and blockchain raises valid ESG concerns which must be addressed since businesses are increasingly held accountable for their environmental impact, social responsibility, and corporate governance practices. Looking first at the environmental question, blockchain technology, particularly public blockchains like Bitcoin and Ethereum, has faced heavy criticism for its high energy consumption. AI raises similar concerns. However, newer blockchain technologies are moving toward more energy-efficient mechanisms which significantly reduce the environmental footprint, but organizations with strong ESG commitments may still be reluctant to adopt combined AI / blockchain solutions.

With regard to data privacy and security, GenAI relies on large datasets to train its models. If GenAI is used in contract generation or analysis, particularly with sensitive contract data, organizations will need to ensure compliance with privacy laws like GDPR in Europe or CCPA. In this context, both blockchain and AI may raise concerns. For example, blockchain may offer security and immutability, but it also presents challenges related to data storage and governance. Once data is recorded on a blockchain, it becomes difficult or impossible to alter, which can conflict with data protection regulations that require the ability to delete personal data upon request (the "right to be forgotten").

There are also concerns around the social impacts of adopting high-tech solutions like AI and blockchain, particularly around job displacement and equitable access. As contracting processes become increasingly automated, there is a risk that traditional roles—such as contract managers, legal advisors, and procurement specialists—could become less relevant, leading to workforce disruption. In addition, the adoption of blockchain and AI at scale may disadvantage smaller businesses or organizations in regions with limited access to advanced technology infrastructure. This could add to existing inequalities in global business environments, raising governance issues for organizations that have committed to inclusive practices.

Hence the move toward digital contracts will depend upon secure, adaptable, and flexible systems. Private versions of GenAI will play a critical role in ensuring that digital contracts can be generated, managed, and updated securely within an organization's own ecosystem, creating confidence on the issues of privacy and security.

Therefore, while acknowledging that the convergence of Generative AI and blockchain represents a highly likely future for contracting, it is by no means the only possible direction. Technological, regulatory, and ethical concerns could influence or even limit the convergence needed for a digital future.

An alternative to the AI and blockchain solution is a future where AI remains focused on supplementing traditional contracting systems without extensive integration with blockchain technology. In this scenario, GenAI would be used primarily within traditional Contract Lifecycle Management (CLM) systems, streamlining drafting, negotiation, and analysis, but contracts would remain largely document-based.

Here, smart contracts and blockchain would not necessarily become dominant, but AI would help create more flexible, dynamic versions of traditional contracts, improving efficiency and accuracy. For industries that are highly regulated or resistant to decentralized systems, this might be a more feasible and acceptable model.

Hybrid contracting systems, where businesses use a mix of traditional contracts and smart contracts is another possible model. In this scenario, AI would handle contract creation, risk management, and performance monitoring, while certain high-risk, high-stakes aspects of contracts (like financial settlements or compliance measures) might be executed using smart contracts. This approach would allow businesses to integrate blockchain and smart contracts where they are most useful, without overhauling the entire contract ecosystem.

10 Humans and AI: Competitors or Collaborators?

AI is already here, and we interact with it more than we realize. GenAI is different because its accessibility means that the interaction is more obvious and is often a matter of choice. The effectiveness and value of human interaction with GenAI is in many cases dependent on human actions and intelligence. For example, if we ask badly-worded or ambiguous questions, we are likely to receive sub-standard replies—very much like we would if talking with another human.

For a variety of reasons, some level of human oversight will remain integral to contracting processes. Organizations might adopt AI-assisted contracting, where humans collaborate with AI systems to generate and manage contracts, but the final decision-making and contract execution remain largely human-driven.

This model would mitigate the risks associated with full automation, especially in industries that rely heavily on negotiation and complex human relationships—such as healthcare, government contracts, and high-value professional services. In these fields, AI might assist with analysis, prediction and performance oversight, but contracts would still be executed through traditional means.

11 In Conclusion: Will GenAI Help Us Move Away from Traditional Contracts?

GenAI undoubtedly has the potential to move us away from traditional forms of contracts with all their limitations. The ability of GenAI to draft, analyze, and optimize contracts in real time introduces a much more dynamic, flexible, and intelligent approach to contract management. By allowing contracts to evolve in response to changing business conditions, digital contracts can become more aligned with real-world operations.

However, while there are hopeful signs and some positive use cases, the full abandonment of traditional contracts is unlikely in the near term, for several reasons:

- Many legal systems still require contracts to be written, signed, and stored in traditional formats. Moving to fully digital, AI-generated contracts would require significant regulatory changes, and industries like law, finance, and government are likely to adopt new methods cautiously.

- Businesses and legal professionals still place a great deal of trust in traditional contracts, which provide a familiar and proven framework for managing relationships and obligations. While AI can help draft and negotiate contracts more efficiently, the acceptance of fully AI-generated contracts by a range of critical stakeholders remains a major hurdle.
- High-value, complex, or sensitive agreements will continue to benefit from human judgment and negotiation. Contracts that involve nuanced relationships, bespoke terms, or intricate business considerations may always require a human touch to ensure all parties are aligned.

Ultimately, while GenAI is providing a vision of how we might move toward more dynamic, digital contracts, the transition will not be a wholesale replacement of traditional contracting methods. Organizations need to balance the efficiency and automation that AI offers with the legal, regulatory, and ethical considerations that ensure contracts remain fair, transparent, and sustainable. They will also need to train their staff in effective use of the technology, especially in areas such as prompting.

The future of contracting depends upon the effective intersection of the insights which come from AI-powered internal systems and the expanded potential of the outsights provided by Generative AI. AI tools embedded within internal systems are already proving effective in improving contract management processes, yet adoption is slow, largely because of the challenges associated with inaccurate data and fragmented processes. GenAI offers the potential to take contract creation, review, and negotiation to new levels of efficiency and effectiveness, but may be constrained or delayed by similar factors. Ultimately, the ability of GenAI to draft contracts, provide negotiation insights, and generate dynamic content will transform the way businesses approach contracting. The contracting process will evolve to become more intelligent, adaptive, and aligned with organizational goals, ultimately reducing complexity and enhancing the value that contracts deliver across industries.

References

Cummins T, Jensen K (2024) Friend or foe? AI and negotiation. Int J Commerce Contract 8(1–2):35–43. https://doi.org/10.1177/20555636241256852

Greenstein B, Light C, Likens S (2024) The path to generative AI value: setting the flywheel in motion. PwC. https://www.pwc.com/gx/en/issues/technology/path-to-generative-ai-value.html. Accessed 23 Sep 2024

IACCM (2015) Commercial excellence: ten pitfalls to avoid in contracting. International Association for Contract and Commercial Management. https://www.worldcc.com/portals/iaccm/Resources/3972_0_8414_10_pitfalls_to_avoid_in_contracting.pdf. Accessed 23 Sep 2024

IACCM (2017) The purpose of a contract: an IACCM research report. International Association for Contract and Commercial Management. https://www.worldcc.com/Portals/IACCM/resources/files/9876_j18069-iaccm-purpose-of-contract-a4-2017-11-14-v1-webready.pdf. Accessed 23 Sep 2024

International Swaps and Derivatives Association (2024) GenAI in the derivatives market: a future perspective. ISDA Future Leaders in Derivatives (IFLD). https://www.isda.org/a/PbwgE/GenAI-in-the-Derivatives-Market-A-Future-Perspective.pdf. Accessed 23 Sep 2024

Nguyen CT, Liu Y, Du H, Hoang DT, Niyato D, Nguyen DN, Mao S (2024) Generative AI-enabled blockchain networks: fundamentals, applications, and case study, vol 1. https://doi.org/10.48550/arXiv.2401.15625. Accessed 23 Sep 2024

The Royal Swedish Academy of Sciences (2016) Press release regarding the nobel prize in economics awarded to Oliver Hart and Bengt Holmström. https://www.nobelprize.org/prizes/economic-sciences/2016/press-release/. Accessed 23 Sep 2024

WorldCC (2023a) CCM: The journey to operational excellence—benchmark report 2023. World Commerce and Contracting. https://www.worldcc.com/Portals/IACCM/Reports/Benchmark-report-2023.pdf

WorldCC (2023b) The ROI of contracting excellence. World Commerce and Contracting. https://www.worldcc.com/portals/iaccm/Resources/11560_0_ROI-of-contracting-excellence.pdf. Accessed 23 Sep 2024

WorldCC (2024a) AI in contracting: from untapped revolution to emerging evolution. https://www.worldcc.com/Portals/IACCM/Reports/AI-in-Contracting.pdf. Accessed 23 Sep 2024

WorldCC (2024b) The purpose of contracts: how clarity of purpose is required to measure contract quality and effectiveness. World Commerce and Contracting. https://www.worldcc.com/Portals/IACCM/Reports/Purpose-of-Contracts.pdf. Accessed 23 Sep 2024

AI as a Financial Coach—Promoting Sustainable Financial Management with Generative AI

Marika Salo-Lahti, Mikko Ranta, Nina Toivonen, and Helena Haapio

Abstract In this chapter we will explore and analyze how generative AI tools designed with a human-centered approach can help companies with financial management and contribute to sustainable finance. The chapter begins with an introduction to the EU regulation related to sustainable finance, aiming to help achieve the objectives of the Green Deal. According to the Triple Bottom Line theory, the three parts of sustainability—environmental, social, and economical—are strongly interlinked. However, economic efficiency and sustainability are often perceived as conflicting goals. We will look at practical ways to reconcile the two perspectives. We will do this with the help of AI crew, a group of AI agents that are specialized in their specific fields. We will test and review how this crew can be used as a financial coach to create solutions for some of the key challenges in sustainable financial management. We will also consider the issue from the perspective of an example company, a European textile firm. The chapter concludes with a summary of our key findings and ideas for future research on AI, sustainable financial management and the law.

Keywords Financial management · Sustainability · Sustainable finance · Generative AI · AI agents · AI crew

---

M. Salo-Lahti (✉)
School of Accounting and Finance, Business Law, University of Vaasa, Vaasa, Finland
e-mail: marika.salo-lahti@uwasa.fi

M. Ranta
School of Accounting and Finance, Accounting, University of Vaasa, Vaasa, Finland
e-mail: mikko.ranta@uwasa.f

N. Toivonen
Faculty of Law, University of Helsinki, Helsinki, Finland
e-mail: nina.toivonen@helsinki.fi

H. Haapio
Institute: Lexpert Ltd, Helsinki, Finland
e-mail: helena.haapio@lexpert.com

© The Author(s), under exclusive license to Springer Nature Singapore Pte Ltd. 2025

M. Corrales Compagnucci et al. (eds.), *Generative AI, Contracts, Law and Design*, Perspectives in Law, Business and Innovation,
https://doi.org/10.1007/978-981-95-2058-9_4

1 Introduction

The European Green Deal poses ambitious goals that aim at climate-neutrality and a sustainable economy. Additional investments of about 700 billion euros annually are needed to achieve the green transition.[1] Despite the great importance of sustainable finance, there are still a number of challenges that hinder the flow of capital towards ESG (Environmental, Social, Governance) goals. The problems include lack of transparency and comparability.[2] The EU has recently introduced a wealth of new sustainability legislation in order to cure these problems. However, there are still many challenges related to its implementation. Investors may struggle to find important sustainability information, and companies may have difficulties complying with the new requirements. Many of the challenges in implementing sustainability regulations are largely due to the increasingly complex and tense operating environment that companies face during the green transition.

While navigating new sustainability obligations, companies must also manage their existing commitments and pursue profitable business operations. A company that is not financially sustainable surely cannot achieve other sustainability goals either. Although research indicates that green investments are often profitable,[3] their benefits are realized in the long term, while maintaining day-to-day profitability often requires quick-return investments. This creates a challenge for companies to commit to the necessary investments for the green transition. Especially for many micro, small, and medium-sized enterprises (SMEs)[4] choosing the risk of a long-term sustainability investment over a short-term gain can be a matter of survival. In practice, this may mean that a company is reluctant to renew its operations to be more environmentally friendly, if it simultaneously results in reduced production and turnover, and therefore a risk of insolvency. On the other hand, cutting costs by ignoring environmental regulations might boost profits temporarily but can lead to severe consequences like reputational damage and even legal action. Conversely, sustainability management can be seen as a cost center, where the immediate financial benefits are unclear. Given that SMEs represent more than 99% of all European businesses and play a crucial role in advancing the green transition, it is essential to address the tensions between financial and ecological sustainability that the majority of businesses face.[5]

---

[1] European Commission (2023a).

[2] OECD (2022), p. 2.

[3] Rahko (2023), p. 8, Gonçalves et al. (2023), p. 1, Ameer and Othman (2012).

[4] SMEs are defined in the EU recommendation 2003/361. For example, a medium-sized business has less than 250 employees, a turnover of 50 million euros or less, and a balance sheet equivalent to a maximum of 43 million euros. European Commission (2003), p. 39.

[5] European Commission (2022c). About the discussion, see also Kaave (2023), p. 2.

Recent developments in artificial intelligence (AI), sophisticated language models, and advanced reading tools offer possible solutions to address the uncertainties related to financial decision-making in the context of social and environmental sustainability. These technologies can potentially help businesses find meaningful information, compare it to their own data, and provide company-specific analysis. Further, they can simplify complex information, translate it into different languages and styles, and present it visually to facilitate communication and decision making.[6] One of the most recent developments include AI crews, collaborative working systems of multiple AI agents resembling an interdisciplinary team of experts. Unlike other AI tools, AI crews enable designing specific artificial intelligent experts that work together, making it possible to accomplish more complex tasks.[7] These tools hold thus interesting possibilities for providing help for businesses to address issues that have both financial, social, and environmental dimensions.

In our previous work, we have explored how AI can be used to help individuals in financial distress.[8] We have also studied how AI tools can help make sustainability information more actionable for its users, and how they can help companies meet their disclosure requirements.[9] In this chapter, we explore the capabilities, applications and tangible benefits of AI tools for businesses striving for both economic, social and ecological sustainability. Our exploration consists of three main parts. The first part focuses on setting the scene for AI facilitated sustainable financial management. We view the systemic-level tensions between economic, social and environmental interests and take a look at the regulatory tools promoting sustainable finance at EU level. In the second part we review existing research on LLMs to understand the current trends and technological possibilities with AI for financial management on tasks such as data analysis, risk assessment, and regulatory compliance. In the third part we build our own sustainable financial coach, or should we say a group of coaches, for our example textile company using the AI crew creation tools. This company, representative of companies in high sustainability risk sectors, provides an example of how AI can help address practical challenges related to tensions between financial, social and environmental sustainability. For the experiment, we use the OpenAI API and Python programming environment with the CrewAI library, which provides capabilities for creating teams of autonomous AI agents with specialized tasks.[10] We conclude our chapter with key insights and hypotheses for future research on AI, sustainable financial management and the law.

[6] See, e.g., Toivonen et al. (2024), Salo-Lahti et al. (2023), Salo-Lahti and Haapio (2024).

[7] CrewAI (2024).

[8] Toivonen et al. (2024). See also Toivonen et al. (2025) in this Book.

[9] Salo-Lahti et al. (2023), Salo-Lahti and Haapio (2024).

[10] CrewAI (2024).

2 Sustainable Financial Management

2.1 The Tension Between Profit-Making and Sustainability

In the past, the role of companies was to generate as much profit as possible. This shareholder-centric thinking has been inspired by Milton Friedman's idea according to which "there is one and only one social responsibility of business—to use its resources and engage in activities designed to increase its profits".[11] Even today, company law principles often define the purpose of a company as profit-making. While the issue of whether or not companies are meant *exclusively* to make profit is discussed as a shareholder vs stakeholder value debate, Porter and Kramer bring in a third aspect, shared value.[12] It means creating economic value in a way that also creates value for society. However, they explicitly state that shared value is not social responsibility, or sustainability. They come more as a side-product from profit-making.

Nowadays, the value chain that leads to profit-making has become longer. When aiming at profit-making, the interests of other stakeholders must be considered. This paradigm shift can also be called enlightened shareholder value, which is underlying, for instance, the UK Companies Act.[13] Section 172 of the Act defines the "duty to promote the success of the company." According to it, company directors must regard, among others, the interests of the company's employees; the need to foster the company's business relationships with suppliers, customers and others; and the impact of the company's operations on the community and the environment. Currently, it is no longer a question of whether other stakeholders and the environment should be taken into account—the new EU sustainability regulation *forces* companies to promote sustainability, which we will soon discuss further.

The Triple Bottom Line idea refers to the three dimensions of sustainability: environmental, social, and economic.[14] While these all are important, economic sustainability is a crucial prerequisite for environmental and social sustainability, and the three are meaningfully interlinked. While economic sustainability is needed to achieve the other sustainability goals, enhancing environmental sustainability can also contribute to economic sustainability, at least in the longer term. According to a Finnish study, industrial plants with environmental investments show significantly better economic performance. In addition to other metrics, investing in environmental protection produces an increase in turnover and labor productivity.[15] Similar results have been obtained with STOXX Europe 600 companies. Sustainability performance

[11] Friedman (1970).

[12] Porter and Kramer (2011), p. 4.

[13] UK Companies Act (2006), Explanatory Notes, note 325: This duty codifies the current law and enshrines in statute what is commonly referred to as the principle of "enlightened shareholder value."

[14] On Triple Bottom Line, see e.g. Elkington (2006).

[15] Rahko (2023), p. 8.

and economic performance have strong positive associations, channeled through profit margin and turnover.[16]

However, despite the shifting understanding of the purpose of a company and the increasing awareness of the benefits of green investments, there remains a tension between the idea of a business as a profit-generator and the new sustainability requirements. Systems theories provide frameworks through which it is possible to observe and explain this paradox. According to the theory of systems intelligence, for instance, the inherent human capability to adapt to different social environments can sometimes contribute to the development of systems that actually serve nobody's interests. In such systems people display behaviors they would change if they only could have a holistic understanding of the setting they are in. Hämäläinen and Saarinen call them *systems of holding back*, Meadows as *systemic traps* and Johnston as *polar fallacies*.[17] The negative system of textile waste generation in the fashion industry provides one example of such systemic failures. While most consumers and companies would like to make less textile waste, nonetheless more and more waste is produced. The first step in tackling negative systems requires becoming aware of how one contributes to creating them, for example by using collaborative and reflective methods that help expand one's individual perspective.[18]

Further, systems theories provide a lens that enables zooming in and out of different systems and their multidimensional interactions. According to Luhmann's theory of social systems, society is an increasingly complex communication-based system comprising various functionally differentiated sub-systems, such as law, economy, and science. These systems communicate through distinct binary codes and have their own subordinate structures, mediums, and operations.[19] This differentiation means that the systems are operationally closed and, by default, do not understand each other's communications. This also means that the systems cannot be steered from the outside by the communications of other systems. Law does not determine what is economically suitable, nor does economy define what is legal. According to Luhmann, this is also the reason why regulatory interventions sometimes fail.[20] Businesses are organizational systems that are primarily part of the economic system. A business can only steer itself by its own communicational operations, such as by organizational decision-making processes. Also, as part of the economic system businesses function through the generation and exchange of economic value.[21]

In the context of the sustainability transition this means that policy instruments such as EU regulations and national legislation can only set goals for businesses in

---

[16] Gonçalves et al. (2023), p. 1.

[17] Hämäläinen et al. (2014), p. 16, Meadows (2008), p. 111, Johnston (2021), p. 331.

[18] Hämäläinen and Saarinen (2004), p. 12, Johnston (2021), p. 360.

[19] According to Luhmann, the system of law communicates what is "legal" or "illegal," the system of economy when a "payment" or "no-payment" is received, and the system of science is about finding what is "true" or "untrue," Luhmann (1989), pp. 11, 36.

[20] Luhmann (1997), p. 46.

[21] Luhmann (1996), pp. 3, 206.

the adoption of sustainability requirements, but achieving the goals happens through businesses' internal everyday measures. Using the insights from systems theories, a successful sustainability transition, therefore, requires that companies, as well as other stakeholders in the business ecosystem, become aware of their own roles and the impact their operations have on the system, and make necessary changes to create a more purposeful impact. Addressing the tension between financial and sustainability objectives also requires innovative approaches, adaptive strategies, and collaborative efforts that help overcome the communicational boundaries between different social systems. Designing fit-for-purpose artificial intelligence tools can be considered one of them.

2.2 EU Legislation to Promote Sustainable Finance and Corporate Sustainability

Several pieces of EU legislation aim to promote sustainable finance, corporate sustainability and related communication. The EU Sustainable Finance Framework, which aims to enhance sustainable finance, is based on three pillars: (1) the EU Taxonomy, which provides a classification of environmentally sustainable economic activities, (2) a comprehensive disclosure regime, and (3) a set of investment tools. The aim of the taxonomy is to provide an objective classification system with which investors can have a common understanding of their investments. The common criteria also prevent greenwashing.[22] The EU Taxonomy Regulation (EU) 2020/852 forms the cornerstone of the EU's framework for sustainable finance. It provides the criteria to determine which economic activities qualify as environmentally sustainable. For companies, the taxonomy is a tool to help them access finance for their green transition. For the financial sector, it provides measures to assess the sustainability of investments.[23]

The Corporate Sustainability Reporting Directive (EU) 2022/2464 (CSRD) and the European Sustainability Reporting Standards (ESRS) are essential in enhancing transparency and comparability of sustainability information. They form the key pillars of the disclosure regime of sustainable finance, together with the Sustainable Finance Disclosure Regulation (EU) 2019/2088 (SFDR).[24] Sustainability reporting can improve access to financial capital, while also helping to identify and manage sustainability risks and opportunities.[25] Although the sustainability reporting requirements are mainly aimed at larger companies, SMEs can also benefit from the voluntary use of sustainable finance tools and thus gain access to sustainable finance.[26]

[22] European Commission (2023b), pp. 3–4.

[23] European Commission (2023a), pp. 6–7.

[24] European Commission (2023b), p. 6.

[25] European Commission (2023a), p. 9.

[26] European Commission (2023a), pp. 4–5.

The European Single Access Point Regulation (EU) 2023/2859 aims to improve the accessibility of sustainability disclosures by gathering them in one place. Tools of sustainable finance, the third pillar in the EU's sustainable finance framework, include EU climate benchmarks of the Regulation on the EU Climate Transition Benchmarks (EU) 2019/2089, and the European Green Bond Regulation (EU) 2023/2631. The latter sets a gold standard for the use of green bonds and helps investors assess and compare the sustainability of investments.[27]

In the future, the EU still aims to enhance the usability of the taxonomy. Some companies have had challenges with implementation. They have struggled to demonstrate and report their taxonomy alignment. The difficulties also relate to other disclosure requirements beyond taxonomy.[28] The Commission has recently launched a set of online tools and guidance in its new EU Taxonomy Navigator website. They are designed to help companies assess and report on their taxonomy alignment.[29]

The Corporate Sustainability Due Diligence Directive (EU) 2024/1760 (CSDDD), when implemented into national legislation, will impose obligations on large companies in relation to human rights, labor rights, and environmental impacts throughout their value chains. Although the Directive is not directly applicable to SMEs, its requirements can extend to them indirectly. This happens when large companies impose similar obligations on their suppliers, who in turn may require these standards to be passed along to their own suppliers.

The new Ecodesign for Sustainable Products Regulation (EU) 2024/1781 (ESPR) is the cornerstone of the EU Commission's approach towards more sustainable and circular products. It builds on and will replace the Ecodesign Directive 2009/125/EC, which has been driving improvements in the energy efficiency and circularity of energy-related products for over a decade. The ESPR will apply to a wide range of physical goods, including textiles, with a focus on improving their environmental sustainability aspects. The regulation aims to establish specific ecodesign requirements aimed at improving product durability, reusability, reparability, energy, and resource efficiency, among others.[30]

The ESPR places obligations and requirements on companies of all sizes, unlike the CSDDD and the CSRD, which primarily target larger enterprises. The ESPR applies broadly to all companies that place products on the EU market. Effective communication and accessible information on sustainability issues is also crucial for companies of all sizes, as it helps companies and consumers make better choices. Similarly, effective communication is essential between actors in companies' value chains. As false sustainability claims are common, the proposed Directive on False Green Claims can help to tackle the problem. Channeling private investment into sustainable products is also at the core.[31]

[27] European Commission (2023b), p. 8.

[28] European Commission (2023b), pp. 2, 9.

[29] European Commission (2023b), p. 9.

[30] European Commission (n.d.).

[31] European Commission (2022a), pp. 5–6, 11.

If used effectively, the sustainable finance framework can help companies access sustainable finance by providing tools to demonstrate their sustainability efforts. Financial products, such as green loans and sustainability-linked loans (SLLs) create practical links between sustainability and economic interests. The loan can be obtained at a lower interest rate if a company operates in a sustainable manner. The market for sustainable financial instruments has grown in the past years. However, the market also faces some challenges. For example, the UK's Financial Conduct Authority (FCA) has raised several concerns related to SLLs.[32] These include weak incentives, conflicts of interest, low ambition and poor design of the Sustainable Performance Targets and Key Performance Indicators (KPIs). Such problems may also involve greenwashing. Building trust and transparency in sustainable finance is crucial. Requiring only sustainability reporting risks confining sustainability to the realm of paperwork rather than fostering real-world impact. To achieve genuine sustainability, loan terms must be based on the attainment of meaningful KPIs, such as reductions in emissions, rather than merely on reporting. Later in this chapter, when we provide examples of using AI tools, the AI team will reflect on the terms of a green loan.

2.3 A Co-Regulatory Approach is Needed

Achieving the goals of sustainable finance and corporate sustainability requires a co-regulatory approach, combining EU and national legislation with industry self-regulation. This approach requires the embedding of policy objectives in legislation and the incorporation of legal requirements into business practices. Loan terms, KPIs, contracts and Codes of Conduct play a crucial role in this process. In order to translate them into action, it is essential to first make them visible, tangible and actionable.

We propose to view loan agreements and contracts as proactive tools that can help parties (1) achieve their goals and promote mutual success, (2) advance sustainability objectives, and (3) prevent issues from escalating into legal problems, conflicts, or litigation. This is the essence of Proactive Contracting. Initially, this approach aimed to use contracts and related documents to promote better business. More recently, it has expanded to promote societal goals, with responsible and sustainable contracting becoming increasingly visible in both research and practice.[33]

A proactive contract has been described as one that is "designed for the parties, especially those responsible for its implementation, rather than for a judge assessing the parties' failures."[34] Supply chain contracts and loan agreements based on this approach can balance the goals and needs of the various parties with the broader interests of society.

[32] Financial Conduct Authority (FCA) (2023), pp. 1, 3.

[33] See, e.g., Saloranta and Hurmerinta-Haanpää (2022).

[34] Berger-Walliser et al. (2011), p. 61.

The CSDDD embodies a co-regulation approach aimed at ensuring that companies comply with sustainability due diligence requirements throughout their supply chains. According to Recital 66 of the CSDDD, the Commission is mandated to provide guidance on model contractual clauses in order to provide companies with the tools to comply. The Commission's guidance should facilitate a clear division of responsibilities between the parties to the contract. It is explicitly stated that the guidance should reflect the principle that mere reliance on contractual assurances is not sufficient to meet the due diligence standards set out in the Directive. Contracts will play a critical role in achieving sustainability goals in supply chains, but words on paper will not be enough.

Generative AI can contribute to effective communication and sustainable financial management. In the next section, we explore existing AI solutions for financial management. We will then build our own examples from the perspective of our example company, a European textile company.

3 Review of Existing Research on LLMs for Financial Management

To manage financial and sustainability objectives effectively, businesses need to adopt a holistic approach. This means creating strategies that recognize the interdependence of economic, social, and environmental factors. By handling them together, companies can achieve sustainable growth that benefits both the bottom line and the broader community. Generative AI tools and related technologies hold the potential to help achieve these objectives. They can analyze vast amounts of data from various sources, including financial reports, sustainability metrics, and market trends. By synthesizing this information, AI can identify patterns and gain insight that might be missed by human analysts. For instance, AI can uncover how sustainable practices impact financial performance and vice versa, guiding strategic decision-making. These models can forecast the long-term financial benefits of sustainable investments, helping businesses make informed decisions that align with both economic and environmental goals. Moreover, generative AI could be useful in scenario planning, helping businesses anticipate the financial and sustainability outcomes of different strategies, and thus, enabling companies to evaluate the potential risks and rewards of their decisions. These tools can also enhance reporting and compliance to meet regulatory requirements and communicate their sustainability efforts transparently to stakeholders.

In a way, generative AI can be seen as a major democratization tool in many applications. Companies that lack resources for sophisticated financial and sustainability knowledge can now utilize generative AI in their planning and get a similar advantage that has previously been available only for those with enough resources. Several research papers have already analyzed the possibilities of generative AI for the financial and sustainability management of companies. Niszczota and Abbas examine the financial literacy capabilities of generative AI models and how individuals utilize their advice in financial contexts. They find that the latest iterations of GPTs are financially literate and suggest that these models can potentially serve effectively as financial advisors. They also argue that as GPT models improve, they can provide reliable financial advice, which could be particularly beneficial for companies with lower financial literacy. However, the study also notes the risk of overreliance on these AI systems due to their tendency to deliver confident answers even when incorrect (hallucination).[35]

Gupta investigates the possibilities of using LLMs to analyze the annual reports of publicly listed companies, aiming to enhance stock investment strategies. His study demonstrates how integrating advanced language models with traditional financial analytics can potentially transform investment strategies by providing a deeper understanding of company fundamentals through the automated analysis of extensive textual data.[36] Some research also calls for caution when utilizing LLMs for financial analysis. Callanan et al. investigate the capabilities of LLMs in tackling financial reasoning problems using sophisticated prompting techniques like few-shot learning and chain-of-thought. They find that while generative AI shows potential in acting as a financial analyst, it currently still needs further specialization and training specific to financial content to fully meet professional standards in finance.[37]

In the future, LLMs optimized for narrow specific tasks might be more efficient solutions than current general LLMs. Pavlyshenko explores enhancing the LLAMA2 LLM for financial news analysis tasks using parameter-efficient fine-tuning techniques. His research demonstrates the potential of fine-tuned language models to significantly impact financial analytics by automating the extraction of useful information from large datasets, thereby supporting more informed decision-making in financial contexts.[38] Kim and Yoon fine-tune an LLM to enhance bankruptcy prediction using LLM-based sentiment analysis on corporate disclosure data. They demonstrate that context-specific linguistic analysis using LLMs can significantly enhance the prediction of corporate bankruptcies.[39]

Several papers have also investigated the possibilities of using AI in sustainability management. However, the research on LLMs is much more limited. Ni et al. introduce CHATREPORT, a tool that uses AI to automatically analyze corporate sustainability reports, making this information more accessible and transparent.[40] Zechiel et al. develop a strategic framework to integrate AI with sustainability goals. The research analyzed AI initiatives from major tech companies like Microsoft and Google, revealing varying strategic approaches. The study also surveyed clients, and

---

[35] Niszczota and Abbas (2023).

[36] Gupta (2023).

[37] Callanan et al. (2023).

[38] Pavlyshenko (2023).

[39] Kim and Yoon (2021).

[40] Ni et al. (2023).

offers theoretical insights and practical guidance for tech companies to align AI and sustainability efforts effectively.[41]

Several papers analyze AI in sustainability management from a more general perspective. Schöggl et al. investigate how digital technologies are implemented to promote a circular economy and manage sustainability in the manufacturing sector. The study highlights significant differences in digitalization levels across industries and company sizes, suggesting that tailored strategies are needed to effectively leverage digital technologies like LLMs for sustainability.[42] Rahman et al. examine how ready B2B firms are to adopt technology, particularly in using AI for customer relationship management, and how this affects their social sustainability performance. The study finds that firms with higher technology readiness and better ICT capabilities are more successful in implementing AI-CRM systems. These systems improve relationship performance with customers and, ultimately, enhance the firm's social sustainability performance. The study emphasizes the importance of ICT capabilities in mediating the relationship between technology readiness and AI-CRM effectiveness.[43]

As discussed, there is a growing body of research on the use of LLMs for both financial management and sustainability transition purposes. In the following section we examine what easy-to-access practical solutions for financial and sustainability management already exist. We then conclude with a discussion on domain-specific solutions that utilize companies' own data in a secure environment and provide tools that are more controllable, should hallucinate less, and have a deeper understanding of each company's situation.

4 Testing AI as a Financial Coach

4.1 The Textile Industry as an Example

In this chapter, our example company is a European textile company with international value chains, for example in material sourcing. We look at the potential of AI tools specifically from the perspective of this company. The textile industry is considered a high-risk sector in terms of sustainability. In the EU, textile consumption has the fourth highest negative impact on the environment and climate, and the third highest impact on water and land use. Overproduction and overconsumption are major problems—each of us in the EU discards about 11 kg of textiles every year, and garments are used for increasingly shorter periods before they are discarded. Extending the life of textile products could significantly reduce the negative environmental impact. Complex and diverse global value chains in the textile sector also

[41] Zechiel et al. (2024).

[42] Schöggl et al. (2023).

[43] Rahman et al. (2023).

typically present social challenges, such as child labor, discrimination, occupational health and safety concerns, unfair wages and forced labor.[44]

Recently, the textile industry has been facing economic sustainability challenges related to high energy and raw material supply, demand for more sustainable products, and attracting a talented workforce. The EU already has sustainability instruments tailored to the needs of the textile industry. These include, for instance, the EU Ecolabel criteria for textile products and the EU GPP criteria for textile products and services. The EU has also proposed extended producer responsibility rules for textiles with eco-modulation of fees in its revision of the Waste Framework Directive. In the future, EU waste legislation may also set mandatory targets for preparing textile waste for reuse and recycling. Digital tools can help transform the design and production of textiles by allowing customers and retailers to interact in new ways, creating flexibility and responding to consumer needs.[45]

4.2 Exploring the Potential of AI Crew with an Example Company

How should a company interested in employing AI for financial management get started? Easy first steps for companies to experiment with the possibilities of AI is by using prompting with standard versions of LLMs and then moving into specialty GPTs. For example, the ChatGPT platform provided by OpenAI[46] offers numerous GPTs specifically modified for aiding companies in financial and sustainability management. For companies new to leveraging LLMs for financial and sustainability management, prompting and specialty GPTs allow to explore the capabilities of LLMs without the immediate need for extensive investments, offering a low-risk introduction to AI-driven solutions.[47]

Prompting involves providing the LLM with specific queries or tasks in natural language to obtain useful responses. This method can be effective for companies looking to obtain immediate insights or automate routine tasks without the necessity of model customization.[48] For instance, a financial analyst can prompt an LLM to generate a market analysis report, summarize financial statements, or predict stock price movements based on recent trends. Similarly, a sustainability manager can use the model to suggest eco-friendly practices, analyze carbon footprint data, or prepare first drafts of sustainability reports based on company data. Most current LLMs allow for small amounts of company and other relevant data to be provided in the chat for more specific guidance. However, this approach requires careful consideration of confidentiality and security issues.

[44] OECD (2018).

[45] European Commission (2022a), pp. 2, 4, 7.

[46] OpenAI (2024).

[47] Zhao et al. (2024).

[48] Zhao et al. (2024).

Prompts can help companies quickly realize the value of LLMs. However, for a more detailed analysis, the next useful step would be to use specialty GPTs that offer tailored capabilities out of the box compared to general-purpose models.[49] These models can be useful for companies needing domain-specific insights without the immediate need for investments in domain-specific LLMs. Within the ChatGPT environment, companies can access various specialty GPTs designed for financial analysis, regulatory compliance, sustainability reporting and more. These models are pre-configured to "understand" and respond to domain-specific queries, providing a quick and efficient way to leverage AI for specialized tasks.[50]

For companies planning to adopt specialty GPTs for their financial and sustainability management, the following guidelines provide a framework for getting started. First, companies should identify specific areas within financial and sustainability management where AI can add value. This could be routine reporting, data analysis or strategic planning. Second, companies should search for specialty GPTs that align with the identified needs. For instance, select a GPT focused on financial analytics for budgeting and forecasting or a sustainability-focused GPT for ESG reporting. Third, companies should start with simple prompts to understand the model's capabilities and gradually move to more complex queries using the insights gained to refine the use of GPTs and integrate them into regular workflows.

We provide an example of using specialized GPTs for the purposes of our sample European textile company. For the experiment, we use the OpenAI API and the Python programming environment. The key library used is the CrewAI library, which provides functions for creating teams of autonomous AI agents with specialized tasks. The library allows for the detailed definition of each agent's goals, backstories and tasks. Furthermore, the library allows to specify whether the agents have memory and how they share information with each other. Our example includes four specialized agents working together: *a financial management expert* with in-depth knowledge from the company's annual reports, *a sustainability management expert* with in-depth knowledge from the company's sustainability reports, *a legal expert* with in-depth knowledge of EU green regulation, and *a reporting expert* specialized in creating reports for management. All agents have memory, and all but the reporter agent can delegate tasks to other agents. The details of the agents are shown in Fig. 1.

We test the usability of our AI crew by asking it to analyze the KPIs of a green loan. All agents are given the loan terms provided by a large multinational bank. We ask the crew to work sequentially, passing their findings to the next agent. The specific task assigned to the AI crew was: "Analyze in detail the KPIs provided in Schedule 7 of the file Sustainability_terms_- generic.txt. Create a list of actions that the company would need to do to fulfill the requirements for those KPIs." The results are shown in Fig. 2, illustrating the first steps of the crew's reasoning process, and in Fig. 3, which shows an extract from the final report output.[51]

---

[49] OpenAI (2024).

[50] Zhao et al. (2024).

[51] The Python code for this example is available upon request from the authors.

Fig. 1 Our AI crew that works in sequential order and has memory capabilities

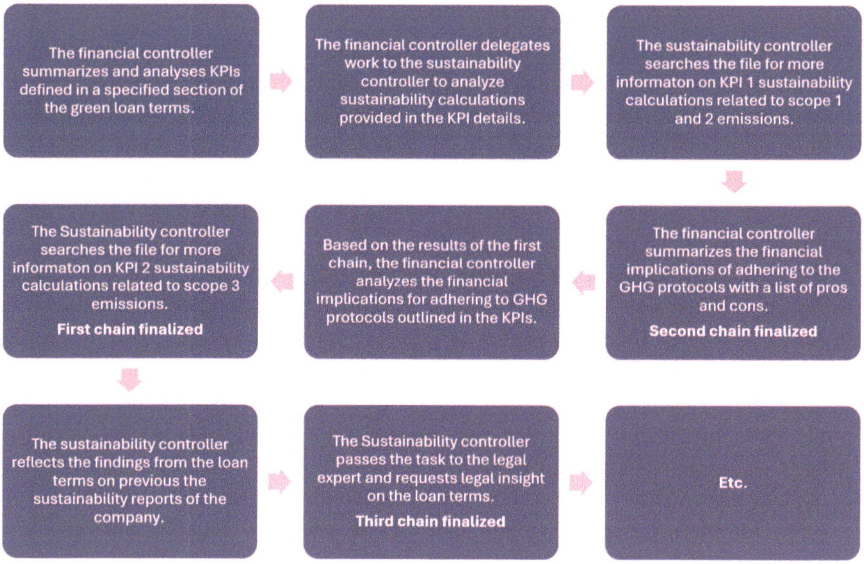

Fig. 2 First steps of the reasoning process of our AI crew

```
**Key Performance Indicators**

The KPIs in Schedule 7 are comprehensive and revolve around different aspects of sustainability. They encompass environmental factors like energy consumption, waste generation, and water usage, social factors like worker safety, diversity and inclusion, and governance factors such as compliance with regulations and ethical business practices. Failure to meet these KPIs could lead to significant legal and financial consequences for *********.

**Recommended Actions**

To comply with these KPIs, ********* needs to adopt the following measures:

1. **Monitoring and Reporting System:** ********* should establish a robust system to track and report its progress against the KPIs. This would involve setting up strong data collection and management systems and regular reporting mechanisms.

2. **Compliance Program:** A program ensuring all employees are aware of the KPIs and their role in achieving them should be implemented. Regular training and updates on the KPIs should be part of this program.

3. **Engage External Experts:** To ensure the accuracy and validity of its reporting, ********* should hire an independent professional services firm or environmental consultancy.

4. **Sustainability Amendment Strategy:** Lastly, ********* should have a plan in place to deal with events that could significantly affect any KPI or SPT, like asset sales, acquisitions, or corporate restructuring.

**Potential Benefits and Risks**

While these actions require upfront investment, they can potentially prevent significant legal and financial repercussions and boost *********'s reputation. However, ********* should also consider potential risks. Non-compliance with KPIs can result in penalties or legal actions, and data collection and reporting requirements could strain resources.
```

Fig. 3 An extract of a report from our AI crew. The crew shared knowledge and sequentially analyzed the topic through several rounds before arriving at a final conclusion and compiling the report

The complete reasoning process of the crew is complex, encompassing well over 10,000 words. Due to space constraints, we qualitatively describe the initial steps of the process in Fig. 2. The agents iterate the task in chains, where the output of the previous chain serves as a prompt for the next. This sequential process demonstrates an interesting evolution in reasoning with each expert contributing their specialized knowledge and iterating on the output before passing it to the next expert. After numerous iterations, the final findings are handed to the reporter agent, who compiles the final report for company management.

Due to space constraints, Fig. 3 shows an extract of the final report created by our AI crew. The entire work process included much more detailed information and reasoning. However, this example extract already demonstrates how the crew is able to identify KPIs from the document and provide actionable recommendations for management. Additionally, there are numerous parameters that can be adjusted to modify how the AI crew operates. For example, instead of sequential processing, the crew could be organized to work hierarchically, which more closely resembles how human teams function. Another way to obtain more specific information would be to provide more preliminary data, for example, on green loans, as our input data contained only one generic loan term document.

By starting with prompting and GPTs, companies can build confidence in using LLMs for financial and sustainability management. This approach provides immediate value with minimal investment, allowing organizations to familiarize themselves with AI capabilities and identify potential areas for deeper integration. As companies experiment with these tools, they can gather valuable data on how LLMs perform in real-world scenarios. This learning phase is crucial for understanding their strengths and limitations.

With this knowledge, companies can gradually move towards more sophisticated approaches, such as fine-tuning LLMs with proprietary data. Another possibility for further developing financial AI coaches is using design personas to address the effect of AI agents on user experience. As AI agents partner with their human users and their businesses, it is necessary to ensure that their behavior supports AI–human collaboration and aligns with company and industry-specific goals. These possibilities will be discussed in more detail in the following sections.

4.3 Fine-Tuning LLMs

When companies are ready, a promising step forward is the use of LLMs fine-tuned with proprietary data.[52] LLMs, such as GPT-4, are trained on large datasets encompassing diverse topics and languages. While these models exhibit impressive generalization capabilities, their true potential is unlocked through fine-tuning, which involves further training the pre-trained LLMs on domain-specific datasets, which could include a company's historical financial records, sustainability reports,

[52] Minaee et al. (2024).

and industry-specific documents. Fine-tuning enables the model to understand the unique language, terminologies and patterns inherent to the company's operations. This customization not only improves the accuracy of predictions and insights but also ensures that the model's outputs are aligned with the company's specific goals and regulatory requirements. Many efficient solutions are available for fine-tuning[53] ranging from standard supervised methods to advanced approaches such as Reinforcement Learning with Human Feedback (RLHF), Direct Preference Optimization (DPO), Low-Rank Adaptation (LoRA), Quantized Low-Rank Adaptation QLoRA, and Odds Ratio Preference Optimization (ORPO).

Supervised fine-tuning trains a pre-trained language model on a labeled dataset specific to tasks like financial or sustainability analysis. This process starts by collecting and preprocessing the dataset, then loading the model and adding task-specific layers, such as a classification layer for risk assessment. The model is trained, tested on a separate dataset, and then deployed. The advantages of this approach include tailored task performance, faster convergence, and leveraging pre-trained knowledge for enhanced results. RLHF fine-tunes language models using human evaluations to better align with human preferences. It involves sampling outputs from a pre-trained model, gathering feedback, training a reward model to predict feedback scores, and then using reinforcement learning to fine-tune the model based on these scores. The process is iterative, continuously refining based on new feedback. RLHF excels in tasks requiring human judgment. DPO streamlines this by directly optimizing models based on human preferences gathered by comparing output pairs and training a preference model to predict favored outcomes. This approach is simpler and more computationally efficient than RLHF, foregoing complex reinforcement learning by directly fine-tuning the language model to align with human preferences.

LoRA and QLoRA are fine-tuning techniques that optimize computational and memory efficiency while preserving model performance. LoRA reduces trainable parameters by inserting small, trainable low-rank matrices into each layer of a pre-trained model, updating only these matrices instead of the entire weight matrix. QLoRA enhances this by adding quantization and lowering the precision of model weights (e.g., from 32-bit to 8-bit), which decreases memory use and computational demands. It integrates these lower-precision weights with low-rank matrices that are fine-tuned, keeping the original model's quantized weights fixed. ORPO is a fine-tuning method that enhances preference alignment using an odds ratio-based penalty without needing a reference model or a warm-up phase. It calculates the odds ratio between favored and disfavored responses to an input, incorporating this ratio into the loss function alongside conventional supervised fine-tuning loss. This method penalizes undesired outputs while promoting preferred ones, improving computational efficiency by requiring fewer training passes.

Fine-tuning LLMs can significantly boost their performance in financial and sustainability management. For example, supervised fine-tuning can improve financial forecasting accuracy by leveraging historical data and market trends. Risk assessment benefits from RLHF, which refines models through expert feedback to better

[53] Han et al. (2024).

predict risks. DPO could enhance sustainability reporting by aligning outputs with human preferences. Additionally, LoRA and QLoRA increase efficiency by reducing computational demands, facilitating the deployment of advanced models in resource-limited settings. Fine-tuned LLMs excel in specific tasks, closely align with human judgments, and support better decision-making in complex business environments. They can adapt to a company's data trends and contextual changes. In sustainability, fine-tuned models provide insights for strategic planning, suggesting innovations like energy-efficient technologies and sustainable practices that align with corporate goals, thus promoting environmental and social impact while enhancing profitability.

Fine-tuned LLMs can also automate the creation of detailed financial reports, ensuring adherence to specific regulatory standards and reducing the risk of non-compliance and potential penalties. Similarly, as sustainability reporting becomes crucial, fine-tuned LLMs can efficiently handle the collection, analysis, and reporting of ESG metrics, producing comprehensive sustainability reports. Overall, fine-tuning LLMs with proprietary data enhances financial and sustainability management, providing more accurate and actionable insights than generic models. This customization helps businesses meet their sustainability objectives more effectively, positioning fine-tuned LLMs as key tools for future innovative and sustainable business practices.

4.4 Designing an AI Crew with Personas

In addition to fine-tuning the LLMs for businesses' financial and sustainability management needs, it is also important to pay attention to the way this information is gathered, conveyed and communicated to their human clients. In other words, the user-interface of the AI tool plays an essential role in determining its practical usability. Research indicates that humanizing machines can positively affect their user-experience and the level of trust people bestow upon them.[54] Furthermore, research suggests that people prefer interacting with artificial agents that have a personality complementary to their own.[55] However, it must be noted that personalized AI–human interactions also come with many constraints, such as potential misalignment of preferences or the amplification of certain individual characteristics over others.[56] As the personality of an AI agent is nevertheless a crucial part of its functionality, it becomes critical to design AI agents that complement the personality types of their users responsibly and transparently, supporting users' autonomy. The persona method used in design can help identify both the behavioral patterns and styles of the human users, as well as personalize AI agents with characteristics relevant to achieving the user's goals.[57]

[54] See e.g. deVisser et al. (2016).

[55] See e.g. Lee et al. (2006).

[56] Valenzuela et al. (2024).

[57] Karahasanović et al. (2021), p. 229.

In design practice, personas are both a communication aid and a tool that helps designers empathize with different kinds of users in various design contexts. A persona represents the characteristics of a typical user: how the user behaves, what they feel and think and what kind of needs and frustrations they may have in relation to the target of the design. Personas are often created based on research data, such as user interviews or surveys.[58] However, as design authors have pointed out, there are some risks considering their usability. It has been argued that as simplified representations of real humans, personas might reinforce existing biases and stereotypes, rather than help understand what people actually need and want. This is the case especially if personas are created based on invalid data, or if they describe the user in a manner that emphasizes irrelevant or too general factors.[59]

As noted in previous research, personas may have particular potential in the design of AI agents.[60] In the context of this chapter, this could mean creating an AI crew for financial management purposes, where each agent has specific characteristics, personalities and mindsets that support not only the performance of their individual tasks, but also their interactions with each other and with the user. For example, in our example presented in Sect. 4.2, the "Financial Controller" might have either a risk-averse or a risk-taking personality, depending on how much financial risk the company is willing to take in its green investments. The "Sustainability Controller" might be sympathetic to particular sustainability concerns relevant to the company's business, such as avoiding child labor in the textile company's materials supply chain. The "Legal Expert" might have the mindset of a proactive lawyer who not only helps identify legal risks and comply with mandatory requirements, but also seeks to promote what is desirable and find new opportunities for the company under the applicable sustainability laws. Finally, "The Reporter" might not only be friendly and use understandable language, but also have the characteristics of a true communication specialist and information designer, including the ability to adapt communication styles to different audiences and align them with the company's goals.

5 Conclusions

In this chapter, we have explored the transformative potential of generative AI as a tool for financial and sustainability management. We began with an overview of sustainable finance and its critical role in achieving the objectives of the European Green Deal, emphasizing the importance of economic sustainability as a foundation for environmental and social sustainability, particularly in the context of

[58] Stickdorn et al. (2018), pp. 124–126.

[59] Comprehensively about the benefits and pitfalls of the persona method see, e.g., Mardsen and Haag (2016).

[60] Karahasanović et al. (2021), p. 230.

the Triple Bottom Line framework.[61] We identified key challenges that companies face in balancing profitability and sustainability, highlighting the tension between immediate financial returns and long-term sustainability investments, as well as the systemic nature of both business operations and sustainability challenges.

Next, we examined the role of EU sustainability legislation. While essential, it also poses compliance challenges, particularly for SMEs, which play a key role in the green transition. Achieving sustainable finance and corporate sustainability goals requires a co-regulatory approach that integrates EU and national legislation with industry self-regulation, such as loan agreements and supply chain contracts. However, none of these will automatically translate into action: making loan terms, contracts and their KPIs visible, tangible and actionable is critical to translating goals into reality.

Finally, we explored the practical applications of generative AI in financial and sustainability management. We looked at how AI tools can support businesses by simplifying complex information, providing tailored analysis and offering strategic insights. The example case of a European textile company illustrated the potential of AI to enhance both financial and environmental sustainability in a high-risk sector.

While AI assistants are already widely used for various purposes, they are not always designed or built with legal needs or requirements in mind. In a complex context such as sustainable financial management, it is crucial to integrate the legal, sustainable and financial aspects, as well as user experience and accessibility. AI crews and their building tools can help capture this complexity by allowing AI assistants from different domains to work together. In the future, design patterns could also be used to help encode legal or other specific knowledge into AI tools.[62]

In conclusion, generative AI can serve as a powerful financial and sustainability coach, helping businesses align their financial metrics with sustainability goals. By leveraging AI, companies can overcome many of the traditional barriers to sustainable finance, ensuring that they not only comply with regulatory requirements but also contribute to a more sustainable and resilient economy. Future research should continue to explore the evolving capabilities of AI in financial management, and consider the ethical and practical implications of its use. For example, more research is needed on the risks and opportunities of developing efficient and autonomous AI crews. As AI technologies advance, they hold the promise of further democratizing access to sophisticated financial advice, thereby fostering a more inclusive and sustainable financial landscape.

[61] See, e.g., Elkington (2006).

[62] For legal knowledge, see Dickhaut et al. (2023), pp. 3–4.

References

Ameer R, Othman R (2012) Sustainability practices and corporate financial performance: a study based on the top global corporations. J Bus Ethics 108(1):61–79. https://doi.org/10.1007/s10551-011-1063-y. Accessed 25 Jun 2024

Berger-Walliser G, Bird RC, Haapio H (2011) Promoting business success through contract visualization. J Bus Ethics 17:55–76

Callanan E, Mbakwe A, Papadimitriou A, Pei Y, Sibue M, Zhu X, Ma Z, Liu X, Shah S (2023) Can GPT models be financial analysts? An evaluation of ChatGPT and GPT-4 on mock CFA exams, vol 1. https://doi.org/10.48550/arXiv.2310.08678. Accessed 25 Jun 2024

European Commission (n.d.) Ecodesign for Sustainable Products Regulation. https://commission.europa.eu/energy-climate-change-environment/standards-tools-and-labels/products-labelling-rules-and-requirements/sustainable-products/ecodesign-sustainable-products-regulation_en. Accessed 25 Jun 2024

Council of the European Union (2024) Proposal for a directive of the european parliament and of the council on corporate sustainability due diligence and amending directive (EU) 2019/1937—letter to the chair of the JURI committee of the European parliament. Brussels, 15 March 2024

CrewAI (2024). https://crewai.net/. Accessed 25 Jun 2024

Dettmers T, Pagnoni A, Holtzman A, Zettlemoyer L (2023) QLoRA: efficient finetuning of quantized LLMs, vol 1. https://doi.org/10.48550/arXiv.2305.14314. Accessed 25 Jun 2024

deVisser EJ, Monfort SS, McKendrick R, Smith MA, McKnight PE, Krueger F, Parasuraman R (2016) Almost human: anthropomorphism increases trust resilience in cognitive agents. J Exp Psychol Appl 22(3):331–349. https://doi.org/10.1037/xap0000092. Accessed 25 Jun 2024

Dickhaut E, Janson A, Söllner M, Leimeister JM (2023) Lawfulness by design—development and evaluation of lawful design patterns to consider legal requirements. Eur J Inf Syst 2023:1–28. https://doi.org/10.1080/0960085X.2023.2174050. Accessed 25 Jun 2024

Elkington J (2006) Governance for sustainability. Corp Gov 14(6):522–529. https://doi.org/10.1111/j.1467-8683.2006.00527.x. Accessed 25 Jun 2024

European Commission (2003) Commission Recommendation of 6 May 2003 Concerning the definition of micro, small and medium-sized enterprises. Official Journal L 124, 20 May, 36–41. https://eur-lex.europa.eu/legal-content/EN/TXT/?uri=CELEX:32003H0361. Accessed 25 Jun 2024

European Commission (2022a) EU strategy for sustainable and circular textiles. COM(2022) 141 final. Brussels, 30 March

European Commission (2022b) Proposal for a directive of the European parliament and of the council on corporate sustainability due diligence and amending directive (EU) 2019/1937. COM(2022) 71 final. Brussels, 23 February

European Commission (2022c) Annual Report on European SMEs 2021/2022 SMEs and Environmental Sustainability. https://single-market-economy.ec.europa.eu/document/download/9e7fd906-c5b0-46c5-9b9e-4b62f6bce98f_en. Accessed 25 Jun 2024

European Commission (2023a) A Sustainable Finance Framework That Works on the Ground. COM(2023) 317 final. Strasbourg, 13 June

European Commission (2023b) Enhancing the usability of the EU taxonomy and the overall EU sustainable finance framework. SWD(2023) 209 final. Strasbourg, 13 June

Financial Conduct Authority (FCA) (2023) Review of the sustainability-linked loans (SLL) Market. https://www.fca.org.uk/publication/correspondence/sll-letter-june-2023.pdf. Accessed 25 Jun 2024

Friedman M (1970) A friedman doctrine—the social responsibility of business is to increase its profits. The New York Times. https://www.nytimes.com/1970/09/13/archives/a-friedman-doctrine-the-social-responsibility-of-business-is-to.html. Accessed 25 Jun 2024

Gonçalves TC, Louro D, Barros V (2023) can corporate sustainability drive economic value added? Why we eat, how we eat: contemporary encounters between foods and bodies. Evidence from larger European firms. J Risk Finan Managem 16(4):215. https://doi.org/10.3390/jrfm16040215. Accessed 25 Jun 2024

Gupta U (2023) GPT-InvestAR: enhancing stock investment strategies through annual report analysis with large language models, vol 1. https://doi.org/10.48550/arXiv.2309.03079. Accessed 25 Jun 2024

Hämäläinen R, Jones R, Saarinen E (2014) Being better better. Living with systems intelligence. Aalto ARTS Books, Helsinki

Hämäläinen R, Saarinen E (2004) Systems intelligence: discovering a hidden competence in human action and organizational life. Helsinki University of Technology, Helsinki

Han Z, Gao C, Liu J, Zhang J, Zhang SQ (2024) Parameter-efficient fine-tuning for large models: a comprehensive survey, vol 5. https://doi.org/10.48550/arXiv.2403.14608. Accessed 25 Jun 2024

Hong J, Lee N, Thorne J (2024) ORPO: monolithic preference optimization without reference model, vol 2. https://doi.org/10.48550/arXiv.2403.07691. Accessed 25 Jun 2024

Hu EJ, Shen Y, Wallis P, Allen-Zhu Z, Li Y, Wang S, Wang L, Chen W (2021) LoRA: low-rank adaptation of large language models, vol 2. https://doi.org/10.48550/arXiv.2106.09685. Accessed 25 Jun 2024

Johnston CM (2021) In: Creative systems theory: a comprehensive theory of purpose, change and interrelationship in human systems. The Institute for Creative Development (ICD) Press, Seattle, WA

Kaave P (2023) Proactive legal design—making sustainability visible and monitorable in SME loan agreements. J Strateg Contract Negot 7(3–4):100–124. https://doi.org/10.1177/20555636231209217. Accessed 25 Jun 2024

Karahasanović A, Følstad A, Schittekat P (2021) Putting a face on algorithms: personas for modelling artificial intelligence. In: Degen H, Ntoa S (eds), Artificial intelligence in HCI. Second international conference, AI-HCI 2021, Held as part of the 23rd HCI international conference, HCII 2021, Virtual Event, July 24–29, 2021, Proceedings. Springer, Cham

Kim A, Yoon S (2021) Corporate bankruptcy prediction with domain-adapted BERT. SSRN Scholarly Paper 4191690, 10 November, https://papers.ssrn.com/abstract=4191690. Accessed 25 Jun 2024

Lee KM, Peng W, Jin S-A, Yan C (2006) Can robots manifest personality?: An empirical test of personality recognition, social responses, and social presence in human-robot interaction. J Commun 56(4):754–772. https://doi.org/10.1111/j.1460-2466.2006.00318.x. Accessed 25 Jun 2024

Luhmann N (1989) Ecological communication. The University of Chicago Press, Chicago

Luhmann N (1996) Social systems (trans: Bednarz J Jr, Baecker D). Stanford University Press, Stanford

Luhmann N (1997) Limits of steering. Theory Cult Soc 14(1):41–57

Mardsen N, Haag M (2016) Stereotypes and politics: reflections on personas. In: Proceedings of the 2016 CHI conference on human factors in computing systems (CHI '16). Association for Computing Machinery, New York, NY. https://doi.org/10.1145/2858036.2858151. Accessed 25 Jun 2024

Meadows DH (2008) In: Wright D (ed) Thinking in systems. a primer. Chelsea Green Publishing, Vermont

Mecklenburg N, Lin Y, Li X, Holstein D, Nunes L, Malvar S, Silva B, Chandra R, Aski V, Yannam PKR, Aktas T, Hendry T (2024) Injecting new knowledge into large language models via supervised fine-tuning, vol 2. https://doi.org/10.48550/arXiv.2404.00213. Accessed 25 Jun 2024

Minaee S, Mikolov T, Nikzad N, Chenaghlu M, Socher R, Amatriain X, Gao J (2024) Large language models: a survey, vol 2. https://doi.org/10.48550/arXiv.2402.06196. Accessed 25 Jun 2024

Ni J, Bingler J, Colesanti-Senni C, Kraus M, Gostlow G, Schimanski T, Stammbach D, Vaghefi SA, Wang Q, Webersinke N, Wekhof T, Yu T, Leippold M (2023) CHATREPORT: democratizing sustainability disclosure analysis through LLM-based tools. vol 2. https://doi.org/10.48550/arXiv.2307.15770. Accessed 25 Jun 2024

Niszczota P, Abbas S (2023) GPT Has become financially literate: insights from financial literacy tests of GPT and a preliminary test of how people use it as a source of advice. Finan Res Lett 58(Part A):104333. https://doi.org/10.1016/j.frl.2023.104333. Accessed 25 Jun 2024

OECD (2018) OECD due diligence guidance for responsible supply chains in the garment and footwear sector. OECD Publishing, Paris. https://doi.org/10.1787/9789264290587-en. Accessed 25 Jun 2024

OECD (2022) Policy guidance on market practices to strengthen ESG investing and finance a climate transition. OECD business and finance policy papers, No. 13. OECD Publishing, Paris, https://doi.org/10.1787/2c5b535c-en. Accessed 25 Jun 2024

Ouyang L, Wu J, Jiang X, Almeida D, Wainwright CL, Mishkin P, Zhang C, Agarwal S, Slama K, Ray A, Schulman J, Hilton J, Kelton F, Miller L, Simens M, Askell A, Welinder P, Christiano P, Leike J, Lowe R (2022). Training language models to follow instructions with human feedback. vol 1. https://doi.org/10.48550/arXiv.2203.02155. Accessed 25 Jun 2024

Pavlyshenko BM (2023) Financial news analytics using fine-tuned Llama 2 GPT model, vol 2. https://doi.org/10.48550/arXiv.2308.13032. Accessed 25 Jun 2024

Porter ME, Kramer MR (2011) Creating shared value. How to reinvent capitalism—and unleash a wave of innovation and growth. Harvard Business Rev 89(1–2):62–77

Rafailov R, Sharma A, Mitchell E, Ermon S, Manning CD, Finn C (2023) Direct preference optimization: your language model is secretly a reward model. vol 2. https://doi.org/10.48550/arXiv.2305.18290. Accessed 25 Jun 2024

Rahko J (2023) The effects of environmental investments on the economic performance of industrial plants—Evidence from Finland. J Cleaner Prod 394:136142. https://doi.org/10.1016/j.jclepro.2023.136142 Accessed 25 Jun 2024

Rahman MS, Bag S, Gupta S, Sivarajah U (2023) Technology readiness of B2B firms and ai-based customer relationship management capability for enhancing social sustainability performance. J Business Res 156:113525. https://doi.org/10.1016/j.jbusres.2022.113525. Accessed 25 Jun 2024

Salo-Lahti M, Haapio H (2024) Possibility-driven design and responsible use of AI for sustainability. In: Ducato R, Strowel A, Marique E (eds), Design(s) for law. Ledizioni, Milan

Salo-Lahti M, Ranta M, Haapio H (2023) AI tools for sustainability—actionable information for both humans and machines. Jusletter IT, 30 March

Saloranta J, Hurmerinta-Haanpää A (2022) Proactive contract theory in the context of corporate sustainability due diligence. J Strateg Contract Negot 6(3–4):221–236. https://doi.org/10.1177/20555636231165901. Accessed 25 Jun 2024

Schöggl J-P, Rusch M, Stumpf L, Baumgartner RJ (2023) Implementation of digital technologies for a circular economy and sustainability management in the manufacturing sector. Sustain Prod Consump 35:401–420. https://doi.org/10.1016/j.spc.2022.11.012. Accessed 25 Jun 2024

Stickdorn M, Hormess ME, Lawrence A, Schneider J (2018) This is service design doing. O'Reilly Media Inc., Sebastopol, CA

Toivonen N, Salo-Lahti M, Ranta M, Haapio H (2024) AI-enhanced fresh starts: proactive financial health care with AI as a personalized coach. Jusletter IT, 15 February

Toivonen N, Salo-Lahti M, Ranta M, Haapio H (2025) Beyond debt: the intersection of justice, financial wellbeing and AI. In: Corrales Compagnucci M, Haapio H, Fenwick M (eds), Generative AI, contracts, law and design. Springer, Singapore

UK Companies Act (2006) Explanatory notes. https://www.legislation.gov.uk/ukpga/2006/46/notes/division/6/2. Accessed 25 Jun 2024

Valenzuela A, Puntoni S, Hoffman D, Castello N, De Freitas J, Dietvorst B, Hildebrand C, Huh YE, Meyer R, Sweeney ME, Talafair S, Tomaino G, Wertenbroch K (2024) How artificial intelligence constrains the human experience. J Assoc Consum Res 9(3):241–256. https://doi.org/10.1086/730709. Accessed 4 Mar 2025

Zechiel F, Blaurock M, Weber E, Büttgen M, Coussement K (2024) How tech companies advance sustainability through artificial intelligence: developing and evaluating an AI × sustainability strategy framework. Ind Mark Manage 119:75–89. https://doi.org/10.1016/j.indmarman.2024.03.010. Accessed 25 Jun 2024

Zhao H, Liu Z, Wu Z, Li Y, Yang T, Shu P, Xu S, Dai H, Zhao L, Mai G, Liu N, Liu T (2024) Revolutionizing finance with LLMs: an overview of applications and insights 1:22. https://doi.org/10.48550/arXiv.2401.11641. Accessed 25 Jun 2024

Generative AI, Can You Help Us Bridge the Implementation Gap in Contracting?

Robert Waller, Helena Haapio, and Patrick Shone

Abstract Traditional contracts are written with disputes and litigation or arbitration in mind. This tends to prioritise a precise form of legal drafting that is coded for legal purposes, rather than for the practical purposes of performing the contract. The resulting disconnection is known as the implementation gap. Bridging the gap requires, among other things, an understanding of the objectives and what information is of most relevance to each type of business user. The ability of generative AI (GenAI) to simplify the language of contracts is well established, but in this chapter we explore what else it can do to bridge the gap and how well it can anticipate the needs of particular audiences—including people responsible for implementation in the field, without a background in law. We begin by using Anthropic's Claude and OpenAI's ChatGPT4o as our brainstorming and ideation partners in the problem-framing and solution-finding phases. While they provide significant support, we also evaluate how much help they can be as our contract assistants. We give ChatGPT4o contract simplification tasks and test how good it is at creating a contract guide: a tool that is often used to help contract implementation personnel to do their job. We use de Beaugrande and Dressler's classic standards of textuality to challenge ChatGPT, asking it to explain its own limitations, and the level of human oversight required. Finally, we discuss how effective prompting can help us get the most usable results from our AI assistants.

R. Waller (✉)
School of Design, University of Leeds, Leeds, UK
e-mail: r.h.waller@leeds.ac.uk

H. Haapio
School of Accounting and Finance, Business Law, University of Vaasa, Vaasa, Finland

JARGONFREE Contract Language Research Group, Tampere University, Tampere, Finland

Lexpert Ltd, Helsinki, Finland

H. Haapio
e-mail: helena.haapio@lexpert.com

P. Shone
OpenDialog AI Ltd, London, UK
e-mail: pat.shone@opendialog.ai

© The Author(s), under exclusive license to Springer Nature Singapore Pte Ltd. 2025

M. Corrales Compagnucci et al. (eds.), *Generative AI, Contracts, Law and Design*, Perspectives in Law, Business and Innovation,
https://doi.org/10.1007/978-981-95-2058-9_5

Keywords Contract design · AI · Implementation gap · Human oversight · Textuality · Prompt engineering

1 Introduction: The Risks of Writing About AI While It's Still Revealing Itself

The implementation gap describes the disconnection between the written terms of contracts and their practical implementation. We focus on the big picture—what can AI assistants do to bridge this gap and just how sensitive are they to the needs of different audiences?

Writing a chapter on AI at the present moment feels like something of a risk. It seems that every week a new product is announced, and our individual explorations reveal new capabilities and wonders. So you might regard this chapter as a snapshot of a point in time during the development of AI as a tool for writers and designers.

And the more we find out, the more we realise how little we know—or perhaps even, how much can be known—about how AI actually works. Even among the developers of AI, there appears to be a surprising level of uncertainty about what is actually going on inside the artificial brains they have created.

When we wonder how AI manages to write so well, the Large Language Model (LLM) is deployed as the explanation. We are told that it's all about massive computing power trained on huge databases of text, picking the next word on the statistical probability that it is appropriate. For example, blogger and AI pundit Ethan Mollick[1] writes that LLMs work by

> analyzing a piece of text and predicting the next token, which is simply a word or part of a word. Ultimately, that is all ChatGPT does technically – act as a very elaborate autocomplete like you have on your phone.

But this seems too simple to explain why any AI-produced text makes sense as an argument, not just a string of sentences. Or why it passes as part of a conversation between two people, with particular motives and histories, who would normally bring a lifetime's experience of human interaction to its interpretation.

Geoffrey Hinton, winner of the 2024 Nobel prize for Physics and often called the "godfather of AI," was interviewed recently on the BBC.[2] He seemed to dismiss the LLM as the sole explanation:

> Some people think that these things don't really understand, that they're different from us, just using statistical tricks. That's not the case. [Take] these big language models for example. The early ones were developed as a theory of how the brain understands language – they are the best theory we've got about how the brain understands language. We don't understand either how they work, or how the brain works in detail, but we think probably they work in fairly similar ways.

[1] Mollick (2024), p. 9.

[2] BBC Newsnight (2024).

In other words, the creators of AI have simulated the neural networks in our human brains, and set them in motion to think, to plan, to advise, and to communicate with an apparently accurate sense of audience—in fact, to pass the Turing Test with ease. But what happens inside these simulated brains seems to be a mystery.

An article in the New Yorker explains Hinton's realisation that AI had more creativity than he'd credited it with. Journalist Joshua Rothman[3] reports that Hinton wrote a one-liner joke "Fox News is an oxy moron:"

> Then, on a lark, he asked ChatGPT if it could explain his joke. The system told him his sentence implied that Fox News was fake news, and, when he called attention to the space before "moron," it explained that Fox News was addictive, like the drug OxyContin. Hinton was astonished. This level of understanding seemed to represent a new era in A.I.

AI expert Stephen Wolfram makes a similar point.[4]

> But in the end, the remarkable thing is that all these operations – individually as simple as they are – can somehow together manage to do such a good "human-like" job of generating text. It has to be emphasized again that (at least so far as we know) there's no "ultimate theoretical reason" why anything like this should work. And in fact, as we'll discuss, I think we have to view this as a – potentially surprising – scientific discovery: that somehow in a neural net like ChatGPT's it's possible to capture the essence of what human brains manage to do in generating language.

As long ago as 1981 Margaret Boden[5] wrote.

> We now have machines with a subjective model (representation) of the world and their own actions in it by means of which they deliberate more or less carefully about what they should do and what they should not have done and why.

So even the early experimental systems developed forty years ago were much more than parrots that we can teach to speak, but which have no idea what they are saying.

In another forty-year-old quote, Geoff Simons[6] wrote:

> The spectrum of AI has traditionally been concerned with a group of well-defined cognitive functions – memory, learning, problem-solving, decision-making, language understanding, game playing, visual perception, etc. In the future these various activities will become more sophisticated and, in many ways, more humanlike. These processes represent, in some sense, an initial phase of AI evolution. Increased understanding of the various theoretical concerns and technological progress will combine to extend the spectrum of AI to such phenomena as intuition, creativity and emotion.

In addition to language understanding, and language generation, then, the AI research agenda has since its origins included game playing, learning, problem-solving, and decision-making—all aspects of thinking and social interaction that involve a sense of context, options, strategy, together with an awareness of other actors and their own intentions and perspectives.

---

[3] Rothman (2023).

[4] Wolfram (2023).

[5] Boden (1981), p. 293.

[6] Simons (1984), p. 233.

These factors are of course at the heart of contracting and explain why it is such a challenging and fascinating field. Contracts embody (or should embody) the intentions of the contracting parties, a record of their rights, obligations, and responsibilities and also address their concerns about each other's motives—the games they may be playing, we might say.

In this chapter, we explore how AI assistants can serve as brainstorming and ideation partners in the problem-framing and solution-finding phases. By harnessing their capabilities, we aim to find inspiration, explore different perspectives and stimulate creativity. While AI offers significant support, it is clear that humans cannot completely hand over responsibility to machines. Therefore, we also examine the extent of human oversight required and discuss how effective prompting can improve the quality of AI-generated results.

2 Claude and ChatGPT Tell Us How to Bridge the Implementation Gap

This chapter records conversations between its co-authors and two AI assistants: Claude from Anthropic, and ChatGPT4o from OpenAI. First, we ask them in general terms about the potential for using generative AI in bridging the implementation gap in contracting. Next, we set ChatGPT4o two contract simplification tasks, to check how much help it might be as our assistant. Then, we present ChatGPT4o with a sceptical point of view about its capabilities and challenge it to offer counter arguments.

We started with the assumption and experience that AI systems are very good at writing and editing, so this did not need to be verified. AI has been built into writers' helps such as Grammarly and DeepL Write for some time now, and it is brilliant at simplifying language, or applying styles to it. AI can pick out the main themes in a document and suggest headings or summaries. And one of us has successfully asked ChatGPT to suggest FAQ-style headings and apply a layered structure to a contract text.[7] So in this chapter we go a little further and test whether AI can help us frame our problem, find solutions and address the needs of different audiences.

First, we prompted Claude and ChatGPT to address the topic of our chapter by asking: "Can you help us bridge the implementation gap in contracting?" We didn't have to explain what the implementation gap is—Claude and ChatGPT already knew it (not a surprise, as a quick online search reveals plenty of uses of the term). But Claude went on to suggest some quite comprehensive solutions[8]:

> The "implementation gap" in contracting refers to the disconnect that often exists between the terms agreed to in a written contract and what actually happens in practice during the execution and operationalization of that contract. Contracts are often long, complex documents

[7] Autto et al. (2024a, 2024b).

[8] Our conversations with ChatGPT and Claude are documented and can be obtained on request from the authors.

full of legalese that the average person finds difficult to fully understand. Key obligations, deliverables and procedures outlined in the contract don't always get clearly communicated to or followed by the personnel responsible for carrying out the contract.

This is where I believe generative AI language models could help. These models, when trained on large datasets of contracts, have the ability to read and understand the content and key terms of contracts. They could potentially be used to:

- Automatically extract and highlight the most important terms, obligations, deliverables, timelines etc. from a complex contract into a more digestible summary. This summary could be shared with relevant stakeholders to improve understanding and alignment.
- Generate simple, plain-language versions of contracts or contract clauses to improve comprehension by a broader audience. The AI could "translate" legalese to everyday language.
- Proactively identify potential risks or points of confusion in draft contracts and suggest clarifying language or flag issues for further discussion between the parties. This could help produce clearer, more complete contracts.
- Generate checklists, process flows, or other job aids based on the procedures and requirements captured in the contract, to guide proper execution.
- Power chatbots or virtual assistants that could interactively answer employee and contractor questions about their contractual responsibilities in a particular scenario.

However, there are challenges and risks to be managed:

- AI models can hallucinate or make mistakes, so any outputs would need careful human review, especially for high-stakes contracts. The AI is not a substitute for human legal and subject matter expertise.
- Training AI models requires access to large amounts of contract data, which may be proprietary or sensitive. Proper data governance is essential.
- Using AI to interpret contracts does not replace the need for the parties to a contract to invest time upfront to ensure there is true mutual understanding and agreement. The AI could give a false sense of "figuring it out later."
- There may be concerns about using AI in contexts where explainability and accountability for decisions are important, as the AI's reasoning is often a "black box."

So in summary, I believe generative AI has real potential to help organizations improve the execution of contracts and reduce implementation gaps, when used carefully as an assistive tool to augment and scale human expertise. But it's not a magic bullet and comes with challenges to proactively address. Organizations should experiment incrementally to build comfort and validate value.

ChatGPT, for its part, began by noting that bridging the implementation gap in contracting requires a shift from contract creation as a legal formality to contract execution as a strategic, operational tool: ensuring that contracts not only capture agreements in writing but also guide behaviour, decision-making, and collaboration throughout their lifecycle. It then told us *how*, under five main headings: designing contracts for action, not just documentation; improving contract language and structure; embedding contracts in workflows and digital systems; ensuring contracts drive behaviour and decision-making; and linking contracts to business outcomes. Bridging the gap, it said, involves designing contracts that are clear, jargon-free, and structured to facilitate understanding by all stakeholders. It also suggested incorporating visuals and modular components that can improve usability and ensure contracts serve as effective management tools. Ultimately, it noted, this approach shifts the perception of contracts from mere control mechanisms to collaborative tools that foster trust, transparency, and continuous improvement.[9]

We were impressed by Claude's and ChatGPT's summaries of the potential solutions. Both have gone straight to ideas that this chapter's authors, and others in the field of contract design and legal information design, have advocated for many years.[10] However, we observe that Claude, presumably because it is trained on existing documents, is quite conservative in its suggestions. It did not suggest digital channels, graphic formats or design patterns borrowed from other genres such as user guides, FAQs, or comic strips—all of which have been experimented with by contract and legal information designers, including the authors of this chapter.[11] Yet these alternative formats have all been developed to make documents usable and actionable.

In addition to the conventional legal and risk management concerns, modern contracts are also expected to act as a framework for a mutually successful business outcome, and as an effective communication tool for those who need operational guidance.[12] So it is encouraging to see that Claude and ChatGPT have moved beyond the simple translation of legalese, to suggest summaries and job aids based on the requirements of the contract. And Claude has clearly taken on board the well-known criticisms of AI, that it can hallucinate, and lacks accountability.

We noticed that our two AI assistants focused on different issues. In fact, an important caveat to bear in mind is that you can ask your AI assistant to do the same task on separate occasions, and get different responses—so on another day, each system will have produced still different outcomes.

We experimented with prompting ChatGPT and Claude to take on different personas, varying from an academic researcher to a contract practitioner. The answers varied considerably. When we wanted to see how ChatGPT would respond to our prompt to bridge the implementation gap in contracting through the role of a contract practitioner, it took a hands-on, practical approach that ensures contracts are not just created but effectively executed and responded, dividing its responses into 11 different topics and giving its why and how for each:

Here's how I would approach the challenge:

1. **Understand the Context and Stakeholders**
    - **Why**: The implementation gap often arises from mismatched expectations or lack of clarity about roles and responsibilities.
    - **How**: Begin every engagement with stakeholder workshops or interviews to deeply understand:

---

[9] Our conversation with ChatGPT 4.o is available at https://chatgpt.com/share/67bf3250-bf98-800d-a8ad-5d2d9ebad3c4. For the sake of brevity, we have summarised it here.

[10] Waller (2022), Waller et al. (2022), Passera (2017), Waller et al. (2017), Waller et al. (2016), Haapio (2013), Passera and Haapio (2013).

[11] See, e.g., the resources listed in Notes 7 and 10.

[12] WorldCC (2024).

  - The business goals.
  - The operational realities of all parties.
  - Potential risks and constraints.

- Translate this understanding into clear, actionable contract language.

2. **Draft for Action, not just Agreement**

- **Why**: Contracts are often seen as legal safeguards rather than operational tools.
- **How**: Focus on designing contracts that emphasize:

  - Clear obligations and timelines.
  - Specific success criteria (e.g., "Deliverable X must meet Quality Standard Y by Date Z").
  - Flexibility for change management (e.g., mechanisms for renegotiation or amendments).

3. **Co-Create Contracts with Stakeholders**

- **Why**: People are more likely to follow agreements they've helped shape.
- **How**: Use collaborative drafting sessions where all parties have input into the terms, facilitated by tools like interactive templates or contract platforms. This process can:

  - Clarify expectations.
  - Surface misunderstandings early.
  - Build trust and buy-in.

4. **Embed Usability and Accessibility**

- **Why**: Contracts are often too dense for operational teams to use effectively.
- **How**: Redesign contracts to be user-friendly:

  - Use plain language and clear headings.
  - Include visuals like timelines, flowcharts, or responsibility matrices.
  - Provide summaries or quick-reference guides for key obligations.

5. **Integrate Technologyfor Monitoring and Execution**

- **Why**: Many obligations fail due to a lack of follow-up or visibility.
- **How**: Use Contract Lifecycle Management (CLM) tools to:

  - Automate reminders for deadlines and obligations.
  - Provide dashboards to track performance metrics.
  - Generate alerts for potential breaches or disputes.

6. **Focus on Communication and Education**

- **Why**: Teams implementing contracts may not fully understand their roles or risks.
- **How**: Conduct kickoff meetings or training sessions where:

  - Key terms and obligations are explained.
  - Teams can ask questions or raise concerns.
  - A "contract champion" is identified in each organization to monitor compliance and resolve issues.

7. **Create Feedback Loops**
    - **Why**: Static contracts often fail to adapt to real-world conditions.
    - **How**: Establish mechanisms for regular review and adjustment:
        - Schedule quarterly reviews of contract performance.
        - Encourage parties to document challenges and successes for future improvements.
        - Include escalation paths for resolving issues collaboratively before they escalate to disputes.

8. **Adopt Proactive Legal Strategies**
    - **Why**: Many contracts are reactive, focusing on mitigating disputes rather than achieving results.
    - **How**: Shift the focus toward:
        - Preventive clauses that foresee common pitfalls.
        - Collaborative clauses that promote shared problem-solving.
        - Incentives for positive performance, such as bonuses for exceeding targets.

9. **Make Success Measurable**
    - **Why**: Vague contracts make it hard to assess performance.
    - **How**: Incorporate measurable outcomes:
        - Define clear KPIs for each party.
        - Specify how success will be tracked and validated.
        - Align payment milestones with deliverable acceptance.

10. **Leverage Dispute Prevention and Early Resolution**
    - **Why**: Implementation gaps often lead to disputes, which derail contracts.
    - **How**: Include:
        - Early warning systems for potential disputes (e.g., regular status updates).
        - Tiered resolution processes, such as mediation before arbitration or litigation.
        - Clear definitions of force majeure or other exceptions to prevent unnecessary conflict.

11. **Document Lessons Learned**

- **Why**: Each contract offers insights that can improve future agreements.
- **How**: At the end of each contract lifecycle:
    - Conduct a post-mortem to assess what worked and what didn't.
    - Create templates or playbooks based on best practices.
    - Use this feedback to refine both contracting processes and clauses.

By emphasizing **collaboration, usability, monitoring, and adaptability**, I would ensure contracts are not just signed but lived documents that guide successful outcomes. This approach bridges the gap between intent and execution, ensuring contracts serve as tools for mutual success. Would you like to explore any of these steps in more depth?

It was encouraging to see that in all our conversations, Claude and ChatGPT had taken “contract” to mean more than the contract document—they looked at what the document says about the business relationship and how it will be managed. ChatGPT gave us valuable suggestions on how to manage and monitor contracts and contract portfolios, and how to integrate them into enterprise workflows and systems such as Contract Lifecycle Management (CLM) tools. While GenAI has great potential in these contexts,[13] our chapter focuses on the contract documents themselves, and how GenAI can help us guide human users in their use.

So our next step was to take two actual sets of contract documents—in this case standard terms and conditions—that one of us had worked on for commercial clients, to see if GenAI could find the same points of relevance to the workplace. In both client projects, the goal was to bridge the implementation gap, and to make sure that important practical actions were noticed rather than being hidden in a fog of legalese and small print. In both projects, we applied principles normally associated with user guides: plain language, headings, summaries, and visualisations of complex processes.

2.1 Writing a Contract Guide

We first experimented with the General Terms and Conditions of Purchase from a technology company. We wanted to see if ChatGPT could create a separate user guide section that summarises various types of practical action that was scattered through the document. We wanted it to list all the clauses that set up.

- a requirement to keep records,
- a requirement to communicate information,
- or a requirement for both parties to agree.

We asked ChatGPT to read the General Terms and Conditions (GTCs) and list all the clauses that contained the listed topics—essentially to do the same work as the human had done, resulting in the redesigned document, excerpts of which are shown in Fig. 1.

ChatGPT proved for the most part capable of this task, although the results were slightly different from the human:

- Sometimes the human and ChatGPT disagreed about whether a particular requirement belonged in the communication requirement section or the to-be-agreed section.
- ChatGPT occasionally over-interpreted a clause. For example, it thought that the confidentiality clause required “confidentiality records” to be kept, whereas the clause actually just required data to be kept confidential.

[13] Cummins and Guyer (2025) in this Book.

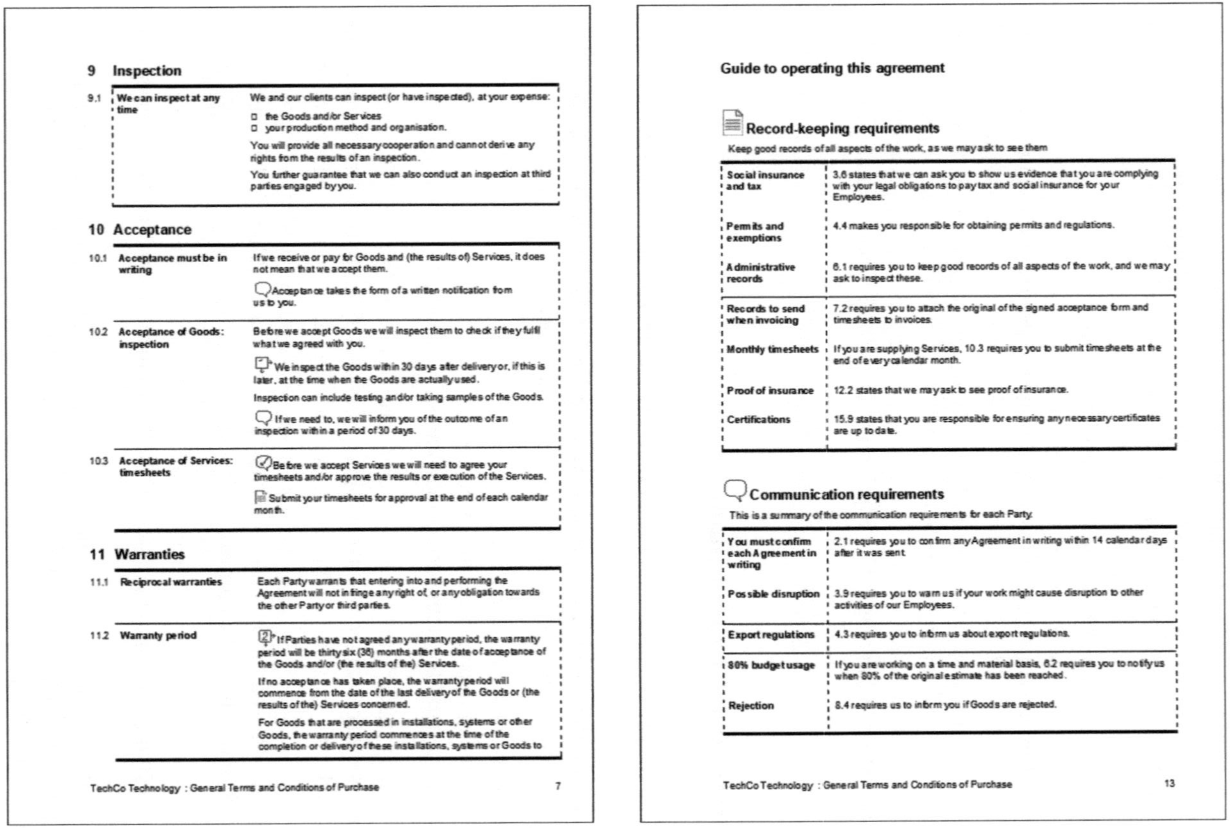

9 Inspection

9.1	**We can inspect at any time**	We and our clients can inspect (or have inspected), at your expense: □ the Goods and/or Services □ your production method and organisation. You will provide all necessary cooperation and cannot derive any rights from the results of an inspection. You further guarantee that we can also conduct an inspection at third parties engaged by you.

10 Acceptance

10.1	**Acceptance must be in writing**	If we receive or pay for Goods and (the results of) Services, it does not mean that we accept them. Acceptance takes the form of a written notification from us to you.
10.2	**Acceptance of Goods: inspection**	Before we accept Goods we will inspect them to check if they fulfil what we agreed with you. We inspect the Goods within 30 days after delivery or, if this is later, at the time when the Goods are actually used. Inspection can include testing and/or taking samples of the Goods. If we need to, we will inform you of the outcome of an inspection within a period of 30 days.
10.3	**Acceptance of Services: timesheets**	Before we accept Services we will need to agree your timesheets and/or approve the results or execution of the Services. Submit your timesheets for approval at the end of each calendar month.

11 Warranties

11.1	**Reciprocal warranties**	Each Party warrants that entering into and performing the Agreement will not infringe any right of, or any obligation towards the other Party or third parties.
11.2	**Warranty period**	If Parties have not agreed any warranty period, the warranty period will be thirty six (36) months after the date of acceptance of the Goods and/or (the results of the) Services. If no acceptance has taken place, the warranty period will commence from the date of the last delivery of the Goods or (the results of the) Services concerned. For Goods that are processed in installations, systems or other Goods, the warranty period commences at the time of the completion or delivery of these installations, systems or Goods to

TechCo Technology : General Terms and Conditions of Purchase 7

Guide to operating this agreement

Record-keeping requirements

Keep good records of all aspects of the work, as we may ask to see them

Social insurance and tax	3.6 states that we can ask you to show us evidence that you are complying with your legal obligations to pay tax and social insurance for your Employees.
Permits and exemptions	4.4 makes you responsible for obtaining permits and regulations.
Administrative records	6.1 requires you to keep good records of all aspects of the work, and we may ask to inspect these.
Records to send when invoicing	7.2 requires you to attach the original of the signed acceptance form and timesheets to invoices.
Monthly timesheets	If you are supplying Services, 10.3 requires you to submit timesheets at the end of every calendar month.
Proof of insurance	12.2 states that we may ask to see proof of insurance.
Certifications	15.9 states that you are responsible for ensuring any necessary certificates are up to date.

Communication requirements

This is a summary of the communication requirements for each Party.

You must confirm each Agreement in writing	2.1 requires you to confirm any Agreement in writing within 14 calendar days after it was sent.
Possible disruption	3.9 requires you to warn us if your work might cause disruption to other activities of our Employees.
Export regulations	4.3 requires you to inform us about export regulations.
80% budget usage	If you are working on a time and material basis, 6.2 requires you to notify us when 80% of the original estimate has been reached.
Rejection	8.4 requires us to inform you if Goods are rejected.

TechCo Technology : General Terms and Conditions of Purchase 13

Fig. 1 Excerpts from the human-generated, redesigned general terms and conditions of purchase from a technology company (anonymized here). The icons in the main pages (left) alert the reader to contract requirements, which are then listed in a user guide at the end of the document (right)

- ChatGPT spotted a couple of things missed by the human—for example, the Force Majeure (FM) clause required the other party to immediately inform the buyer of a FM event.

Overall, then, the results looked much the same as if a human assistant had done the work—it was useful but needed checking.

Next, we asked ChatGPT to read the original GTCs and write its own guide to them. So it did. It produced something that seemed at first sight to be an excellent job. We liked, for example, the translation of "Definitions" into "Key terms to know." One of these terms was "Contract," which in ChatGPT's guide was defined as "The legally binding agreement formed by our order, your acceptance, and the GTC." However, this was not something it found in the original document. Instead ChatGPT was seeking to educate the reader, using its general knowledge.

It also used its general knowledge to introduce guidance about how to accept an order, but this time it may have over-reached:

> **How to Accept**: To accept an order, confirm receipt and indicate that you'll fulfill it according to the GTC. Often, starting to fulfill the order or shipping goods means you've accepted it.

The problem is that how to accept an order was not mentioned anywhere in the original document. ChatGPT introduced this process and added its own advice in the sentence starting with "often." This may or may not be right under the applicable law. So at this point, we thought that ChatGPT had possibly provided us an example of what Claude predicted might happen, when it said:

> AI models can hallucinate or make mistakes, so any outputs would need careful human review, especially for high-stakes contracts. The AI is not a substitute for human legal and subject matter expertise.

To check this, we tested the possibility that ChatGTP was not hallucinating but in fact was basing its advice about how to accept an order on its knowledge of the applicable law. So we asked it from where it had derived this advice. This extended conversation produced more detail than we can report here, and in the spirit of the sort of dialogue two humans might have, both parties modified their view. The humans had more confidence, while ChatGPT backtracked somewhat. In the end it modified this item of guidance to read:

> Note that under some interpretations of contract law, starting to fulfill the order (e.g., shipping goods) may sometimes imply acceptance, but it's best to provide written confirmation to avoid ambiguity.

At this point we could have continued the discussion and asked whether a written confirmation would be "best" from the supplier's or the buyer's point of view, but we decided to leave the discussion of possible Battle of Forms issues and applicable law for a later date.

2.2 *Organising Content by Audience: Does GenAI Understand What Different People Need?*

We then gave ChatGPT a second test, using a set of General Terms and Conditions of Sale from a different company. In this case, we asked it to create a guide and organise it into separate sections aimed at operational, financial, and legal audiences.

It did an excellent job of sifting through the information of relevance to these different audiences. For example, it knew that Safe Offloading is of interest to operational people but not to accountants, and that Governing Law is of interest to lawyers and Credit Terms to accountants. We will not go into detail here of exactly what it did, but instead want to reflect on what this implies about its capabilities generally.

With these tests, we reached a point where we were impressed by our AI assistant's ability to go beyond just rewriting the text that is there. It was clearly capable of generating useful guidance for different audiences. So our next challenge was framed more theoretically: we asked ChatGPT's help in explaining its insights into human intentions in communication.

3 Grammaticality and Textuality: Does AI Achieve Both?

For language to communicate in a purposeful way, it needs qualities of textuality as well as grammaticality. To explain the distinction, consider three similar sentence pairs, which all obey the rules of English grammar:

- I have a bicycle. I enjoy riding it.
- I have a bicycle. I want fish for lunch.
- I have a bicycle. Napoleon died in 1821.

We have no problem at all with the first sentence pair, but the second pair only makes sense with interpretative effort by the reader. We have to imagine a scenario such as that there is a fish restaurant at a suitable distance for cycling to, and then we have to infer a third sentence such as "So I will ride down to the harbour to get some."

However, no amount of interpretation would make sense of the third pair if it appeared in a normal conversation.[14] It is grammatical, but that is not enough to make it a valid text.

Grammar describes the rules for combining words in sentences, but it says little about the meaning and impact of language in use. In their classic work on text linguistics, Robert de Beaugrande and Wolfgang Dressler[15] contrast the two approaches, and define seven standards of textuality – qualities needed for language to work as part of a useful conversation:

---

[14] Although, ever confident, ChatGPT had a go when I asked it. It wrote an elaborate story in which the protagonist reflects on history while on a bike ride.

[15] De Beaugrande and Dressler (1981), p. 37.

- **Cohesion**: Grammatical dependencies on the text surface. *AI can definitely do this.*
- **Coherence**: Conceptual dependencies in the textual world. *AI is pretty good at this—an LLM would be unlikely to generate the third sentence pair because it is so improbable.*
- **Intentionality and Acceptability**: The attitudes of the participants towards the text. Can AI correctly anticipate the motives of writers and readers, and the effect of the text on its readers? *Our user guide test presented in Sub-section 2.2 above suggests that it is good at knowing what information will be seen as relevant by particular types of user.*
- **Informativity**: The incorporation into the new and unexpected into the old and expected. In the case of business contracts, this might take the form of signalling ways in which a particular contract departs from the expected norm. *Does AI bring this perspective?*
- **Situationality**: The setting. The identification of a text as a contract establishes its setting, and the expected roles and concerns of its users. *Does AI bring this perspective? Claude's account of the implementation gap shows an impressive understanding of the context.*
- **Intertextuality**: The mutual relevance of separate texts. Contracts often consist of and exist in a universe of related documents and references, such as general terms and conditions, specifications, price lists, orders, confirmations, and legal and regulatory frameworks. *Again, does AI bring this perspective? Claude mentioned "checklists, process flows, or other job aids," so is aware of different document types, so it gives confidence that with the right prompting it could check on how contracts work alongside other genres.*

4 Knowledge that's not Written Down

The tasks we set ChatGPT and its output reassure us that GenAI can make apparently accurate assumptions about intentions, situations, and the like. But if it is in fact dependent on LLMs for its world knowledge, what about all the knowledge that is not written down?

In a famous ethnomethodological study, the sociologist Étienne Wenger spent an extended time in an insurance claims office observing the use of information by staff. This is a particularly interesting study in the context of legal information design, because the insurance industry is famously governed by contracts in the form of the "small print." The handling of insurance claims, we might think, is amongst the most rigid of business processes. But Wenger's observations led him to conclude that written information is just one component of the knowledge that is collectively held and used amongst groups of people who work together—he calls them "communities of practice."

Wenger describes the types of knowledge used in such communities:

> It includes what is said and what is left unsaid; what is represented and what is assumed. It includes the language, tools, documents, images, symbols, well-defined roles, specified criteria, codified procedures, regulations, and contracts that various practices make explicit for a variety of purposes. But it also includes all the implicit relations, tacit conventions, subtle cues, untold rules of thumb, recognizable intuitions, specific perceptions, well-tuned sensitivities, embodied understandings, underlying assumptions, and shared world views. Most of these may never be articulated, yet they are unmistakable signs of membership in communities of practice and are crucial to the success of their enterprises.[16]

Wenger describes written knowledge as "reified,"[17] which he contrasts with the "participatory" knowledge held informally within communities of practice. This depends on trust, continuity of experience, and reflective expertise.

So, when we ask an AI system to rewrite a contract document for us, to what extent is it reliant solely on reified knowledge (that is, the written information it is tasked to simplify), or can it step back and reflect on its own limitations and imagine the other types of tacitly held knowledge that humans use in their interactions. In other words, can it be aware that there is knowledge that lies outside the data available to it? We asked ChatGPT to tell us.

5 AI's Understanding of Textuality and of Its Own Limitations

We prompted ChatGPT as follows:

> I am writing a paper on the potential for AI to help rewrite business contracts. I know you can produce correct and grammatical language, but I want to know to what extent you can imagine the motives of the writer and the reader. This has been termed "textuality" as distinct from "grammaticality," in a book published by Robert de Beaugrande and Wolfgang Dressler. Please comment on the extent to which you take them into account when rewriting a business contract. I will paste their six[18] standards in next.

Well, ChatGPT didn't wait for the quote from de Beaugrande and Dressler. It already knew it, and off it went:

> The distinction between "textuality" and "grammaticality" is an important concept in understanding how AI like me approaches language tasks, especially when it comes to rewriting business contracts. While I can certainly generate correct and grammatically sound text, understanding the motives of the writer and the interpretation by the reader – both key elements of textuality – requires a broader comprehension of the context, the relationship between the parties, and the desired outcomes of the contract.
>
> In a business contract, the intentions of the writer are often to clearly outline the terms of an agreement, avoid ambiguity, protect legal rights, and ensure that obligations are clearly

---

[16] Wenger (1998), p. 47.

[17] "Reified" here means to fix an abstract concept in a permanent or solid form, from the Latin *res* (thing).

[18] There are in fact seven standards, but de Beaugrande and Dressler in some places join Intentionality and Acceptability, reducing the list to six.

stated. On the other hand, the reader (often the other party or a legal advisor) will be focused on interpreting the contract in a way that aligns with their own interests, searching for clarity, fairness, and the minimization of risk. The concept of textuality, as Robert de Beaugrande and Wolfgang Dressler describe, involves recognizing the communicative function of the text – understanding not just the literal meaning of the words, but also the pragmatic and discursive layers involved in communication.

When I rewrite a business contract, my approach currently focuses more on maintaining precision, clarity, and consistency in language, as these are critical to the enforceability and legal integrity of a contract. However, I can incorporate elements of textuality by paying attention to…

ChatGPT then listed and accurately explained the standards. And finished by explaining its own limitations (we added italics for emphasis):

While I can simulate an understanding of motives to an extent – such as crafting text that protects one party's interests or reflects an equitable agreement – *there are still nuances in human intention and negotiation dynamics that may escape my grasp*, particularly in highly specific or emotionally charged scenarios. Understanding the strategic choices that a writer or a reader might make, or how certain phrasing might influence interpretation, can be difficult for AI because it requires a deep comprehension of human psychology, negotiation tactics, and unspoken norms.

ChatGPT sensed we might want to know more about these limitations and suggested.

Feel free to paste the six standards from de Beaugrande and Dressler's work, and I can elaborate further on how I might apply them when rewriting a business contract.

It then went through each standard and explained its own limitations, finishing with wise words about the roles of AI and humans in contract drafting. We have used italics to draw attention to AI's acknowledgement of its need for human help.

Cohesion: grammatical dependencies on the text surface

AI's approach: I can effectively maintain cohesion in business contracts by ensuring that there are clear grammatical ties between sentences and clauses. This includes using conjunctions, references, pronouns, and other linking devices that make the text flow logically. For example, clauses that define terms and conditions can be linked to sections on obligations and remedies in a consistent manner.

Challenge: While I can manage surface-level cohesion well, maintaining nuanced legal connections between clauses that subtly reinforce certain rights or responsibilities *might require human insight*. For example, recognizing when a particular clause needs to be reiterated in later sections for emphasis or legal protection.

Coherence: conceptual dependencies in the textual world

AI's approach: Coherence in a business contract involves structuring the document so that the underlying concepts (such as liabilities, warranties, or payment terms) are presented in a logically ordered way. I can ensure that key concepts are clearly introduced, defined, and related to each other in a way that aligns with the overall purpose of the agreement.

Challenge: Achieving coherence on a deeper level requires understanding the strategic intentions behind the contract. For example, one party might want to subtly introduce a higher degree of protection against unforeseen risks. Ensuring that this intent is conceptually sustained throughout the document (and is balanced against the other party's interests) *requires an understanding of negotiation dynamics, which can be difficult for an AI to fully grasp.*

Intentionality and Acceptability: the attitudes of the participants towards the text

AI's approach: I can be programmed to recognize that a business contract often represents a formal agreement between a Buyer and a Seller. The intent of the Buyer is typically to secure value, manage risks, and ensure that deliverables are provided as expected. The Seller's intent, on the other hand, is to guarantee payment while outlining the scope of their obligations. I can craft text that reflects these standard attitudes and aims for clarity, fairness, and enforceability.

Challenge: Understanding the strategic attitudes of each participant is where AI may fall short. For instance, one party might intentionally leave a clause vague to create negotiation leverage later, or emphasize certain conditions to signal good faith or flexibility. Capturing these subtleties – reflecting not just the surface-level attitudes but also the underlying power dynamics and negotiation tactics – *is difficult for AI to do autonomously.*

Informativity: incorporating the new and unexpected into the old and expected

AI's approach: Informativity is crucial in business contracts, especially when signaling departures from standard templates or introducing novel terms. For example, I can signal changes to standard industry terms by including phrases such as "Notwithstanding the foregoing…" or "Except as otherwise provided…"[19] to clearly mark where a particular clause deviates from established norms. I can integrate innovative clauses that address new circumstances, such as evolving technology or changing market conditions.

Challenge: The challenge here is recognizing when and how to introduce unexpected information without causing confusion or imbalance in the agreement. A human writer might better understand the context and use such deviations strategically to achieve a particular outcome in negotiations.

Situationality: the setting

AI's approach: A business contract operates in a specific context – an agreement between parties typically involving the exchange of goods, services, or money. The roles of Buyer and Seller are clearly defined, with the Buyer focused on obtaining value and minimizing risk, and the Seller focused on delivering the promised goods or services while securing payment. I can write with an understanding of these basic roles, addressing the concerns typically associated with each party (e.g., warranties, liabilities, deadlines, etc.).

Challenge: Situationality also involves understanding the broader social and economic factors that influence the contract. A contract in the tech industry may need clauses around intellectual property and data security, while a construction contract might emphasize timelines and regulatory compliance. Capturing these industry-specific nuances and adapting the contract to reflect them *often requires human experience and insight.*[20]

Intertextuality: mutual relevance of separate texts

AI's approach: Business contracts are rarely isolated; they interact with other legal documents, including NDAs (Non-Disclosure Agreements), Terms and Conditions, and Purchase Orders. I can recognize common legal frameworks and templates, ensuring that rewritten contracts are compatible with related documents. This helps ensure consistency across a business relationship's legal structure.

[19] Here, ChatGPT has clearly forgotten that it is talking to someone who just minutes earlier was asking it to write in plain language.

[20] The authors observe that a human might also intentionally leave certain things unaddressed, relying on general law and its implied terms, which, in the context of liabilities and remedies in a buy/sell situation, typically favour the buyer. See, e.g., Haapio (2009).

Challenge: However, understanding the precise interplay between separate documents – such as how a contract might need to reference an NDA's confidentiality clause or how it aligns with regulatory compliance documents – requires a nuanced understanding of how different texts function together in a specific business setting. AI can assist by suggesting cross-references *but may miss subtle strategic alignments* that a human negotiator would catch.

Conclusion

While AI can incorporate many elements of textuality when rewriting business contracts – especially in terms of coherence, cohesion, and maintaining the basic roles of Buyer and Seller – there are limits to how well it can capture the underlying motives, strategic intent, and negotiation dynamics. The challenges often lie in understanding the deeper, pragmatic layers of communication, such as when to emphasize or de-emphasize certain clauses, how to signal flexibility or rigidity, and when to introduce or depart from standard norms.

Human oversight remains essential in more complex contract drafting, particularly when there are nuances related to power dynamics, industry-specific concerns, or novel legal strategies. Nonetheless, AI can greatly enhance the efficiency of drafting and ensure that contracts meet high standards of clarity, consistency, and precision.

6 Human Oversight

Human oversight is essential, but what form should it take? Our experience of exploring AI in the context of business contracts was instructive. In many ways it drove home the advice that Ethan Mollick[21] summarised in the title of his book: *Co-Intelligence*. He enjoins us to use analogous human roles to help us understand what AI systems can do for us—for example, we can think of them as co-worker, tutor or coach. We like to imagine them as an intern—a colleague who has never worked in the domain before, but is highly qualified and extremely literal. Our prompts need to be clear, specific, and provide enough background information to get the best response.

And even though it's entirely possible to get high quality responses from very simple prompts, a good prompt can make a huge difference to the quality and repeatability of the outputs returned. OpenAI and Anthropic undertake research into what makes an effective prompt, and both provide guides to what has become known as prompt engineering.[22] At a high level, a well-structured prompt will contain some or all of the following elements:

- **Role**: Defining the specific persona or expertise level the AI assistant should adopt
- **Context**: Background information that helps the AI assistant understand the situation
- **Task**: Clear instructions about what you want the AI assistant to do
- **Format**: Specification of how you want the response structured
- **Constraints**: Any limitations or specific requirements

[21] Mollick (2024)

[22] OpenAI (n.d.); Anthropic (n.d.).

- **Examples**: Sometimes it helps to show the AI assistant what good output looks like.

For instance, instead of asking "What's wrong with this contract?," an effectively structured prompt might be something like:

> "You are an experienced contract lawyer reviewing a software licensing agreement. Analyse the following contract excerpt for potential legal issues, focusing particularly on liability clauses and data privacy. Present your findings in bullet points, highlighting critical issues in order of severity.
>
> [CONTRACT TEXT BEGINS] Section 5.2 Data Processing The Provider shall process all Customer Data in accordance with industry standards. Customer agrees that Provider may store data in any jurisdiction of Provider's choosing. Provider shall make commercially reasonable efforts to protect Customer Data.
>
> Section 5.3 Liability Customer shall defend, indemnify and hold harmless Provider against any claims arising from Customer's use of the Services, including but not limited to data breaches, service interruptions, or compliance violations. Provider's total liability shall not exceed the amounts paid by Customer in the previous 12 months. [CONTRACT TEXT ENDS]."[23]

We can explain this level of explicitness by thinking of the difference between writing a detailed recipe and saying something simpler like "please could you make supper." We would need to know someone well enough before we can be sure what a good supper outcome was, and if we don't know them particularly well, we risk serving something they don't like or are allergic to.

Having challenged ChatGPT to evaluate its own understanding of textuality, it makes sense that we would get better outputs by providing some of the key elements of textuality in the prompt—in particular, the context.

7 The Context—Providing Pertinent Information

When interacting with a large language model, the quality and relevance of the prompt is linked to something called the model's context window.

The context window refers to the maximum amount of textual input, measured in discrete units known as tokens, that the model can process simultaneously as it generates a response. Conceptually, it functions somewhat like a working memory buffer, enabling the model to capture and reason about a certain span of recent input before producing an output.

In essence, the prompt dictates how the model's available working memory is initially populated with information. Because the model can attend only to a fixed number of tokens at once, the selection, organisation, and concision of the material

[23] Depending on which side you are on, there are obviously more or less things wrong with the content and language of this contract. For the sake of brevity, we have omitted its definitions and applicable law sections. Unless you are an experienced professional, it is easy to forget these. As legal and regulatory requirements vary, it is important to know what to ask. While AI technologies have advanced, the careful crafting of prompts remains valid to ensure accurate and reliable outputs.

that we include in the prompt directly influences the model's capacity to generate accurate, coherent responses.

There are many ways to incorporate pertinent information and data into prompts. Here are three of the most popular:

7.1 Direct Insertion

In our sample prompt in Sect. 6 we've provided access to the specific contract we care about by inserting it directly in the prompt (it's demarcated using the CONTRACT_TEXT_BEGINS and CONTRACT_TEXT_ENDS boundaries). This works well for short sections of text, but context windows have token limits which means that for longer text this is impractical.

7.2 Retrieval-Augmented Generation (RAG)

RAG is a method for providing information to a prompt that combines the LLM's general knowledge with specific information retrieved from a custom knowledge base.

For example, a corporate legal team might maintain a knowledge base containing sample clauses, previous contracts, applicable regulatory requirements, case law, and internal policies. When analysing a new contract, RAG can automatically retrieve and include the most relevant content into the prompt, enhancing the accuracy, relevance, and specificity of the response.

7.3 Few-Shot Learning

Few-shot learning is a way to train AI through examples showing the AI exactly what we want our output to look like. They might specify:

- The expected level of detail
- The format for presenting issues
- The severity rating system, if contract risk is the focus
- The pattern of issue/analysis/recommendation.

In summary, as we start to pull at the thread of the shortcomings of AI—particularly its inability to fully understand things like negotiation dynamics or tacit human intentions—a focus on human prompting and careful management of context windows can compensate for some of these shortcomings.

And just like our intelligent but inexperienced intern, AI assistants need us to check their work carefully. While they exhibit remarkable linguistic and contextual abilities, they remain fundamentally reliant on the inputs humans provide. Prompt engineering emerges as a practical method for aligning human intent with the output produced by LLMs.

8 Conclusion

As we emphasised in our Introduction, we are all too aware that GenAI is developing very quickly and becoming ever more sophisticated. AI assistants will inevitably become cleverer than us, able to manage hugely more information than we can in our limited working memory—and so increasingly hard for humans to check their work.

Elsewhere we have argued for a layered approach to contract design, in which the full text can exist alongside human-readable explanations and high-level action points.[24] Getting this approach right is key to securing the quality of AI assistance.

AI may already be assisting both parties to a contract, or will soon do so. In procurement we already hear of complex bids that are prepared by sellers with assistance from AI, and then evaluated by buyers also with AI assistance. Given AI's tendency to stray, it will be important for there to be a human readable layer to every document—and not to tolerate AI-generated legalese or code just because another AI system will cope with it. And of course, where humans are in charge of contract performance, a human readable layer is essential to bridge the implementation gap—to make everyone with a need to know, in supplier and buyer companies and their supply chains, aware of what has been agreed, and what constitutes proper delivery of the services or goods and good management of the relationship.

References

Anthropic (n.d.) Prompt engineering overview. https://docs.anthropic.com/en/docs/build-with-claude/prompt-engineering/overview. Accessed 22 Jan 2025

Autto H, Haapio H, Nuottila J (2024a) Contracts rethought and redesigned: a new era with AI. Int J Commerce Contracting 8(1–2):7–34

Autto H, Haapio H, Pappila M (2024b) Artificial intelligence in contract design—biodiversity offset contracts as an example. Liikejuridiikka 3/2024:8–36

BBC Newsnight (2024) "Godfather of AI" on AI "exceeding human intelligence" and it "trying to take over" (Geoffrey Hinton interviewed by Faisal Islam). YouTube, 17 May. https://youtu.be/MGJpR591oaM?si=Y0wnYeUTiZTWXp1U. Accessed 4 Dec 2024

Boden M (1981) Minds and mechanisms. Harvester Press, Brighton

Cummins T, Guyer S (2025) Contracting: is generative AI really making a difference? In: Corrales Compagnucci M, Haapio H, Fenwick M (eds), Generative AI, contracts, law and design. Springer, Singapore

De Beaugrande R, Dressler W (1981) Introduction to text linguistics. Longman, London

---

[24] Waller et al. (2022).

Haapio H (2009) Invisible terms and creative silence: what you don't see can help or hurt you. Contract Management, Sep, 24–35

Haapio H (2013) Next generation contracts: a paradigm shift. Lexpert Ltd, Helsinki

Mollick E (2024) Co-intelligence: living and working with AI. WH Allen, London

OpenAI (n.d.) Promt engineering. https://platform.openai.com/docs/guides/prompt-engineering. Accessed 22 Jan 2025

Passera S (2017) Beyond the wall of contract text—visualizing contracts to foster understanding and collaboration within and across organizations. Aalto University publication series, Doctoral Dissertations 134/2017. https://aaltodoc.aalto.fi/handle/123456789/27292. Accessed 10 Dec 2024

Passera S, Haapio H (2013) Transforming contracts from legal rules to user-centered communication tools: a human-information interaction challenge. Commun Design Quarter 1(3):38–45

Rothman J (2023) Why the godfather of A.I. fears what he's built. New Yorker, 13 Nov. https://www.newyorker.com/magazine/2023/11/20/geoffrey-hinton-profile-ai. Accessed 4 Dec 2024

Simons GL (1984) Introducing artificial intelligence. NCC Publications, Manchester

Waller R (2022) Designing contracts for human readers. In: Corrales M, Haapio H, Fenwick M (eds), Research handbook on contract design. Edward Elgar Publishing, Cheltenham

Waller R, Haapio H, Passera S (2017) Contract simplification: the why and the how. Contract Excellence J, 24 Jul. https://www.worldcc.com/Resources/Blogs-and-Journals/Contracting-Excellence-Journal/View/ArticleID/10867. Accessed 10 Dec 2024

Waller R, Passera S, Haapio H (2022) Layered contracts: both legally functional and human-friendly. In: Jacob K, Schindler D, Strathausen R, Waltl B (eds), Humanization and the law. Springer, Cham

Waller R, Waller J, Haapio H, Crag G, Morrisseau S (2016) Cooperation through clarity: designing simplified contracts. J Strateg Contract Negot 2(1–2):48–68

Wenger É (1998) Communities of practice: learning, meaning, and identity. Cambridge University Press

Wolfram S (2023) What is ChatGPT doing … and why does it work? Blog post, 14 Feb. https://writings.stephenwolfram.com/2023/02/what-is-chatgpt-ng-and-why-does-it-work/. Accessed 4 Dec 2024

WorldCC (2024) The purpose of contracts: how clarity of purpose is required to measure contract quality and effectiveness. https://info.worldcc.com/purpose-of-contracts. Accessed 27 Oct 2024

Generative AI: Can Rule of Law Be Bargained for the Sake of Legal Tech Efficiency?

Ebru Metin and Tanel Kerikmäe

Abstract The threats of generative AI in modernising justice system and lawyering are discussed among stakeholders (judges, members of Bar, IT architects, public offices responsible for innovation etc.). However, the discourse has mostly been limited to the (a) capacities and resources; (b) theoretical technological possibilities; and (c) breaking down the conservativism of judges or clients. The major problems related to "deep fake," biased algorithms, human control etc. are apprehended in the context of European Ethical Charter on the use of AI in judicial systems, and AI Act. In reality, there are several existing and planned use cases of legal tech that are related to generative AI, presented as phenomena of progress. Although the general knowledge of the potential problems and errors exists and the audit by humans is highlighted as a solution, the discussion lacks certain relevant aspect—client's (of innovative services) needs such as transparency and accountability within the scope of Rule of Law. The clear lacuna is the lack of process or lifecycle for adopting the new use-cases prioritising the user-friendly approach and need for more effective access to justice. Innovation in the delicate field of applying legal rules needs analysis of human perception of justice in digital era to avoid the avangard use cases become beneficial rather to the service provider than the client who is left with the illusion of cost and time effectiveness.

Keywords Efficiency · Generative artificial intelligence · Legal technology · Rule of law

(†) Prof. Tanel Kerikmäe passed away during the final stages of this publication. The remaining authors and editors honour his contribution to this article.

E. Metin (✉) · T. Kerikmäe
Department of Business Administration and Department of Law, School of Business and Governance, Tallinn University of Technology, Tallinn, Estonia
e-mail: ebru.metin@taltech.ee

T. Kerikmäe
e-mail: tanel.kerikmae@taltech.ee

© The Author(s), under exclusive license to Springer Nature Singapore Pte Ltd. 2025
M. Corrales Compagnucci et al. (eds.), *Generative AI, Contracts, Law and Design*, Perspectives in Law, Business and Innovation,
https://doi.org/10.1007/978-981-95-2058-9_6

1 Introduction

Artificial intelligence (AI) has an immense impact on all systems, including the justice system.[1] Generative artificial intelligence (GenAI) uses deep learning models which can generate high quality text, image and other outputs based on the data that they were trained on,[2] even has a greater impact in recent years. The rise of GenAI in the justice field has many layers affecting directly judges, lawyers, IT professionals, public offices and other legal content creators. This requires all justice sector actors to at least understand the pros and cons of this technology and how it affects their daily lives in order to sustain, as GenAI also comes with opportunities and threats as any other technology.

Furthermore, GenAI impacts not only the individuals or institutions but the technologies used in the legal sector. Julian Webb defines legal technology as 'the use of digital information and communication technologies to automate all or part of the legal work process, to offer decision support to legal service producers, and to provide legal information and advice directly to clients/end users'.[3] Among many technological advancements, GenAI stands out for its potential due to its huge capacity to automate tasks, enhance decision-making and improving access to legal sources for end users.[4]

However, alongside these promising developments, the integration of GenAI to the justice system raises important ethical and legal questions. Considering these questions, there is the responsible AI approach which is an "approach that aims to consider the ethical, moral, legal, cultural and social-economic consequences, during the development and deployment of AI systems."[5] This chapter explores this GenAI within the realm of legal technology, posing a fundamental question: Can the Rule of Law be compromised for the sake of legal tech efficiency?

2 Current Discourse on Generative AI in Legal Tech

The integration of AI into legal technologies is a topic of significant discussion among stakeholders in the justice system. One example of such discussions of innovating the justice system was the European Union Agency for the Operational Management of Large-Scale IT Systems in the Area of Freedom, Security and Justice (eu-LISA)'s roundtable event during November 2023 in Madrid, Spain. According to the Event Report,[6] the roundtable served as a forum to explore the challenges and opportunities at the intersection of technology and justice where also Member State initiatives in

[1] Alarie et al. (2018), p. 1.

[2] Villasenor (2024), p. 26.

[3] Whalen (2022), p. 49; Webb (2021).

[4] Golbin et al. (2020), p. 2121.

[5] Dignum (2019), p. 119.

[6] eu-LISA (2023), p. 4.

the area of digitalization of justice were presented. Another event was The Athens Roundtable 2023 organised by The Future Society where bridging the gap in AI governance and the rule of law was discussed including a diverse community of policymakers, AI developers, thought leaders, academics and civil society leaders. In one of the sessions, namely "Uncovering the Use of Generative AI in Judicial Contexts," the rise of the GenAI tools and their dual role in the judicial systems worldwide was explored. Experts taking the floor in the panel discussed how GenAI tools by legal operators are used and proposed concrete steps to build capacity, such as the UNESCO AI toolkit for judicial operators.[7] Yet another example of such discussions is the "Generative Artificial Intelligence in the Justice System" conference organized by The European Bars Federation (FBE) in Barcelona, 2024. Panels included topics such as implementing AI in legal decision-making processes, GenAI in the hands of lawyers, Enhancing Access to Justice Through GenAI: Experiences from the CREA II Project and Addressing Public Trust and Confidence in AI-Powered Justice Systems.

In this chapter we will take a look at the current discourse on GenAI in legal tech predominantly focused on three main areas, namely: the capacities and resources required for implementation, the theoretical technological possibilities of GenAI and overcoming conservatism of judges or clients. However, these discussions often miss aspects such as transparency, accountability and the broader implications for the Rule of Law.

2.1 Capacities and Resources Required for GenAI Implementation

The first area of discussion centers around the capacities and resources necessary for the effective implementation of GenAI in legal tech. Stakeholders are concerned with the infrastructure, funding, and technical expertise required to develop and maintain AI systems. According to Goldman Sachs, GenAI could boost annual productivity by 1.5%, driving $7 trillion in added economic value over the next decade.[8] However, the deployment of GenAI systems requires significant investment in infrastructure, including high-performance computing resources, secure data storage and robust cybersecurity measures.[9]

In addition to this, funding is a critical issue, as the development and implementation of AI technologies in the legal sector involve substantial financial commitments. Public and private investment plays a crucial role in supporting these initiatives. According to a CodeX—The Stanford Center for Legal Informatics paper,[10] venture funding for LegalTech startups totalled ~ $700 M between Jan 2023–Feb

[7] Athens Roundtable (2023), p. 6.

[8] Verten (2024), para. 1.

[9] Humphreys et al. (2024).

[10] Ma et al. (2024), p. 3.

2024, leaning towards startups leveraging AI. Furthermore, major startup fund raises included Harvey[11] ($80 M, Series B), EvenUp[12] ($50 M, Series B) and Masttro[13] ($43 M, Series A). Besides the private sector actors, public sector actors have also been actively involved in use of artificial initiatives in the justice systems. One of the examples of such initiatives is Germany where "The Ministry of Justice in Baden-Württemberg recommended using AI with natural language understanding (NLU) and other capabilities to help categorize each case into the different case groups they were handling."[14] In scope of this initiative, IBM created an AI assistant named OLGA that offered case categorization, extracted metadata that bring cases to faster resolution. Another example from the public sector is from Spain where techUK has partnered with the Spanish Ministry of Justice to develop a GenAI-powered judicial search engine called Delfos. Using large language models and the Microsoft Cloud, Delfos enables users to access relevant information quickly and efficiently by searching complex judicial documents with an easy to use user interface.[15]

Technical expertise is another capacity and resource issue that has been widely discussed among legal professionals, academics and members of the judiciary. The integration of GenAI into legal practices necessitates a workforce skilled in AI and machine learning. This includes not only IT professionals but also legal practitioners who understand the capabilities and limitations of AI technologies. UNESCO's "Global Judges' Initiative: Survey on the Use of AI Systems by Judicial Operators"[16] gives solid insights into this matter. According to this report, only 31% of the judicial operators considered themselves experts or very familiar with the subject, 41% declared their knowledge of AI was moderate, 20% believed they knew slightly, and 7% acknowledged knowing nothing about the topic. Furthermore, respondents support mandatory regulations and training on AI use in judicial activities, with 92% calling for such measures. On the other hand, GenAI also challenges private sector legal professionals where some companies bring such tools in-house for reducing reliance on outside suppliers.[17] In regard to this, new AI tools are disrupting especially alternative legal service providers (ALSPs) to bring more of their work back to in-house where in-house legal professionals need to gain skills for handling such AI tools. Continuous training and education programs are essential to keep the legal workforce updated on the latest advancements in AI and their applications in the legal field. On top of these, wide discussions surround the topic of law school students and their abilities to handle AI tools, including the GenAI tools where scholars discuss how to consider new methods to incorporate AI technology into teaching.[18]

[11] Counsel AI Corporation (2024).

[12] EvenUp Inc. (2024).

[13] Masttro (2024).

[14] Schindler (2024).

[15] techUK (2023).

[16] Guttierez (2024).

[17] Moshinsky (2023).

[18] Ajevski et al. (2023).

2.2 Theoretical Technological Possibilities

The second area of focus is the theoretical technological possibilities of GenAI. Stakeholders explore the potential applications of AI in various aspects of the legal system, from automating routine tasks to enhancing decision-making processes.

GenAI can significantly reduce the time and effort required for routine legal tasks[19] such as document drafting, contract analysis, and legal research. By automating these processes,[20] legal professionals can focus on more complex and value-added activities. For instance, drafting legal documents often involves repetitive work, which can be efficiently handled by AI systems trained to recognize and generate appropriate legal language. This not only speeds up the process but also reduces the likelihood of human error.[21]

Contract analysis is another area where AI can make a substantial impact. Traditionally, reviewing contracts for potential risks, compliance issues, and key terms can be time-consuming. AI-powered tools can quickly analyze and highlight crucial elements, ensuring that nothing is overlooked. This allows legal teams to concentrate on negotiating terms and providing strategic advice. According to the World Commerce & Contracting's Report, "AI in procurement, legal, and contract management streamlines transactional tasks through automation, enhances strategic contracting through analytics, optimizes risk assessment, and improves decision-making by analyzing vast data sets, leading to more efficient and informed contract negotiations and compliance monitoring."[22]

Legal research is yet another labor-intensive area of the legal profession. AI systems can explore vast databases of legal texts, case law, and statutes to find relevant information. These systems can provide summaries and highlight pertinent case law, significantly cutting down the research time for lawyers.[23]

AI systems have the potential to assist judges and lawyers in making more informed decisions by providing data-driven insights and predictive analytics. These systems can analyze vast amounts of legal data, identify patterns, and suggest possible outcomes based on historical precedents. On the other side of the justice system, by making legal services more efficient and affordable, GenAI can improve access to justice for underserved populations.[24] Automated legal advice and self-help tools powered by AI can empower individuals to navigate the legal system more effectively.

[19] Brynjolfsson et al. (2023), p. 6.

[20] Villasenor (2024), p. 28.

[21] Orange (2024).

[22] World Commerce & Contracting (2024).

[23] Black (2024).

[24] Chien and Kim (2025), p. 5.

2.3 Breaking Down Conservatism

The third area of discourse involves addressing the conservatism prevalent among judges and/or clients regarding the adoption of AI technologies in the legal field. This conservatism stems from a combination of skepticism about the reliability of AI systems and a preference for traditional legal practices.

Judges[25] and legal practitioners[26] often exhibit skepticism towards AI due to concerns about its reliability, transparency, and accountability. Ensuring that AI systems are explainable and auditable is crucial to building trust among legal professionals. Clients may also be wary of AI-driven legal services, fearing that automated systems might not fully understand their unique situations or provide personalized advice. The legal field is characterized by traditions and practices that are resistant to change. Overcoming this cultural and institutional resistance requires demonstrating the tangible benefits of AI technologies and ensuring that they complement rather than replace human judgment.

The adoption of AI in legal tech must be guided by regulatory and ethical frameworks that address concerns about bias, fairness, and human oversight. These frameworks should ensure that AI systems uphold the principles of the Rule of Law and protect the rights of individuals.

2.4 Missing Elements: Transparency and Accountability

Despite the extensive discussions on capacities, technological possibilities, and conservatism, the discourse often overlooks critical aspects related to transparency and accountability in the use of GenAI in legal tech. Addressing these elements is crucial for ensuring that AI systems are used ethically and in line with the principles of the Rule of Law. Considering the negative aspects of the GenAI tools that are used to create deep fakes,[27] causing discrimination based on the algorithmic biases[28] and hallucinations,[29]transparency and accountability gains even more importance.

Transparency in AI systems is essential for stakeholders to understand how decisions are made. This involves making the underlying algorithms and data sources accessible and comprehensible to legal professionals and clients. Transparency allows stakeholders to evaluate AI decisions where legal professionals need to understand the rationale behind AI-generated decisions to evaluate their validity and relevance. This understanding is crucial for ensuring that AI aids rather than replaces human judgment. Secondly transparency builds trust.[30] Clients and the public need

---

[25] Raymond (2024).

[26] The Economist (2023).

[27] Shoaib et al. (2023).

[28] Zhou et al. (2024).

[29] Magesh et al. (2024).

[30] Larsson and Heintz (2020).

assurance that AI-driven legal services are reliable and fair.[31] Transparency helps build trust in AI systems by providing insight into how they operate and the data they use.

Clear accountability mechanisms are vital to address errors or biases in AI-driven legal processes.[32] Legal frameworks should define the responsibilities of AI developers, legal practitioners, and institutions in ensuring the ethical and lawful use of AI technologies. Key considerations include developer accountability, practitioner responsibility and institutional oversight. In this regard, AI developers should be responsible for ensuring that their systems are designed and tested to meet ethical standards and legal requirements. This includes regular audits and updates to address any identified issues. In addition to this, legal professionals using AI must ensure that they understand the technology and its limitations. They should be trained to interpret AI outputs critically and to integrate these insights into their legal practice responsibly. Finally, institutions should establish governance structures to oversee the deployment and use of AI systems. This includes setting up review boards to monitor AI performance and compliance with legal and ethical standards.

Such issues were also addressed in one of the key documents of European Commission for the Efficiency of Justice (CEPEJ), namely, European Ethical Charter on the use of artificial intelligence (AI) in judicial systems and their environment,' which was adopted in December 2018 by the Council of Europe. According to this Charter, CEPEJ has identified the following core principles to be respected in the field of AI and justice[33]:

- Principle of respect of fundamental rights: ensuring that the design and implementation of artificial intelligence tools and services are compatible with fundamental rights;
- Principle of non-discrimination: specifically preventing the development or intensification of any discrimination between individuals or groups of individuals;
- Principle of quality and security: with regard to the processing of judicial decisions and data, using certified sources and intangible data with models conceived in a multi-disciplinary manner, in a secure technological environment;
- Principle of transparency, impartiality and fairness: making data processing methods accessible and understandable, authorising external audits;
- Principle "under user control:" precluding a prescriptive approach and ensuring that users are informed actors and in control of their choices.

The discourse must prioritize the needs of clients, emphasizing transparency and accountability within the scope of the Rule of Law. Clients should be assured that AI-driven legal services are reliable, fair and transparent. Respectively, reliability is ensuring that AI systems provide accurate and consistent results. This involves strong testing and validation of AI technologies before deployment.[34] Furthermore,

---

[31] Lepri et al. (2018).

[32] Novelli et al. (2023).

[33] Council of Europe (2018).

[34] Dalrymple et al. (2024), p. 3.

in order to ensure fairness, it must be guaranteed that AI does not discriminate against any individual or group. This requires continuous monitoring and adjustment of AI systems to eliminate biases.[35] Lastly, transparency requires providing clients with clear information about how AI systems operate and how decisions are made. This includes offering explanations and justifications for AI-generated recommendations.

3 Ethical and Legal Challenges

GenAI brings a lot of possibilities to legal technology, promising efficiency and innovation. However, it also presents significant ethical and legal challenges that must be addressed to ensure responsible deployment. This chapter delves into these challenges, particularly in the context of transparency, accountability, and the overarching principle of responsible AI (RAI).

3.1 Ethical Challenges

Transparency and explainability are crucial in ensuring that AI systems are understandable and their decision-making processes are traceable. In the legal domain, where the stakes are high, opaque[36] AI systems can undermine trust and accountability. Transparency refers to the clarity with which the functioning and decision-making processes of an AI system are communicated to stakeholders. Particularly, The EU AI Act[37] lays out specific transparency obligations to ensure that AI systems are used and understood in a responsible manner. These regulations are particularly strict for high-risk AI systems. This includes making the underlying algorithms and data sources accessible and comprehensible to legal professionals and clients alike. Explainability goes a step further, requiring that the rationale behind specific AI-driven decisions be clear. This is particularly important in legal contexts, where understanding the "why" behind a decision can impact the perceived fairness and legitimacy of outcomes where the explanation also encourages the trust of users.[38]

Another ethical challenge is the bias issue in AI systems where bias can result from various sources, including biased training data, flawed algorithms, or systemic biases within the legal system itself. Ensuring fairness in AI involves identifying and mitigating these biases to prevent discriminatory outcomes.[39] This can be seen especially in legal contexts, where decisions can significantly affect individuals' lives. AI systems in legal tech must be audited for biases to ensure they do not increase

---

[35] Ibid.

[36] Von Eschenbach (2021), p. 1612.

[37] European Commission (2021).

[38] Vilone and Longo (2020), p. 7.

[39] Kuśmierczyk (2022), p. 6.

existing inequalities. This requires diverse and representative datasets, ongoing monitoring, and the implementation of fairness constraints during the development of AI models.[40]

The use of AI in legal contexts often involves handling sensitive personal data, making privacy protections necessary. The General Data Protection Regulation (GDPR)[41] and other data protection laws provide a framework for ensuring that personal data is processed lawfully, transparently, and securely. Ensuring privacy and data protection involves implementing measures such as data anonymization, encryption, and strict access controls. Moreover, organizations must be transparent about data usage and provide individuals with control over their data, aligning with the principles of consent and data minimization.[42] In addition to these, policy-makers may also consider having specialized regulations in the intersection of data protection and artificial intelligence.[43]

According to the responsible AI (RAI) approach, AI systems should be developed and used in ways that respect human rights, autonomy, and dignity. This involves adhering to ethical guidelines that prioritize fairness, transparency, and accountability.[44]

3.2 Legal Challenges

AI systems including GenAI tools in the legal sector must comply with existing and emerging regulations. The EU AI Act aims to create a regulatory framework for AI that ensures safety, transparency, and accountability. Compliance with such regulations requires legal tech developers to implement robust governance frameworks that oversee AI development and deployment. Legal professionals must stay abreast of regulatory developments and ensure that AI systems adhere to legal standards. This includes conducting regular audits, impact assessments, and implementing necessary adjustments to maintain compliance. Furthermore, RAI approach requires robust governance frameworks which are necessary to oversee AI development and deployment. This includes regular audits, impact assessments, and the establishment of accountability mechanisms.[45]

Determining accountability and liability in AI-driven legal processes is complex.[46] Traditional legal frameworks are often not well-equipped to address the nuances of AI technologies. Establishing clear accountability mechanisms is essential to address errors or biases in AI-driven legal processes. Legal frameworks should define the

[40] Ibid.

[41] European Parliament and Council of the European Union (2016).

[42] Goldsteen et al. (2022).

[43] Kesa and Kerikmäe (2020).

[44] Dignum (2019), p. 51.

[45] Ibid, p. 53.

[46] Janani (2024).

responsibilities of AI developers, legal practitioners, and institutions in ensuring the ethical and lawful use of AI technologies. Accountability mechanisms should include clear protocols for addressing and correcting errors, biases, and other issues that may arise from AI systems. This involves delineating the roles and responsibilities of different stakeholders, from developers to end-users, to ensure a comprehensive approach to accountability.

The use of AI in generating legal documents and advice raises questions about intellectual property rights. For instance, who owns the content created by AI? Addressing these questions requires an understanding of both AI technology and intellectual property law.[47] Ensuring that AI-generated content respects existing intellectual property rights and clarifies the ownership of such content is crucial. Legal frameworks must evolve to address these challenges, ensuring that the rights of all stakeholders are protected while fostering innovation.

The ethical and legal challenges associated with GenAI in legal tech are significant, but they can also be overcome. By adhering to the principles of RAI and implementing robust governance frameworks, the legal field can harness the potential of GenAI while maintaining public trust and ethical standards. Addressing these challenges requires a concerted effort from all stakeholders, including legal professionals, technologists, and policymakers, to ensure that AI systems are developed and used responsibly.

4 Human Perception of Justice in the Digital Era

As the legal field increasingly incorporates digital technologies, particularly GenAI, it is essential to consider how these advancements impact human perceptions of justice. The digital era introduces new paradigms in the administration of justice, raising questions about fairness, accessibility, and trust. This section explores how technological innovations affect the perception of justice among legal professionals, clients, and the general public, and examines the steps needed to ensure that justice remains transparent, fair, and accessible in a digital landscape.

As mentioned in earlier sections, for AI to be effectively integrated into the legal system, it must gain the trust of legal professionals, clients, and the public. This involves demonstrating the reliability, fairness, and transparency of AI systems. Regular audits, bias assessments, and the implementation of robust ethical guidelines can help build this trust. Establishing clear accountability mechanisms is essential to address any errors or biases in AI-driven legal processes. This includes defining the responsibilities of AI developers, legal practitioners, and institutions in ensuring the ethical and lawful use of AI technologies. Accountability also involves providing avenues for redress when AI systems cause harm or produce unfair outcomes.[48]

---

[47] Hristov (2017), p. 431.

[48] Gardner (2022), p. 84.

The adoption of digital technologies in the legal field can exacerbate the digital divide,[49] where certain populations may lack access to the necessary technology or digital literacy to fully benefit from AI-driven legal services. According to Lutz, the digital divide has three levels, namely: Internet access (first-level divide), digital skills, technology uses, online participation (second-level divide), and outcomes in the form of benefits and harms (third-level digital divide).[50] Ensuring equitable access to these technologies at all levels is crucial for maintaining justice.

Furthermore, legal technologies must be designed with the end-user in mind, ensuring that they are user-friendly and accessible to individuals with varying levels of technical proficiency. This includes developing intuitive interfaces and providing adequate support and resources to help users navigate digital legal services. In this regard, one approach could be using legal design[51] principles while designing such interfaces as part of "the vision of legal design" serving the "launch new policy reforms, technology interventions, and service and visual design initiatives that can improve the legal system."[52]

In order to ensure that legal professionals are equipped to navigate the challenges of AI integration, ongoing education and training are essential. This includes training on the ethical use of AI, understanding its limitations, and developing the skills needed to interpret and leverage AI tools effectively. One of the promising developments is that bar associations around the world show eagerness to address this issue through organizing trainings,[53] creating informative content,[54] issuing guidances,[55] and composing task forces.[56]

On the policy-makers' side, they must adopt an inclusive approach when developing regulations and guidelines for AI in the legal field. This involves engaging with a diverse range of stakeholders, including legal professionals, technologists, and representatives of marginalized communities, to ensure that the benefits of AI are distributed equitably and that potential harms are mitigated.

By addressing these challenges through responsible AI practices, continuous education, and inclusive policy-making, the legal system can ensure that justice remains fair and accessible in the digital era. Maintaining a focus on human perception of justice is crucial to upholding the integrity of the legal system as it evolves with technological advancements.

---

[49] Lutz (2019).

[50] Ibid.

[51] According to Margaret Hagan, "Legal design is the application of human-centered design to the world of law, to make legal systems and services more human-centered, usable, and satisfying." See, Hagan (n.d.).

[52] Hagan (2020), p. 6.

[53] Law Association (2024).

[54] Johnson (2023).

[55] Bar Council (2024).

[56] American Bar Association (2024).

5 Recommendations and Future Directions

This chapter has explored the intersection of GenAI and RAI within the context of legal technology, focusing on whether the Rule of Law can be compromised for the sake of legal tech efficiency. The integration of GenAI into legal technology presents significant ethical and legal challenges, including risks associated with deep fakes, biased algorithms, and the necessity of maintaining human oversight. Furthermore, there is a critical need for transparency and accountability in the use of AI in the legal field. Current discourse often overlooks these aspects, which are essential for upholding the Rule of Law. Technological innovations affect the perception of justice among legal professionals, clients, and the public. Ensuring fairness, accessibility, and trust in AI-driven legal processes is crucial. Implementing RAI practices is vital for addressing the ethical and legal challenges of GenAI. These practices emphasize ethical development, robust governance, and stakeholder engagement.

To effectively integrate responsible AI practices into the legal field, the following recommendations are proposed: Firstly, developing transparent and accountable AI systems where AI systems used in legal contexts are transparent and their decision-making processes are explainable. Secondly, mitigating algorithmic bias through conducting regular audits to identify and mitigate biases in AI systems and using diverse and representative datasets during the development of AI models are crucial. Implementing fairness constraints to prevent discriminatory outcomes should also be taken into account. Thirdly, it is important to enhance accountability mechanisms by establishing clear accountability frameworks that define the responsibilities of AI developers, legal practitioners, and institutions. This should be followed by implementing protocols for addressing and rectifying errors, biases, and other issues arising from AI systems and providing avenues for redress when AI systems cause harm or produce unfair outcomes. Fourthly, prioritizing privacy and data protection is essential by implementing measures like data anonymization, encryption, and strict access controls to protect sensitive personal data. Lastly, promoting ongoing education and training everyone involved in the justice system, including law students, is key to covering all aspects of these recommendations.

To further advance the responsible integration of AI in the legal field, future research should focus on several areas. One example can be conducting long-term research to assess the long-term impact of AI on the legal system, particularly concerning fairness, accessibility, and trust. Further investigations can include how AI-driven legal processes evolve over time and their effects on different demographic groups. Further research may focus on investigating effective models of human-AI collaboration in the legal field and finding how AI can best support human decision-making while ensuring that legal professionals retain ultimate control and responsibility. Another area to be explored is focusing on designing AI systems that prioritize user-friendliness and accessibility where we also proposed legal design as a methodology. This may include how different user groups interact with AI-driven legal services and how these systems can be optimized to meet their needs. Finally, the implications of AI on legal education and training can be studied further where curricula can be developed in a way that incorporates AI literacy, ethical considerations, and practical applications in legal practice.

6 Conclusion

The integration of GenAI into the legal field promises transformative potential, enhancing efficiency and accessibility while presenting significant ethical and legal challenges. The discourse among stakeholders, including judges, lawyers, IT architects, and public offices, primarily revolves around the capacities, theoretical possibilities, and the conservatism of judges or clients towards AI adoption. However, crucial aspects such as transparency, accountability, and the broader implications for the Rule of Law often remain underexplored.

The advent of GenAI in the legal sector brings with it a dual narrative of opportunities and threats. On one hand, it holds the promise of automating routine tasks, enhancing decision-making processes, and improving access to legal resources, potentially democratizing access to justice. On the other hand, it raises critical ethical and legal concerns, such as the risks associated with deep fakes, biased algorithms, and the necessity of maintaining human oversight. Addressing these issues is paramount to ensuring that technological advancements do not compromise the Rule of Law.

One of the core challenges highlighted in this chapter is the need for transparency and accountability in AI-driven legal processes. The European Ethical Charter on the use of AI in judicial systems and the AI Act underscore the importance of these principles. Ensuring that AI systems are transparent involves making their underlying algorithms and data sources accessible and comprehensible to legal professionals and clients. This transparency is crucial for building trust, as stakeholders need to understand how decisions are made to evaluate their validity and relevance.

Accountability mechanisms are equally essential. Legal frameworks must define the responsibilities of AI developers, legal practitioners, and institutions to ensure ethical and lawful use of AI technologies. This includes implementing protocols for addressing and rectifying errors, biases, and other issues arising from AI systems. Clear accountability frameworks can help mitigate the risks associated with AI deployment, ensuring that the benefits of technological advancements are realized without undermining legal principles.

The perception of justice in the digital era is another critical consideration. For AI to be effectively integrated into the legal system, it must gain the trust of legal professionals, clients, and the public. This involves demonstrating the reliability, fairness, and transparency of AI systems.

Legal technologies must be designed with the end-user in mind, ensuring that they are user-friendly and accessible to individuals with varying levels of technical proficiency. This includes developing intuitive interfaces and providing adequate support and resources to help users navigate digital legal services.

In conclusion, while the integration of GenAI into the legal field offers immense potential for enhancing efficiency and accessibility, it must be approached with a strong commitment to ethical and legal standards. The Rule of Law cannot be compromised for the sake of technological efficiency. By prioritizing transparency, accountability, and continuous education, the legal system can evolve responsibly, ensuring that justice remains fair, accessible, and trustworthy in the digital era.

References

Ajevski M, Barker K, Gilbert A, Hardie L, Ryan F (2023) ChatGPT and the future of legal education and practice. The Law Teacher 57(3):352–364

Alarie B, Niblett A, Yoon AH (2018) How artificial intelligence will affect the practice of law. University of Toronto Law J 68(supplement 1):106–124

American Bar Association (2024) Task force on law and artificial intelligence. https://www.americanbar.org/groups/leadership/office_of_the_president/artificial-intelligence/. Accessed 20 Jun 2024

Athens Roundtable (2023) Fifth edition of the athens roundtable. https://www.aiathens.org/dialogue/fifth-edition. Accessed 21 Jun 2024

Black N (2024) Legal research tools in the age of generative AI. ABA J. https://www.abajournal.com/columns/article/legal-research-tools-in-the-age-of-generative-ai. Accessed 10 Sep 2024

Brynjolfsson E, Li D, Raymond LR (2023) Generative AI at work (No. w31161). National Bureau of Economic Research, Cambridge, MA

Chien CV, Kim M (2025) Generative AI and legal aid: results from a field study and 100 use cases to bridge the access to justice gap. Loyola of Los Angeles Law Rev 57(4):903–988

Council of Europe (2018) Ethical charter on the use of artificial intelligence in judicial systems and their environment. https://rm.coe.int/ethical-charter-en-for-publication-4-december-2018/16808f699c. Accessed 21 Jun 2024

Bar Council (2024) New guidance on generative AI for the bar. https://www.barcouncil.org.uk/resource/new-guidance-on-generative-ai-for-the-bar.html. Accessed 20 Jun 2024

Counsel AI Corporation (2024) Generative AI for professional services. https://www.harvey.ai/. Accessed 22 Jun 2024

Dalrymple D, Skalse J, Bengio Y, Russell S, Tegmark M, Seshia S, Tenenbaum J (2024) Towards guaranteed safe AI: a framework for ensuring robust and reliable AI systems, vol 2. https://doi.org/10.48550/arXiv.2405.06624. Accessed 21 Jun 2024

Dignum V (2019) Responsible artificial intelligence: how to develop and use AI in a responsible way. Springer, Cham

The Economist (2023) Generative AI could radically alter the practice of law. https://www.economist.com/business/2023/06/06/generative-ai-could-radically-alter-the-practice-of-law. Accessed 22 Jun 2024

eu-LISA (2023) Industry roundtable report—Nov 2023. https://www.eulisa.europa.eu/Publications/Reports/Industry%20Roundtable%20Report%20-%20Nov%202023.pdf. Accessed 25 Jun 2024

European Commission (2021) Proposal for a regulation of the european parliament and of the council laying down harmonised rules on artificial intelligence (Artificial Intelligence Act) and amending certain union legislative acts. EUR-Lex. https://eur-lex.europa.eu/legal-content/EN/TXT/?uri=celex%3A52021PC0206. Accessed 22 Jun 2024

European Parliament and Council of the European Union (2016) Regulation (EU) 2016/679 of the European parliament and of the council of 27 April 2016 on the protection of natural persons with regard to the processing of personal data and on the free movement of such data (General

Data Protection Regulation). Official J Europ Union L 119:1–88. https://eur-lex.europa.eu/eli/reg/2016/679/oj. Accessed 23 Jun 2024
Gardner A (2022) Responsibility, recourse, and redress: a focus on the three R's of AI ethics. IEEE Technol Soc Mag 41(2):84–89
Golbin I, Rao AS, Hadjarian A, Krittman D (2020) Responsible AI: a primer for the legal community. In: 2020 IEEE international conference on big data (Big Data) IEEE
Goldsteen A, Ezov G, Shmelkin R, Moffie M, Farkash A (2022) Data minimization for GDPR compliance in machine learning models. AI and Ethics 2(3):477–491
Guttierez JD (2024) UNESCO global judges' initiative: survey on the use of AI systems by judicial operators. UNESCO.
Hagan M (2020) Legal design as a thing: a theory of change and a set of methods to craft a human-centered legal system. Des Issues 36(3):3–15
Hagan M (n.d.) Legal design. Law by design. https://lawbydesign.co/legal-design/. Accessed 20 Jun 2024
Hristov K (2017) Artificial intelligence and the copyright dilemma. IDEA: The Law Rev Franklin Pierce Center for Intellectual Property 57(3):431–454
Humphreys D, Koay A, Desmond D, Mealy E (2024) AI hype as a cyber security risk: the moral responsibility of implementing generative AI in business. AI and Ethics 4:791–804
EvenUp Inc (2024) AI-powered demands and medical chronologies. https://www.evenuplaw.com/. Accessed 25 Jun 2024
Janani J (2024) Ensuring AI accountability: the need for expedited oversight frameworks based on EU. J Law Legal Res Developm 1(2):25–29
Johnson R (2023) Public-generative AI: the risks and opportunities for in-house teams. International Bar Association. https://www.ibanet.org/public-generative-ai-risks-and-opportunities. Accessed 26 Jun 2024
Kesa A, Kerikmäe T (2020) Artificial intelligence and the GDPR: inevitable nemeses? TalTech J Europ Stud 10(3):68–90
Kuśmierczyk M (2022) Algorithmic bias in the light of the GDPR and the proposed AI act. In: Olejnik M, Wiktoria Morawska W (eds) (In)equality. Faces of modern Europe. Wydawnictwo Centrum Studiów Niemieckich i Europejskich im. Willy'ego Brandta, Wrocław
Larsson S, Heintz F (2020) Transparency in artificial intelligence. Internet Policy Rev 9(2):1–16
Law Association (2024) Navigating the law with generative AI (On Demand). https://thelawassociation.nz/cpd-library/navigating-the-law-with-generative-ai-on-demand/. Accessed 21 Jun 2024
Lepri B, Oliver N, Letouzé E, Pentland A, Vinck P (2018) Fair, transparent, and accountable algorithmic decision-making processes: the premise, the proposed solutions, and the open challenges. Philosophy and Technol 31(4):611–627
Lutz C (2019) Digital inequalities in the age of artificial intelligence and big data. Human Behav Emerg Technol 1(2):141–148
Ma M, Sinha A, Tandon A, Richards J (2024) Generative AI legal landscape 2024. Stanford Law School. https://law.stanford.edu/publications/generative-ai-legal-landscape-2024-2/. Accessed 25 Jun 2024
Magesh V, Surani F, Dahl M, Suzgun M, Manning CD, Ho DE (2024) Hallucination-free? Assessing the reliability of leading AI legal research tools, vol 1. https://doi.org/10.48550/arXiv.2405.20362. Accessed 22 Jun 2024
Masttro (2024) Your platform for wealth in full view. https://www.masttro.com/. Accessed 22 Jun 2024
Moshinsky B (2023) Generative AI's challenge to legal sector's alternative providers. Financial Times. https://www.ft.com/content/dca849c0-09c5-4f73-9950-2c8bbd9d5759. Accessed 26 Jun 2024
Novelli C, Taddeo M, Floridi L (2023) Accountability in artificial intelligence: what it is and how it works. AI and Soc 39:1871–1882
Orange (2024) Decision making: AI can reduce rates of human errors. https://hellofuture.orange.com/en/ai-reduce-human-error-rate/. Accessed 19 Jun 2024

Raymond N (2024) US appellate judge calls bans on AI use by lawyers "Misplaced." Reuters. https://www.reuters.com/legal/transactional/us-appellate-judge-calls-bans-ai-use-by-lawyers-misplaced-2024-04-05/. Accessed 25 Jun 2024
Schindler E (2024) Judicial systems are turning to AI to help manage vast quantities of data and expedite case resolution. IBM Blog. https://www.ibm.com/blog/judicial-systems-are-turning-to-ai-to-help-manage-its-vast-quantities-of-data-and-expedite-case-resolution/. Accessed 28 Jun 2024
Shoaib MR, Wang Z, Ahvanooey MT, Zhao J (2023) Deepfakes, misinformation, and disinformation in the era of frontier AI, generative AI, and large AI models. In: 2023 International conference on computer and applications (ICCA). IEEE
techUK (2023) Helping justice agencies make the jump into GenAI and beyond. https://www.techuk.org/resource/helping-justice-agencies-make-the-jump-into-genai-and-beyond.html. Accessed 24 Jun 2024
Verten D (2024) It's time to focus on the ROI of GenAI. here's how. World Economic Forum. https://www.weforum.org/agenda/2024/05/how-businesses-should-get-the-most-out-of-genai-by-focusing-on-return-on-investment/. Accessed 22 Jun 2024
Villasenor J (2024) Generative artificial intelligence and the practice of law: impact, opportunities, and risks. Minnesota J Law Sci Technol 25(2):25–48
Vilone G, Longo L (2020) Explainable artificial intelligence: a systematic review, vol 4. https://doi.org/10.48550/arXiv.2006.00093. Accessed 22 Jun 2024
Von Eschenbach WJ (2021) Transparency and the black box problem: why we do not trust AI. Philosophy Technol 34(4):1607–1622
Webb J (2021) Legal technology: the great disruption? In: Abel RL, Sommerlad H, Hammerslev O, Schultz U (eds) Lawyers in 21st century societies (vol II). Hart Publishing, Oxford
Whalen R (2022) Defining legal technology and its implications. Int J Law Inform Technol 30(1):47–67
World Commerce & Contracting (2024) AI in contracting. https://www.worldcc.com/Portals/IACCM/Reports/AI-in-Contracting.pdf?ver=P4x9_UqMiBJrHwAdsMFt0g%3d%3d. Accessed 22 Jun 2024
Zhou M, Abhishek V, Derdenger T, Kim J, Srinivasan K (2024) Bias in generative AI, vol 1. https://doi.org/10.48550/arXiv.2403.02726. Accessed 22 Jun 2024

Proactive Privacy Communication Design for Emotional Robots

Hilja Autto, Jouko Nuottila, Anna Hurmerinta-Haanpää, and Yueh-Hsuan Weng

Abstract This chapter discusses a proactive approach to privacy communication and emotional robots, which are becoming an important part of human–machine interaction. These robots use emotional AI and are able to recognize and respond to human emotions. While there are many benefits associated with the mainstreaming of robotics, there are also significant personal data and privacy concerns involved in the use of emotional AI and robots. As a result, several initiatives to regulate the use of (emotional) AI have been made. This chapter argues that in addition to regulation, a proactive approach to privacy communication is needed in order for users of emotional robots to give consent to the collection of personal data. Tools based on the proactive approach and information design research and methods—multichannel communication, plain language, tone of voice, visualization and tailoring—make it possible to communicate personal data and privacy choices effectively to users: when robots communicate clearly through speech, gestures and screens, even less motivated users can make informed choices about whether to give their consent to the processing of their personal data. In addition, these tools make communication more effective, comprehensible and engaging for the user. The goal is that anyone who interacts with robots can do it safely and by making informed choices.

H. Autto (✉) · J. Nuottila
Faculty of Law, University of Lapland, Rovaniemi, Finland
e-mail: hilja.autto@ulapland.fi

J. Nuottila
e-mail: jouko.nuottila@ulapland.fi

A. Hurmerinta-Haanpää
School of Business, Department of Accounting and Business Law, Aalto University, Espoo, Finland
e-mail: anna.hurmerinta-haanpaa@aalto.fi

Y.-H. Weng
Inamori Frontier Program, Institute for Advanced Study, Kyushu University, and FRIS, Tohoku University, Fukuoka, Sendai, Japan
e-mail: weng.yueh.hsuan.647@m.kyushu-u.ac.jp

© The Author(s), under exclusive license to Springer Nature Singapore Pte Ltd. 2025

M. Corrales Compagnucci et al. (eds.), *Generative AI, Contracts, Law and Design*,
Perspectives in Law, Business and Innovation,
https://doi.org/10.1007/978-981-95-2058-9_7

Keywords Emotional robots · Human–robot interaction · Proactive law approach · Information design · Privacy communication

1 Introduction

The emotional robots of the twenty-first century are more advanced than ordinary industrial robots. They are social and programmed to recognize human emotions and to respond appropriately.[1] They can analyze the tone of voice, facial expressions and body language of their users to provide a more human experience when interacting with people.

These robots could have the appearance of, for instance, a pet or some other approachable object. However, users may not be aware that these cute, human- or animal-like robots are collecting their data, and that it involves certain risks. This raises critical questions about how to properly inform users of these risks and how to ensure their understanding and consent.

We argue that a proactive approach offers a suitable way to address privacy communication risks associated with robotization and promotes effective and user-friendly communication. In line with Hagan,[2] we think that privacy communication includes communication about how information is processed and used. Tools based on the proactive approach and information design research and methods—multi-channel communication, plain language, tone of voice, visualization and tailoring—can provide solutions to privacy communication problems and facilitate successful interaction between humans and robots. First, the use of multichannel communication can enhance communication on privacy protection issues. For instance, a robot can display an accessible animation of data protection content on its screen, with speech to clarify the animation and gestures to reinforce the message. This enables the robot user to better understand and engage with the message, contributing to transparent communication and facilitating comprehension of data protection risks and rights. Second, plain language and tone of voice can be applied to clarify both the robot's speech and the on-screen text concerning privacy issues. Third, visualization and design patterns can enhance comprehension of the information presented on the screen. Finally, by tailoring the whole communication to suit the specific needs and characteristics of an individual user, it is possible to optimize the information provided for each robot user.

This chapter proceeds as follows: Sect. 2 introduces operation robots with emotional characteristics; Section 3 the challenges of privacy communication; Section 4 the requirements for emotional robots provided in the EU GDPR and AI Act; Section 5 the proactive approach to privacy communication. Finally, Sect. 6 concludes.

[1] Leite et al. (2008), p. 77.

[2] Hagan (2016), p. 1.

2 Next-Generation Robots and Emotional Functionalities

The term "robot" was officially introduced in 1921 by the Czech writer Karel Capek in his play *R.U.R.—Rossum's Universal Robots*, although a similar concept is mentioned in ancient Greek and Chinese mythology. According to Capek, a robot is a group of human-like artificial workers who lack original thought.[3] Japanese robot lawyer Hirano defines robots as artificial machines that operate based on a "sense-think-act" cycle. In other words, they are machines that can sense information from their environment, process that information, and autonomously decide how to activate their mechanisms (the parts responsible for movement or action) to respond appropriately for achieving their designated tasks.[4]

Twentieth century robots, especially industrial ones, typically operated in isolated environments and were tightly controlled. They were designed to perform well-defined tasks and often operated out of human reach. The next generation of robots are more autonomous and sophisticated. Japanese expectations for the next generation, as set out in the Fukuoka World Robot Declaration of February 2004, include robots that coexist with humans and contribute to a safe and peaceful society.[5] Such robots are designed to support human well-being and facilitate everyday tasks, a significant step forward from their predecessors that were limited to industrial applications. Experts in robotics pioneering countries such as Japan and South Korea believe that humans and next-generation robots will co-exist by 2030. These robots can adapt to complex and unstructured environments, allowing them to operate in a wide range of situations and locations. They will be able to interact with humans and assist them in their daily tasks, providing both physical and mental support.[6] When AI and machine learning are incorporated into robotic systems, these advanced devices will not only be able to adapt to complex task environments, but also support humans in service, transportation, healthcare, and military environments.[7]

In 2016, the Cabinet Office of Japan made an ambitious strategic plan to create Society 5.0, that is, a human-centered society that balances economic development and the resolution of social issues through a system that highly integrates cyberspace and physical space.[8] As a part of the Society 5.0 plan, the Cabinet Office also launched the Moonshot R&D Program that sets ambitious goals to resolve difficult societal issues. One goal (Goal 3) of Moonshot is the "Realization of AI robots that autonomously learn, adapt to their environment, evolve in intelligence and act alongside human beings, by 2050."[9] At the moment, there are eight types of next-generation robots to be developed under Goal 3. One team, led by Tohoku University's

[3] Capek (1920), pp. 5–14, Capek (1923), pp. 3–19.

[4] Hirano (2024), pp. 32–34.

[5] International Robot Fair 2004 Organizing Office (2004).

[6] Weng et al. (2009), pp. 267–268.

[7] Weng et al. (2009), p. 269.

[8] Fukuyama (2018), pp. 47–50.

[9] Moonshot Research and Development Program (2024).

Smart Robot Design Laboratory, is developing next-generation robots for healthcare. Their robots involving adaptable transformative hardware can provide smart healthcare services through enhancing patients' self-efficacy during human–robot interactions. Next-generation robots will need affective computing[10] to help them understand patients' emotional states based on biometric vocal, facial, body gestural, body postural, and physiological data.[11] The co-evolution of affective computing and robotics is a critical trend in creating emotional robots, since many social interactions rely on understanding and responding to the counterpart's emotional states. However, emotional robots also cause new ethical, legal, and social concerns. Next, we focus on the risks that the use of emotional robots poses on privacy.

3 Privacy Risks Related to Emotional Robots

Emotional next-generation robots raise many ethical, legal and social concerns related to mental health,[12] deception[13] and surveillance,[14] but the most intensely discussed risks relate to privacy and data protection.[15] One critical difference between next-generation robots and industrial robots is that the task environments of the former are fully open or semi-open, such as parks, shopping malls, hospitals, etc.[16] The associated risks can be particularly high when dealing with information as sensitive and intimate as people's emotions, which was not a problem in the case of industrial robots. Healthcare often deals with highly sensitive data and very vulnerable subjects, such as elderly and seriously ill people, and therefore represents a "worst case scenario" where potential privacy breaches are particularly serious.[17]

Also, many of the next-generation emotional robots resemble the human body structure; they have limbs. Many of them also imitate the human face, including the eyes, mouth, and ears. Some robots are even able to form facial expressions. These robot features are necessary to make robots more comfortable to use and to increase people's desire to interact and communicate with them. However, the features are likely to increase privacy risks in using robots because of specific, yet universal human characteristics addressed through the studies of religion, anthropology, sociology and psychology. Of particular relevance is the study of animism[18] that deals with the human tendency to attribute life to the lifeless (in the field of sociology and

[10] Picard (2000). Affective computing means development activities to assign computers the human-like capabilities of observation, interpretation and generation of affect features (emotions).

[11] Whang and Lim (2008).

[12] McStay and Rosner (2021).

[13] Coeckelbergh (2012).

[14] McStay (2020).

[15] See, e.g., Katirai (2024).

[16] Saplacan et al. (2024), pp. 250–251.

[17] Van Wynsberghe (2013). See also Lutz and Tamò (2016).

[18] Guthrie (1993), Bird-David (1999), Harvey (2006).

psychology), or even to believe in spiritual entities living inside lifeless objects (in the field of religion and anthropology). In ancient times, people gave names to sacred rocks, mountain peaks, stone idols, rivers, and springs.[19] People also worshipped them for providing life and good luck. Modern, technological animism[20] is an easily recognizable phenomenon all around us. We give names to our cars, computers, and robot vacuum cleaners, and refer to them as she or he. Technological animism also occurs in our relation to artificial intelligence and robots,[21] especially social robots.[22]

Animism often occurs together with anthropomorphism,[23] which means a human tendency to attribute human characteristics to objects, things, and events that are not human. While a great deal of research has been conducted on animism and anthropomorphism in several fields of science, the most relevant field regarding the emotional robot context is psychology.[24] The research results confirm that animism and anthropomorphism are universal human traits that are widely used in creating digital user interfaces[25] and developing user experiences of artificial intelligence and robots.[26] It is often a deliberate design choice to use features facilitating the formation of emotional bonds between humans and technological artefacts.[27] These features may include imitation of human habits and personalities,[28] face animation,[29] human voice imitation,[30] human-like movements,[31] and facial expressions by robots.[32] The reason for developing anthropomorphic robots is widely accepted; they help humans to accept and adopt robots for various service functions, increase the perceived service quality, and improve customer satisfaction.[33] The engagement with robots is also deeper if they imitate emotions, warmth, and empathy.[34]

While the objectives above are reasonable and there are many positive consequences of the design choices, there are also several concerns related to anthropomorphized, emotional robots. Humans have a need to establish and maintain a sense of social connection with others.[35] Individuals who lack social connections and suffer from chronic loneliness tend to anthropomorphize non-human agents and to form

---

[19] See, e.g., Haber (2009), Scarre (2009).

[20] Richardson (2016), Marenko (2021).

[21] Richardson (2016), Pauketat and Anthis (2022).

[22] White and Katsuno (2021).

[23] See, e.g., Guthrie (1993), Harvey (2006), Epley et al. (2008).

[24] Airenti (2018).

[25] Menon et al. (2021).

[26] Alabed et al. (2022), Marenko (2021).

[27] Van Allen et al. (2013), pp. 2250–2251, Menon (2020), pp. 5–7.

[28] Van Allen et al. (2013).

[29] Pandzic et al. (2003).

[30] Natale (2020).

[31] Jang (2024).

[32] Rawal and Stock-Homburg (2022).

[33] Alabed et al. (2022), p. 13.

[34] Alabed et al. (2022), pp 13–14.

[35] Epley et al. (2008), pp. 886–887.

relationships with them, imitating a human social connection.[36] If these perceived relationships are considered deep and meaningful, individuals develop trust and are more likely to disclose their personal and private information to robots.[37] As especially vulnerable user groups such as children, patients and elderly persons who can feel socially disconnected are prone to develop social relationships with robots, this raises serious privacy concerns related to their use of emotional robots.

First, an apparent problem is the humanoid dependency caused by long term interactions between anthropomorphic emotional robots and their users. Humanoid dependency refers here to an unhealthy tendency of relying on humanoid machines to support users caused by people's biased projection of anthropomorphism.

Second, the collection of data by emotional robots and the potential inability of humans to detect it can pose various risks. When a user is at a computer, they may not enter intimate information about their family relationships, health, and other private matters into a search engine. Things may be different if they have a domestic robot with which they are very familiar and which they perceive as a pet rather than a data-collecting AI robot. In this case, the user may discuss private matters with family members, for example, and the data may end up in the robot's data. Furthermore, data collected in a hospital environment can be particularly sensitive. A patient may discuss health-related issues with a doctor or relative, which may be stored in the robot's data. External threats, such as the risk of a data breach, add to the mix, as sensitive data can end up in wrong hands. The use of personal data for commercial purposes can also be problematic, even if the user has given consent to it.

Third, and as will be discussed later, in the EU context, processing of personal data must be lawful. According to Article 6, paragraph 1 (a) and (b) of the General Data Protection Regulation (GDPR), the processing is lawful, for instance, "if the data subject has given consent to the processing of his or her personal data for one or more specific purposes or if the processing is necessary for the performance of a contract to which the data subject is party or in order to take steps at the request of the data subject prior to entering into a contract."[38] The consent is requested only once before the processing of the data starts, which can be problematic when the user starts to form an emotional relationship with the robot; the legal issues may be forgotten or the user may not care about them anymore. This might be especially true if at some point the user perceives the robot as a friend or a trusted pet.

Fourth, privacy communication faces the same problems as any communication involving legal material. It tends to become complex language, so-called "legalese" that is difficult for non-lawyers to understand. The difficulty is compounded by the fact that privacy communication combines legal and technical language, both of which can be challenging for a layperson to understand.[39] This risk is partly addressed

---

[36] Epley et al. (2008), p. 876, Airenti (2018), p. 8.

[37] Alabed et al. (2022), p. 12.

[38] There are also other occasions when the processing of personal data is allowed. See GDPR, Art. 6. These occasions are not, however, relevant in the context of this Chapter.

[39] Autto et al. (2024), Kimble (1996).

in recent EU regulations, namely the AI Act (Regulation (EU) 2024/1689) and the GDPR, which will be discussed next.

4 Requirements for Emotional Robots by the GDPR and the AI Act

In the EU context, emotional robots and the processing of personal data are regulated in reasonably fine detail. To begin with, the robots fall under the category of high-risk AI systems in the recently implemented AI Act.[40] Consequently, they must fulfill special requirements set forth in Sect. 2 of Chapter III of the AI Act. Moreover, emotional robots that "interact directly with natural persons must be designed and developed in such a way that the natural persons concerned are informed that they are interacting with an AI system, unless this is obvious from the point of view of a natural person who is reasonably well-informed, observant, and circumspect, taking into account the circumstances and the context of use."[41] Finally, deployers of robots that are meant to recognize emotions shall inform the natural persons exposed thereto of the operation of the system and shall process the personal data in accordance with the GDPR. According to paragraph 5 of Article 50, all this information "shall be provided to the natural persons concerned in a clear and distinguishable manner at the latest at the time of the first interaction or exposure. The information shall conform to the applicable accessibility requirements."

As discussed earlier in this chapter, emotional robots will need to process many forms of personal data. One form is biometric data that, according to Article 4 (14) of the GDPR, means "personal data resulting from specific technical processing relating to the physical, physiological or behavioural characteristics of a natural person, which allow or confirm the unique identification of that natural person, such as facial images or dactyloscopic data."[42] It is unavoidable that in the data collection performed by next-generation robots, some of these "real world" data are biometric personal data which are processed for supporting emotional human–robot interactions based on facial recognition, voice recognition, gait analysis, eye tracking, etc. These biometric data are identified as a special category of personal data under the GDPR. Processing of personal data that falls under the special category of personal data is in principle

[40] According to ANNEX III of the AI Act, High-risk AI systems pursuant to Article 6(2) are the AI systems listed in any of the following areas:

1. Biometrics, in so far as their use is permitted under relevant Union or national law:

(a) remote biometric identification systems.

This shall not include AI systems intended to be used for biometric verification the sole purpose of which is to confirm that a specific natural person is the person he or she claims to be;

(b) AI systems intended to be used for biometric categorization, according to sensitive or protected attributes or characteristics based on the inference of those attributes or characteristics;

(c) AI systems intended to be used for emotion recognition.

[41] AI Act, Art. 50.

[42] GDPR, Art. 4 (14).

prohibited, unless the data subject has given explicit consent to its processing or there is a reason to defend substantial public interests, or there are other reasons listed in paragraph 2 of Article 9 of the GDPR.[43]

According to Article 4 (11) of the GDPR, "consent of the data subject means any freely given, specific, informed and unambiguous indication of the data subject's wishes by which he or she, by a statement or by a clear affirmative action, signifies agreement to the processing of personal data relating to him or her."[44] Consent can be given by a written statement, including by electronic means, or by an oral statement. This could mean ticking a box when visiting an internet website, choosing technical settings for information society services, or another statement or conduct which clearly indicates in this context the data subject's acceptance of the proposed processing of their personal data. Silence, pre-ticked boxes, or inactivity should not therefore constitute consent. Consent should cover all processing activities carried out for the same purpose or purposes. When the processing has multiple purposes, consent should be given to all of them. If the data subject's consent is to be given following a request by electronic means, the request must be clear, concise, and not unnecessarily disruptive to the use of the service for which it is provided.[45]

Article 7, paragraph 1 of the GDPR stipulates that "where processing is based on consent, the controller shall be able to demonstrate that the data subject has consented to processing of his or her personal data." Recital (42) states that if a declaration of consent is preformulated by the controller, it should be in accordance with Council Directive 93/13/EEC that concerns unfair terms in consumer contracts. Consequently, the declaration should be provided in an intelligible and easily accessible form using clear and plain language, and it should not contain unfair terms.

For consent to be informed, the data subject should be aware at least of the identity of the controller and the purposes of the processing for which the personal data is intended. Consent should not be regarded as freely given if the data subject has no genuine or free choice or is unable to refuse or withdraw consent without detriment.[46]

Finally, although the AI Act and GDPR do not provide it directly, the user needs information about how their data will be processed in order to give explicit consent to the processing.[47] According to Article 12 of the GDPR, this information needs to be given in a concise, transparent, intelligible, and easily accessible form, using clear and plain language. Also, according to Article 12 (7), the information may be provided in combination with standardized icons in order to give in an easily visible, intelligible, and clearly legible manner a meaningful overview of the intended processing. Where the icons are presented electronically, they shall be machine-readable.

[43] GDPR, Art. 9, para. 2.

[44] GDPR, Art. 4 (11).

[45] Recital (32) of the GDPR.

[46] Recital (42) of the GDPR.

[47] For example, Article 13 of the GDPR provides that when personal data is collected from the data subject, information specified in the Article should be given at the time when personal data is obtained.

In sum, both the AI Act and the GDPR require a great deal of information to be given to the users of emotional robots so that they (1) know that they are interacting with an AI system, (2) know how the emotion recognition system operates and (3) can give explicit consent to processing personal data of a special category. Consent can be considered privacy communication for ensuring the accountability of data governance between the data subject and the data controller.[48] The problem with giving consent to processing personal data (or a special category of personal data) is that when someday emotional next-generation robots become popular like what Bill Gates has predicted "A Robot in Every Home"[49] it will not be practical to expect robot companies to have their corporate lawyers visit customers' houses in order to gain their consent. Therefore, emotional robots will need to be designed to engage in consent-related privacy communication with data subjects on behalf of data controllers. It can be seen as an advanced version of the "cookie consent" required from data subjects when interacting with websites and apps.[50] It is still an open question on how to implement the robot consent into daily human–robot interaction.[51] We argue that the proactive law approach and information design tools, such as multi-channel communication, plain language, tone of voice, visualization, and tailoring, offer an efficient means to design privacy communication carried out between data controllers and users of emotional robots. Next, we shortly present the proactive law approach and then describe in more detail the relevant tools for privacy communication.

5 A Proactive Approach to Privacy Communication Design

5.1 Proactive Law Approach

The proactive law approach builds on the proactive contracting approach, which was developed in collaboration between legal practitioners and academics at the turn of the millennium. While the proactive contracting approach focuses on contracts and the contracting process, the proactive approach to law can be applied in any field of law and to any legal communication. The proactive law approach has been endorsed by the European Economic and Social Committee (EESC) in developing better regulation in the European Union (EU).[52] Here, we present its elements that are relevant in the context of privacy communication and emotional robots.

First, the proactive law approach has two dimensions: prevention and promotion. While minimizing legal problems and risks is included in the preventive dimension,

[48] GDPR, Art. 5, para. 2.

[49] Gates (2008), p. 4.

[50] Weng (2023), p. 112.

[51] Lintvedt (2024).

[52] EESC (2009).

the approach also focuses on promoting what is desirable.[53] This has been referred to as the ex-ante approach, meaning that the focus is on ensuring that the law or any legal information is operationally efficient, reflects real-life needs, and is implemented in such a manner that the ultimate objectives are accomplished.[54] In the context of privacy communication between emotional robots and users, the proactive approach would mean that information is provided to the users in such a way that they can give the robot their (explicit) consent to process personal data. It also means that the users of the robots are assisted to become aware of their rights related to privacy.

Second, the proactive law approach highlights the need to include users of legislation and other legal communication in the law-making process.[55] This ensures that the law reflects real-life needs and is acceptable. Laws and other legal communication should therefore be drafted as straightforwardly as possible and as close to their users as possible, ensuring that the language used is readily comprehensible and uncomplicated. Their contents should also be communicated in ways that are meaningful to their intended audiences and use cases, accompanying and guiding their implementation and enforcement in all phases of their life cycle.[56]

Relating to the previous point, the proactive law approach places much emphasis on legal design and user-centricity.[57] The design of legal communication can cover its content, language, presentation, and the very process of creating such communication.[58] To enable user-centricity, it is essential that insights from information design research related to people's literacy skills, memory, information processing and overload, and understanding, are taken into account, and that information design methods, such as experimentation, user-testing and prototyping, are used in the design process.[59]

5.2 *Tools for Better Privacy Communication*

Following the insights from information design research, the privacy communication of emotional robots should be designed with elderly people and other user groups in mind. Also, the functionality of privacy communication should be tested with users. Moreover, we argue that tools based on the proactive approach and information design research and methods—multichannel communication, tone of voice, plain language,

[53] See, e.g., Haapio (2013), pp. 38–39, EESC (2009), para. 5.3.

[54] EESC (2009), para. 6.10.

[55] EESC (2009), para. 2.6.

[56] EESC (2009), para. 6.12.4.

[57] Passera and Haapio (2013), pp. 40–43.

[58] See, e.g., Hurmerinta-Haanpää (2022), pp. 164–165, Haapio (2013), pp. 57–58, Passera (2017), p. 62.

[59] Hurmerinta-Haanpää and Nuottila (2025).

visualization, and tailoring—enable user-friendly and effective privacy communication. The diverse characteristics of robots offer new possibilities for privacy communication, as communication can occur not only through documents, but also through the robot's speech, gestures, and displays. This may also engage robot users who are less motivated to read, as information can be accessed through alternative channels.

5.2.1 Multichannel Communication

Proactive legal thinkers have studied multichannel communication in the context of talking comic contracts. Comic contracts are designed as legally binding contracts in which the contracting parties are portrayed as characters and the terms of the contract are mainly communicated visually. Furthermore, talking comic contracts have a voice, which makes them easy to understand and accessible. The digital combination of the comic contract and audio narration is conveyed by synchronizing the narration with a preset zoom and pan of the relevant images.[60] The objective of comic contracts is to facilitate comprehension by individuals with limited literacy and disadvantages.[61]

Multichannel communication can also enhance the clarity and accessibility of privacy communication, for example, when a user wants to know more about a robot's privacy policy. The robot could display easy-to-read privacy information on its screen using design patterns,[62] or even show an animation of the contents of the privacy policy. At the same time, the robot could explain what is happening in the animation or the voice could be part of the animation. The robot could also use gestures to emphasize important points.[63]

5.2.2 Plain Language

Plain language also provides useful tools for expressing legal and technical information. It is language that is easy to understand and use,[64] involving not only the vocabulary but also the planning of the document, designing it, organizing it, writing clear sentences, using plain words, and testing the document whenever possible on typical readers. Contrary to popular belief, plain language is not the opposite of precise language; even complex issues can be expressed in plain language without

---

[60] Ketola et al. (2024), pp. 167–168.

[61] Ketola et al. (2024), p. 167.

[62] Hagan and Haapio (2016), pp. 1–2. Design patterns are repeatable solutions to commonly occurring usability and understandability problems. They are presented in more detail below. In the context of contracts, there is a contract design pattern library available at: https://contract-design.worldcc.com/. The library is designed for the WorldCC by Helena Haapio and Stefania Passera.

[63] See Gleeson et al. (2013), pp. 355–356. The study demonstrated that users of the robot were able to interpret the robot's gestures with great accuracy and rated them as natural and easy to interpret.

[64] Plain Language Federation (2024).

compromising precision or accuracy.[65] According to Kimble, plain language is more accurate than traditional legal writing because it reveals ambiguities and errors that the traditional style, with all its complexities, tries to hide.[66] In the context of personal data processing by emotional robots, using typical legal (and technical) language that is difficult to understand could lead to misunderstandings and unexpected risks for the user. Therefore, information about robots, privacy, and emotional features should be communicated in plain language to ensure that the message gets through.

For most people, the benefits of plain language are intuitive. Readers are likely to prefer it to the dense and impersonal style of many official documents because they are easier to understand, cause fewer misinterpretations, raise fewer questions, and, ultimately, save the reader's time and the organization's resources.[67] Plain language could also help engage robot users with data protection information and proactively reduce misunderstandings related to privacy issues.

The next generation of robots is still a relatively new phenomenon in people's everyday lives, so understanding and assessing the risks can be challenging. This is because the risks associated with new technologies are not necessarily as obvious as those associated with familiar ones, such as conventional computers. The novelty and unfamiliarity of the new breed of robots significantly increases the need for clear communication. In this context, people need clear, unambiguous and understandable information to make informed decisions and to avoid misunderstandings.

5.2.3 Tone of Voice

When communicating with a user, robots may use a professional, familiar, friendly, or some other tone of voice. The choice of tone can be used to engage specific target groups. The appropriate tone for a given audience can be determined by considering the characteristics of the audience. Tone of voice refers to how you say something, rather than what you say: it can affect the way in which your communication is received and the impression that you make. Tone of voice patterns can help one to consciously choose and shape how things are said and how one is perceived. In legal documents, almost everyone uses a tone that is legalistic, technical, wordy, formal, and impersonal. Certain groups of readers may be put off by this standard tone and may not read or engage with information they need to understand. In many situations, it is strategically wise to encourage readers by using a more informal and approachable tone.[68]

Since robots can have the ability to multichannel communication, it is important to consider tone of voice in both speech and text. This includes a robot's speech and the animations and text that it can show on its display. In addition, gestures

---

[65] Kimble (1996), pp. 1–2, see also U.S. Securities and Exchange Commission (1997), pp. 3152, 3154.

[66] Kimble (1996), p. 2.

[67] Kimble (1996), p. 3.

[68] WorldCC Foundation, Passera and Haapio (2024b).

can enhance the tone of voice, as they can complement and reinforce the message of speech or text, making the communication clearer and more expressive. For example, a friendly smile or a wave of the robot's hand can add a positive tone to the speech, while serious gestures such as a solemn expression or crossed arms can emphasize concerns or the importance of a message.

5.2.4 Visualization

Visualization is an important part of information design. It can be useful in privacy communication because of its attention-grabbing and engaging effect, whereby it can act as a tool to gain the user's specific, informed, and unambiguous consent and thus contribute to the progress of safe robotics. Visualization in this context refers to the visual presentation of documents such as privacy policies and contracts by using diagrams, images, and structured layouts that make the documents more understandable, usable, and effective.[69]

Visualization can be used in various ways in robot communication. It may be done, for example, by displaying images on the robot's screen or using animation and interactive elements. Visuals can help clarify concepts that may be difficult to grasp through text alone. For example, privacy concerns could be illustrated through practical animated situations. An illustration could show a robot collecting emotional data in a hospital setting, demonstrating the risks associated with such scenarios.

5.2.5 Tailoring

Tailoring is also a way to implement effective communication that promotes privacy in robotics. The emotional characteristics of robots can offer new dimensions to tailoring. Robots can use contextual information to better understand the user's situation and emotional experience. This can be achieved by considering previous conversations or utilizing historical knowledge about the user to gain an understanding of the person's emotions. These can be considered in tailoring. By being able to infer and interpret human emotions, robots can improve their interactions with users, making communication more engaging and tailored.[70] These emotional capabilities could also be used to tailor privacy communication to the robot user, promoting comprehensible and user-friendly delivery. Altogether, tailoring means adapting information to the user's needs, preferences, and context.

The language or tone of a robot's communication can also be tailored to the user's preferences. Furthermore, the robot may present information in different formats, such as text, voice, images, or even video, depending on the user's specific needs. It can also continuously learn from the user's interactions, emotions, and reactions and

---

[69] See, e.g., Passera (2017), p. 19.

[70] Spezialetti, Placidi and Rossi (2020), McColl et al. (2016), Cavallo et al. (2018).

adapt its communication style accordingly. If the robot's approach triggers a negative reaction, it may adjust its behavior to work out a more positive outcome.

5.3 Risks of Adopting New Tools

The use of tools for privacy communication introduced here—multi-channel communication, plain language, tone of voice, visualization, and tailoring—may give rise to new problems. First, when information involves more than one dimension, a decision has to be made about the order of precedence between them. For example, the Creative Commons licensing system uses a design pattern referred to as layering[71] with three layers for different readers: machine readable, human readable, and full text. In this case full text has been given priority. In the case of talking comic contracts, a decision has to be made whether to give priority to the speech, images or text of the comic. Ketola, de Rooy and Haapio argue that the comic contract cannot be reduced to just speech, images or text, ignoring the combination of these forms: the legally binding contract is the user's experience of the contract's presentation, consisting of all its elements. Thus, in the event of a conflict, talking comic contracts should be interpreted as a whole and one element should not be prioritized over the other. This is justified from the point of view that comic contracts are intended to make contracts easy to understand by people with low literacy and disadvantages. From the user's perspective, any attempt to introduce a condition where one mode is legally more binding than another would be artificial and introduce unnecessary complexity. Ketola, de Rooy and Haapio aptly ask in their article: "If we cannot predict which of the modes, visual, text or audio, the user understands most easily, in which of the modes do we communicate the fact that one of the modes would be the legally binding mode?"[72] The priority order between the channels needs to be settled. The same applies to robots. In the future, many of their users may have disabilities, as robots may increasingly be employed in hospitals and used as home robots by the elderly. We cannot know which mode would be fair to prioritize from the user's perspective, so the communication should be interpreted as a whole.

In multichannel robot communication, a priority decision must also be made between a robot's characteristics. For example, if the robot's spoken message gives an impression which differs from that given by the information displayed on its screen, causing confusion for the user, how should this be addressed? Problems can also arise from gestures and facial expressions that can be interpreted differently in different cultures. On the other hand, images and animations, for example,

[71] Creative Commons (2024), WorldCC Foundation, Passera and Haapio (2024a), Juro-Privacy (2024). The Creative Commons licensing system and the Juro privacy policy are well-known examples of layering.

[72] Ketola et al. (2024), pp. 191–192.

can help to avoid misunderstandings in multilingual environments.[73] Multichannel communication can therefore bring not only new questions, but also solutions.

The use of tools introduced here is not very common in robot communication, and changing old ways of working can be demanding. The tools can also introduce new interpretation situations, because multichannel communication involves many different forms that need to be addressed. Our proposal to move away from traditional legal and technical writing is, in a sense, a leap into the unknown, but it is also risky to stick to a familiar and well-known language that is opaque, difficult to understand, and does not solve the problems of comprehension.

6 Conclusion

As robotics becomes more mainstream and the capabilities of robots increase, we face new challenges as well as opportunities. Concerns about emotional robots include privacy issues and a need to ensure that people can give their consent to their personal data processing. Giving consent to an emotional robot is very different from giving consent on a regular computer by clicking "I agree." Robot users may develop attachment to robots that exhibit human or pet-like characteristics and are perceived as approachable, potentially leading to a limited understanding of the robot's data collection capabilities. Furthermore, even when users have consented to the collection of their data and comprehended its implications at that time, the gradual development of a close relationship with the robot may lead to situations in which legal and privacy considerations are ignored.

We argue that the proactive law approach and the tools presented in this chapter—multichannel communication, plain language, tone of voice, visualization, and tailoring—can address the issues described above. They will enhance the accessibility of privacy communication in robotics and ensure that robot users understand the information-gathering capabilities of emotional robots and can give their consent to the processing of their data. Using these tools will also enable better compliance with the requirements of both the GDPR and the AI Act.

The next generation of robots may have multiple channels of communication at their disposal, including speech, gestures, and screens. These channels can be optimized by using plain language, appropriate tone of voice and visualization in the communication. Furthermore, tailoring communication to the specific requirements of individual robot users, for instance, by considering their individual needs and personalities, can ensure a highly targeted and personalized approach. This, in turn, increases the likelihood of user engagement and the user's awareness of data protection rights and the associated risks.

---

[73] Haapio has discussed how visualizations can reduce contractual misunderstandings in multilingual environments. See Haapio (2013), p. 139.

References

Airenti G (2018) The development of anthropomorphism in interaction: intersubjectivity, imagination, and theory of mind. Front Psychol 9:2136

Alabed A, Javornik A, Gregory-Smith D (2022) AI anthropomorphism and its effect on users' self-congruence and self–AI integration: a theoretical framework and research agenda. Technol Forecast Soc Chang 182:121786

van Allen P, McVeigh-Schultz J, Brown B, Kim HM, Lara D (2013) AniThings: animism and heterogeneous multiplicity. In: McKay WE (ed) CHI '13 extended abstracts on human factors in computing systems. Association for Computing Machinery, New York

Autto H, Haapio H, Weng Y-H (2024) AI-assisted design for better privacy communication in human-robot co-existence. In: Schweighofer E, Eder S, Costantini F, Schmautzer F, Pfister J (eds) Sprachmodelle: Juristische Papageien oder mehr?/Language models: legal parrots or more? Proceedings of the 27th international legal informatics symposium IRIS 2024. Editions Weblaw, Bern

Bird-David N (1999) "Animism" revisited: personhood, environment, and relational epistemology. Curr Anthropol 40(S1):S67–S91

Bohnenkamp LM, Abramov O, Kopp S (2024) Are robots' gestures understood? A study on the factors influencing how humans perceive information present in robot gestures. In: HRI '24: companion of the 2024 ACM/IEEE international conference on human-robot interaction. Association for Computing Machinery, New York

Brondi S, Pivetti M, Di Battista S, Sarrica M (2021) What do we expect from robots? Social representations, attitudes and evaluations of robots in daily life. Technol Soc 66:101663

Capek K (1920) R.U.R.—Rossum's universal robots: Kolektivní drama o vstupní komedii a třech aktech. Aventinum, Prague

Capek K (1923) R.U.R.—Rossum's universal robots: a fantastic melodrama in three acts and an Epilogue. (English version by Selver P and Playfair N). Samuel French, New York

Cavallo F, Semeraro F, Fiorini L, Magyar G, Sinčák P, Dario P (2018) Emotion modelling for social robotics applications: a review. J Bionic Eng 15:185–203. https://doi.org/10.1007/s42235-018-0015-y

Coeckelbergh M (2012) Are emotional robots deceptive? IEEE Trans Affect Comput 3(4):388–393. https://doi.org/10.1109/T-AFFC.2011.29

Creative Commons (2024) About CC licences. https://creativecommons.org/share-your-work/cclicenses/. Accessed 30 Sep 2024

EESC (2009) Opinion of the European economic and social committee on "The proactive law approach: a further step towards better regulation at EU level." Off J Eur Union C175(05):26–33

Epley N, Waytz A, Akalis S, Cacioppo JT (2008) When we need a human: motivational determinants of anthropomorphism. Soc Cogn 26(2):143–155

Fukuyama M (2018) Society 5.0: aiming for a new human-centered society. Japan SPOTLIGHT 37(4):47–50

Gates B (2008) A robot in every home. Scient Amer Special Editions 18(1s):4–7

Gleeson B, MacLean K, Haddadi A, Croft E, Alcazar J (2013) Gestures for industry: intuitive human-robot communication from human observation. In: Kuzuoka H, Evers V, Imai M, Forlizzi J (eds) Proceedings of the 8th ACM/IEEE international conference on human robot interaction. IEEE Press, New Jersey

Guthrie SE (1993) Faces in the clouds: a new theory of religion. Oxford University Press, New York

Haapio H (2013) Next generation contracts: a paradigm shift. Lexpert, Helsinki

Haber AF (2009) Animism, relatedness, life: post-western perspectives. Camb Archaeol J 19(3):418–430

Hagan M, Haapio H (2016) Design patterns for contracts. In: Schweighofer E, Kummer F, Hötzendorfer W, Borges G (eds) Networks. Proceedings of the 19th international legal informatics symposium IRIS 2016. Österreichische Computer Gesellschaft OCG, Wien

Hagan M (2016) User-centered privacy communication design. In: Paper presented at the twelfth symposium on usable privacy and security (SOUPS) 2016, Denver, 22–24 June 2016
Harvey G (2006) Animism: respecting the living world. Columbia University Press, New York
Hirano S (2024) Robot law, 2nd edn. Kobundo, Tokyo
Hurmerinta-Haanpää A (2022) The functional contracting framework: assessing the impacts of contract functions, framing, and regulatory focus. In: Corrales Compagnucci M, Haapio H, Fenwick M (eds) Research handbook on contract design. Edward Elgar Publishing, Cheltenham
Hurmerinta-Haanpää A, Nuottila J (2025) The proactive contracting approach: The first 25 years and beyond. In: Masson A, Bouthinon-Dumas H, Voss WG, Do Carmo Silva JM (eds) Handbook on law and management. Oxford University Press, Oxford
International Robot Fair 2004 Organizing Office (2004) World robot declaration. http://prw.kyodonews.jp/prwfile/prdata/0370/release/200402259634/index.html. Accessed 9 Sep 2024
Jang S (2024) Why make atlas dance? Colonial Utopia that persists in contemporary robotics. Junctions 8(1):38–53
Juro-Privacy (2024) free-privacy-notice/design-first privacy notice template. Github. https://github.com/juro-privacy/free-privacy-notice. Accessed 30 Sep 2024
Katirai A (2024) Ethical considerations in emotion recognition technologies: a review of the literature. AI and Ethics 4:927–948. https://doi.org/10.1007/s43681-023-00307-3
Ketola A, de Rooy R, Haapio H (2024) Comic contracts 2.0—contracts that have (and Give) a voice. In: Ducato R, Strowel A, Marique E (eds) Design(s) for law. Ledizioni, Milan
Kimble J (1996) Writing for dollars, writing to please. Scribes J Legal Writing 6(1):1–37
Leite I, Pereira A, Martinho C, Paiva A (2008) Are emotional robots more fun to play with? In: Proceedings of RO-MAN 2008—the 17th IEEE international symposium on robot and human interactive communication. IEEE
Lintvedt N (2024) A critical analysis of consent in human–robot interaction. In: Barfield W, Weng Y-H, Pagallo U (eds) The Cambridge handbook of the law, policy, and regulation for human–robot interaction. Cambridge University Press, Cambridge
Lutz C, Tamò A (2016) Privacy and healthcare robots—an ANT analysis. In: Paper presented at the we robot 2016 conference, University of Miami, Coral Gables, 1–2 April 2016
Marenko B (2021) Hybrid animism: the sensing surfaces of planetary computation. New Format 2021(104 & 105):183–197
McColl D, Hong A, Hatakeyama N, Nejat G, Benhabib B (2016) A survey of autonomous human affect detection methods for social robots engaged in natural HRI. J Intell Rob Syst 82:101–133. https://doi.org/10.1007/s10846-015-0259-2
McStay A, Rosner G (2021) Emotional artificial intelligence in children's toys and devices: ethics, governance and practical remedies. Big Data Soc 8(1). https://doi.org/10.1177/205395172199 4877
McStay A (2020) Emotional AI, soft biometrics and the surveillance of emotional life: an unusual consensus on privacy. Big Data Soc 7(1). https://doi.org/10.1177/2053951720904386
Menon AR, Hedin B, Erikson E (2021) Expanding affective computing paradigms through animistic design principles. In: Ardito C, Lanzilotti R, Malizia A, Petrie H, Piccinno A, Desolda G, Inkpen K (eds) Human-computer interaction—INTERACT 2021. Lecture notes in computer science, vol 12932. Springer, Cham
Menon AR (2020) Animism and anthropomorphism in living spaces—designing for "Life" in spatial interactions. KTH Royal Institute of Technology, Stockholm
Moonshot Research and Development Program (2024). https://www.jst.go.jp/moonshot/en/program/goal3/index.html. Accessed 14 Sep 2024
Natale A (2020) To believe in Siri: a critical analysis of AI voice assistants. Working Paper no. 32. Communicative figurations research network, ZeMKI, Centre for Media, Communication and Information Research, Bremen
Pandzic IS, Ahlberg J, Wzorek M, Rudol P, Mosmondor M (2003) Faces everywhere: towards ubiquitous production and delivery of face animation. In: Ollila M, Rantzer M (eds) Proceedings

of the 2nd international conference on mobile and ubiquitous multimedia. Linköping University Electronic Press, Linköping

Passera S (2017) Beyond the wall of contract text: visualizing contracts to foster understanding and collaboration within and across organizations. Aalto University, Helsinki

Passera S, Haapio H (2013) Transforming contracts from legal rules to user-centered communication tools: a human-information interaction challenge. Commun Design Quarter Rev 1(3):40–43. https://doi.org/10.1145/2577389.2577395

Pauketat JVT, Anthis JR (2022) Predicting the moral consideration of artificial intelligences. Comput Hum Behav 136:107372. https://doi.org/10.1016/j.chb.2022.107372

Picard RW (2000) Toward computers that recognize and respond to user emotion. IBM Syst J 39(3.4):705–719

Plain Language Federation (2024) Plain language. https://www.iplfederation.org/plain-language/ Accessed 22 May 2024

Rawal N, Stock-Homburg RM (2022) Facial emotion expressions in human-robot interaction: a survey. Int J Soc Robot 14(7):1583–1604

Richardson K (2016) Technological animism: the uncanny personhood of humanoid machines. Soc Anal 60(1):110–128

Saplacan D, Pajalic Z, Tørresen J (2024) Should social and assistive robots integrated within home- and healthcare services be universally designed? In: Barfield W, Weng Y-H, Pagallo U (eds) The Cambridge handbook of the law, policy, and regulation for human–robot interaction. Cambridge University Press, Cambridge

Scarre C (2009) Stones with character: animism, agency and megalithic monuments. In: O'Connor B, Cooney G, Chapman J (eds) Materialitas: working stone, carving identity. Oxbow Books, Oxford

U.S. Securities and Exchange Commission (1997) Plain english disclosure, 62 Federal Register. https://www.sec.gov/rules-regulations/1998/01/plain-english-disclosure. Accessed 30 Sep 2024

Spezialetti M, Placidi G, Rossi S (2020) Emotion recognition for human-robot interaction: recent advances and future perspectives. Front Robot AI 7:532279. https://doi.org/10.3389/frobt.2020.532279

van Wynsberghe A (2013) Designing robots for care: care centered value-sensitive design. Sci Eng Ethics 19(2):407–433

Weng Y-H, Chen C-H, Sun C-T (2009) Toward the human-robot co-existence society: on safety intelligence for next generation robots. Int J Soc Robot 1(4):267–282

Weng Y-H (2023) A comparative data protection analysis of healthcare robots: on informed consent in human–robot interaction. In: Hakli R, Mäkelä P, Seibt J (eds) Social robots in social institutions. IOS Press, Amsterdam

Whang M, Lim J (2008) A physiological approach to affective computing. In: Or J (ed) Affective computing. I-Tech Education and Publishing. https://doi.org/10.5772/6174

White D, Katsuno H (2021) Toward an affective sense of life: artificial intelligence, animacy, and amusement at a robot pet memorial service in Japan. Cult Anthropol 36(2):222–251

WorldCC Foundation, Passera S, Haapio H (2024a) Layering. Contract design pattern library. https://contract-design.worldcc.com/library/layering. Accessed 23 May 2024

WorldCC Foundation, Passera S, Haapio H (2024b) Tone of voice. contract design pattern library. https://contract-design.worldcc.com/library/tone-of-voice. Accessed 23 May 2024

Generative AI for Individuals' Financial Well-being and Debt Rehabilitation

Nina Toivonen, Marika Salo-Lahti, Mikko Ranta, and Helena Haapio

Abstract Technology plays a significant role in today's over-indebtedness. However, its potential to help people overcome debt problems and maintain good financial health remains largely untapped. The need for alternative, personalized solutions to over-indebtedness is becoming increasingly pressing worldwide, especially since many people struggling with debt do not have access to judicial debt rehabilitation programs. This chapter explores how generative AI (GenAI) could support individuals in financial distress. Using the behavioral COM-B model as a framework for designing effective interventions, we discuss how AI could help improve individuals' capabilities, opportunities, and motivation to achieve financial well-being, and what solutions already exist for these purposes. Inspired by fitness applications that offer personalized advice, we used OpenAI's GPT Builder to create "Finance Friend," a simple prototype of a financial adviser, and explored its potential as a personalized financial coach. While the tool shows great promise for the future of financial coaching, we also emphasize the need for trustworthy technology and regulatory frameworks that promote responsible design, implementation, and use of AI in the context of debt rehabilitation.

N. Toivonen (✉)
University of Helsinki, Helsinki, Finland
e-mail: nina.toivonen@helsinki.fi

M. Salo-Lahti · H. Haapio
School of Accounting and Finance, Business Law, University of Vaasa, Vaasa, Finland
e-mail: marika.salo-lahti@uwasa.fi

H. Haapio
e-mail: helena.haapio@lexpert.com

M. Ranta
School of Accounting and Finance, Accounting, University of Vaasa, Vaasa, Finland
e-mail: mikko.ranta@uwasa.fi

H. Haapio
JARGONFREE Contract Language Research Group, Tampere University, Tampere, Finland

Lexpert Ltd, Helsinki, Finland

© The Author(s), under exclusive license to Springer Nature Singapore Pte Ltd. 2025
M. Corrales Compagnucci et al. (eds.), *Generative AI, Contracts, Law and Design*,
Perspectives in Law, Business and Innovation,
https://doi.org/10.1007/978-981-95-2058-9_8

Keywords Access to justice · Artificial intelligence · COM-B model · Debt rehabilitation · Financial health · Fintech

1 Introduction

1.1 The Challenge: Over-Indebtedness and Tech-Driven Debt Traps

The reasons behind over-indebtedness are many. According to studies, major life events, such as unemployment, divorce, illness, having a child, or becoming a single parent, often explain consumers' unexpected debt problems.[1] However, studies also indicate that over-indebtedness is typically correlated with a variety of economic, social, and psychological factors, from the debtor's socioeconomic status to his or her personal behavior. People with serious debt problems often have lower incomes, are less likely to own a home, and also know more people who are in debt, highlighting how over-indebtedness can become normalized within a social reference group.[2] In addition to external life events and social factors, over-indebtedness is also connected to debtors' behavioral capacities and tendencies, such as lack of financial management or literacy skills, compulsive buying or gambling addiction, criminal behavior, or as proposed in economic psychology, lack of self-esteem and unhappiness.[3]

In the past few decades, payment problems have been increasingly linked with the rise of online trade, streaming and subscription services, purchases in games and apps together with easy access but high-interest consumer loans, also known as instant loans.[4] Instant loans are typically small amounts of money that can be applied for by a mobile phone or via the Internet. The term "instant" refers to an automated process that enables a loan decision and the money transfer to the consumer's account within minutes. Research suggests that the often persuasive and even aggressive marketing style of instant loans has led especially young adults to loan recklessly.[5] The improved access to high-interest consumer loans is also reflected in the statistics. For example, according to the Finnish payment default statistics, nearly 8% of Finnish adults had a payment default entry in 2023, and the number of persons having a payment default has been rising each year.[6]

However, especially for young adults and low-income consumers, it is not only easy access nor the persuasive advertising that explains the popularity of instant loans. Borrowing in general may be the only way for some consumers to cover

---

[1] See, e.g., Autio et al. (2009), p. 408.

[2] Lea et al. (1993), p. 100.

[3] Townley-Jones et al. (2008), pp. 204–208; Guven (2012), p. 702.

[4] Carlsson et al. (2017), p. 76; Autio et al. (2009), p. 407.

[5] Valkama and Muttilainen (2008), p. 76; Autio et al. (2009), p. 408.

[6] Suomen Asiakastieto Oy (2024).

essential living expenses, particularly during economically turbulent times.[7] Also, individuals with limited financial resources, or people who are already over-indebted, are often forced to borrow from predatory companies that charge higher commissions and higher interest rates than banks or mainstream credit card companies. Research indicates that particularly the use of these types of credit can eventually develop into a self-sustaining cycle of indebted lifestyles with negative social, psychological and health impacts.[8]

While technology plays a significant role in creating the cycles of indebtedness, or in other words "tech-driven debt traps," its potential to assist in overcoming debt problems and maintaining financial well-being has remained somewhat unleashed. Government entities charged with designing and providing debt rehabilitation policies and services have not yet fully leveraged modern technological capabilities in their interventions. This leaves the arena open for private operators, some of whom may exploit debtors' vulnerabilities, use biased algorithms, or provide misleading information. Although many government and nonprofit agencies are increasingly adopting more innovative, user-friendly methods to improve their digital services,[9] people who seek personalized advice typically find themselves navigating outdated government websites or digital guidebooks with overly general content. When public digital solutions fail to meet the need for personalized and practical information, people turn to peers and private operators for assistance.[10] According to global statistics from the World Justice Project, however, most people seeking advice for their legal and financial problems report not receiving sufficient help.[11]

Another concern is that national debt recovery schemes are typically not designed to assist all debtors in need, nor do they provide targeted solutions for the various underlying causes of over-indebtedness or support sustainable behavior change in financial management. For example, many national models for dealing with over-indebtedness in Europe are based on following a judicially authorized programme that adjusts the debts according to the debtor's ability to pay, aiming at achieving debtor's "rehabilitation."[12] However, not all debtors are legally qualified or know how to access these procedures, leaving especially many vulnerable people, such as young adults who are not in education, employment, or training (also called "NEETs"), without a solution to their debt problems.[13]

---

[7] For example, 3.9% of people in the EU had to borrow money to cover their living expenses during the pandemic year of 2020, Eurostat (2023); see also Demertzis et al. (2020), p. 15.

[8] Townley-Jones et al. (2008), p. 206.

[9] For example, the Guarantee Foundation in Finland provides an online service to monitor everyday spending and a web chat to discuss money and debt related concerns, see Guarantee Foundation (2024).

[10] Hagan (2024), p. 366; Sillence and Briggs (2007), p. 746.

[11] World Justice Project (2024).

[12] Frade (2012), pp. 53–54. For an overview of different personal insolvency procedures of the Member States of the European Union, see European e-Justice Portal (2023).

[13] In Finnish context, Linna (2015), p. 40.

Also, not all who enter debt adjustment programs become debt-free or learn how to avoid over-indebtedness in the future. For example, in Finland, about 40% of individual debtors who went through the debt adjustment procedure under the Act on the Adjustment of Debts of a Private Individual (57/1993) between the years 2008 and 2013 had new payment defaults at the end of the debt adjustment process.[14] Although the statistics are not recent, they nevertheless underline that a successful debt rehabilitation does not happen only by cutting down the number of debts, but requires tackling the root causes of over-indebtedness. As proposed in previous research, in contrast to current mechanical debt rehabilitation models, a more human-centric (or "debtor-centric"), systemic, and proactive approach is needed to build fresh starts that can last a lifetime.[15]

1.2 Responding to the Challenge with AI Tools

This chapter explores the promise of generative AI (GenAI) tools in helping over-indebted individuals recover from debt and sustain good financial health.[16] The chapter begins with an introduction to some of the main challenges of access to justice in personal debt rehabilitation. Our examples primarily focus on the Finnish debt rehabilitation system, while acknowledging that over-indebtedness is a universal phenomenon. In the second section we also discuss how behavioral approaches, focusing on the behavioral COM-B model theory that highlights individuals' capabilities, opportunities and motivation as the core foundation for behavior change, could be used as a framework for designing personalized technological interventions that can help overcome debt. In the third section, we discuss what kind of AI solutions already exist in the market for financial management and debt rehabilitation, and experiment with "Finance Friend," a simple prototype of a personal financial coach we created using OpenAI's GPT Builder. Finally, we also highlight some of the current legal concerns in building trustworthy AI for financial management purposes. We conclude our exploration with a summary of our key findings and a list of potential research questions for further investigation on the topic.

---

[14] Fredriksson (2014).

[15] See, e.g., Townley-Jones et al. (2008), p. 209; Carlsson et al. (2017), p. 91; Demertzis et al. (2020), p. 15; Linna (2015), p. 41.

[16] This chapter is an updated version of our papers Toivonen et al. (2023, 2024).

2 From Tech-Driven Debt Traps to Proactive Financial Health Care

2.1 The Justice Gap in Debt Recovery Systems

Debt rehabilitation, also known as debt restructuring or debt adjustment, is a legal process typical for many European jurisdictions, designed to help individuals or entities manage and overcome their financial difficulties resulting from excessive debt.[17] The purpose of debt rehabilitation is to provide a structured and sustainable plan to address the debt burden, improve financial stability, and ultimately achieve a "fresh start." The typical debt rehabilitation model in Europe is designed around following a judicially authorized process where the debtor's liabilities are adjusted according to the debtor's ability to pay.[18] The process typically begins with a debt settlement phase, where the debtor attempts to reach a voluntary agreement with their creditors. If the negotiations fail, the debtor can petition the court for a debt adjustment process, including a personal payment plan. In Finland, the plan generally lasts 3–5 years but can extend up to 10 years depending on the debtor's financial and other circumstances.[19]

Worryingly for individuals seeking sustainable debt relief, the nature of the debt as well as the way it was acquired can become obstacles to accessing a debt rehabilitation program. Judicial debt recovery proceedings, such as the one in Finland, are in principle only available to so-called "responsible" or "sincere" debtors.[20] Since one of the main means of the debt rehabilitation is to cut down the amount of the debt, the debtor must meet certain criteria in order to earn their debts to be "forgiven." For example, according to the Finnish Act on the Adjustment of Debts of a Private Individual (57/1993), a private person may be granted debt adjustment if the main reason for the insolvency is an essential decline in their ability to pay due to illness, disability, unemployment or other "change of circumstances not primarily the fault of the debtor," or there are other "good reasons" for debt adjustment.[21] However, becoming over-indebted mainly through consumer credit has not been considered a valid reason for debt rehabilitation.[22] In European jurisdictions in general, consumption-based payment failures have traditionally been regarded as the result of frivolous behavior, reflecting a debtor's reckless attitude toward social morals and the consequences of

[17] In the United States and other Anglo-American countries, the equivalent to debt-rehabilitation is bankruptcy, a process where debtors' assets are liquidated to cover possible debts. Once the debts are discharged, the debtor is not personally liable to pay them, see, e.g., United States Code (2023) Title 11—Bankruptcy, Chapter 7; also Frade (2012), p. 54.

[18] Frade (2012), p. 54.

[19] Finnish Act on the Adjustment of Debts of a Private Individual (57/1993), section 30.

[20] Linna (2015), p. 31; Frade (2012), p. 52.

[21] Finnish Act on the Adjustment of Debts of a Private Individual (57/1993), section 9.

[22] Linna (2015), p. 39.

their choices. As a result, over-indebtedness is heavily stigmatized, and people with debt problems often face significant barriers when seeking help.[23]

In the light of multidisciplinary research showing that over-indebtedness is driven by a complex interplay of social, economic, and psychological factors—particularly in the context of the e-commerce era, where financial decisions are increasingly pressured—viewing indebtedness from a highly moralistic perspective appears both unscientific and unhelpful.[24] It is of course the task of insolvency systems to discourage opportunistic use of debt recovery and uphold social ethics in consumer behavior, including addressing the moral implications of over-consumption during a global sustainability crisis. However, leaving over-indebted individuals completely outside of the debt rehabilitation system on punitive grounds is socially unsustainable, especially given that over-indebtedness often negatively affects debtors' well-being, health and agency in society, and can even have negative over-generational impacts.[25] Instead, insolvency systems should more effectively seek solutions that address the diverse causes of over-indebtedness, particularly among young adults and other vulnerable groups nudged into debt traps by digital tools, and create alternative pathways out of them.

Currently, the only option for many debtors who are left outside of judicial debt rehabilitation processes is to try to improve their financial situation on their own. In many countries, however, public or non-profit organizations provide free debt counseling or finance education for debtors. In Finland, debtors can seek debt counseling from state legal help offices or nonprofits like the Guarantee Foundation, which provides digital self-help tools and social loans for instant debt relief.[26] Research indicates that debt counseling can be effective particularly for debtors who have a positive attitude toward overcoming debt and the control mechanisms, such as budgeting, needed to achieve their goal. However, the challenge lies in motivating those debtors who perceive their chances of overcoming debt as low, especially if debt recovery is not anticipated in the foreseeable future.[27] For example, Finnish debtors who are ineligible for debt rehabilitation must pay their due debts through payment enforcement, a process that can last up to 20 or even 25 years.[28] Given the length of the process, some debtors may feel unmotivated to improve their financial situation through work or education if these efforts do not result in visible short-term gains to their overall situation.[29]

Considering that tackling over-indebtedness is a complex challenge that takes determination, time and knowledge, there is a serious demand for different types of interventions beyond legal regulation to assist over-indebted individuals in achieving debt recovery and financial wellbeing. Debtors could benefit from well-tailored

[23] Frade (2012), p. 49.

[24] Similarly Lea et al. (1993), p. 115.

[25] Frade (2012), p. 56; Linna (2015), p. 41; Östergren (2022), p. 7.

[26] Financial and Debt Counseling (2024); Guarantee Foundation (2024).

[27] Xiao and Wu (2008), pp. 39–40.

[28] Finnish Act on the Limitation of Debts (728/2003), section 13a.

[29] Linna (2015), p. 35.

technological solutions that are either integrated to the judicial debt rehabilitation processes and counseling services, or, complement the system by providing "a third way" to debt recovery. The latest developments in artificial intelligence, such as GenAI tools, offer a compelling vision of what these solutions could be. What if debtors could rely on personalized AI coaches that not only address their unique financial circumstances and teach how to manage credit and consumption but also motivate them to persevere through the process of change? Although AI-enhanced self-help tools may not suit all debtors, they could help fill the justice gap in current insolvency systems, particularly for those who are excluded from judicial proceedings or need extra motivation or support to take action.

Ideally, AI tools would not only promote access to debt recovery but also help prevent future debt problems. This goal aligns with the philosophy of proactive and preventive law, which emphasizes the importance of fostering attitudes, tools, and skills to promote desirable outcomes and prevent undesirable ones. That includes enhancing awareness of one's rights and responsibilities as well as increasing people's opportunities for self-care.[30] Richard Susskind, a recognized UK expert in law and technology, argues that improving access to justice encompasses a broader scope than just making dispute resolution faster, more affordable, and less adversarial. He outlines four key components of access to justice: (1) dispute resolution, (2) dispute containment, (3) dispute avoidance, and (4) legal health promotion.[31] Following Susskind's suggestion, we argue that access to justice in the context of over-indebtedness extends beyond debt recovery; it also encompasses becoming a financially competent and conscious consumer.

2.2 *Better Financial Health by Supporting Debtors' Capabilities, Opportunities and Motivation*

Designing an AI tool that supports debtors on their journey towards sustainable debt recovery is an interdisciplinary mission. It requires consideration of many legal, financial, social, and technological aspects, but perhaps most importantly, human factors. Designs that aim to influence behavior may fail because of the wrong assumptions about behavioral causalities. Therefore, design interventions aimed at influencing human behavior should draw from design frameworks grounded in psychological and behavioral theories.[32] The scope of this chapter does not allow introducing all possible behavioral frameworks that could apply here. To underscore the need for scientifically informed human-centric solutions, this section will briefly introduce the established COM-B model as an example of how behavioral frameworks can offer strategic guidance in designing the features of an AI tool.[33] However, it's

[30] Haapio et al. (2021), p. 58.

[31] Susskind (2019), pp. 66–70.

[32] Michie et al. (2014b), p. 20.

[33] Michie et al. (2014a).

important to recognize that, like any theoretical frameworks, behavioral models are always somewhat simplified representations of complex reality. Therefore, behavioral design literature recommends complementing these models with user research, data analysis, and pragmatic product development.[34]

It must also be noted, that especially in the context of helping people with financial distress, extra caution is needed to make sure that the behavioral designs are transparent, respect the user's autonomous decision making and truly support the development of healthy behaviors as defined by the user.[35] "The tech-driven debt traps" provide one extreme example of how using behavioral insights in design to persuade, mislead or manipulate people into specific behaviors, like buying something, can have harmful and unjust consequences.[36] On the other hand, well-meaning but too persuasive design interventions easily commit to the paternalistic fallacy that there is only one "right" way to do things. As Dorresteijn and Verbeek remind us, "well-being only comes about when users of technologies have the ability to formulate their own answers to the question of the good life."

The Behavioral COM-B Model.

The COM-B model is a behavioral change theory developed by Michie, Atkins and West. The theory conceptualizes behavior as a part of a system of interaction elements that involves capability, opportunity and motivation. According to the model, for any behavior to occur at any given moment, a person must have the capability and opportunity to engage in the behavior, and the strength of motivation to engage in it must be greater than for any competing behaviors.[37] The model thus suggests that to change a behavior both individual and environmental factors must be targeted. For example, if a debtor needs to make a payment plan, to succeed in this task, he or she needs to have both the knowledge, skills, and stamina (capabilities), as well as time, resources, and physical access to the necessary materials (opportunities) and enough interest (motivation) to take such action. What else the application of the COM-B model could mean in the context of debt-recovery will be discussed next.

Capabilities.

According to the COM-B model theory, capabilities refer both to physical and psychological capacities. Physical capability includes strength and stamina, and psychological capability encompasses knowledge and skills.[38] Supporting financial management capabilities requires addressing especially the latter. Research indicates that consumers who end up with debt problems do recognize flaws in their own money management skills, and lack of money management skills is also one of the central indicators for financial problems.[39] Improving individuals' financial

[34] Wendel (2014), p. xxii.

[35] De Francisco and Casai (2018), p. 10; Dorresteijn and Verbeek (2013), p. 54.

[36] Wendel (2014), p. xxv; Potel-Saville (2024), p. 432.

[37] Michie et al. (2014b), p. 85.

[38] Michie et al. (2014a), pp. 59–60.

[39] Autio et al. (2009), p. 408.

competence is, therefore, a central behavior change objective when designing solutions that help overcome debt problems. Supporting capabilities in the context of debt rehabilitation means especially improving the debtor's financial literacy skills. Financial literacy is defined as the combination of knowledge, skills, attitudes, and behaviors needed to make sound financial decisions that ultimately lead to financial well-being.[40] The results of financial literacy studies show that financial knowledge and behavior are linked. They also show that there are particularly vulnerable groups of people who may need more guidance to foster their financial well-being, such as women, young adults aged 18–24, seniors, people with a low level of education, and manual workers.[41]

Opportunities.

Opportunities are all the factors extrinsic to a person that either prompt or allow the behavior. This includes both physical opportunities created by the environments, such as time and access to resources, as well as social opportunities, like cultural norms.[42] Research suggests that the causes of over-indebtedness are more external than internal, correlating with factors such as socio-economic status, education and use of technologies.[43] Therefore, addressing different opportunity elements related to over-indebtedness, such as access to correct information and health and social services as well as social support is necessary in overcoming debt. Time and timing are also important opportunity factors. Following a payment plan or saving money often takes years, but setting short-term goals helps decomposing the challenge into more achievable steps, which, in turn, may help maintain motivation when the goals are achieved.

Motivation.

Motivation can, first of all be reflective, referring to, for example, self-conscious planning and evaluation of beliefs about what kind of behavior is desirable and what is not. It can also be automatic, thus stemming from debtors' impulses, emotions and reflex responses in financial decision-making.[44] Strong motivation also stems from the experience of self-regulation and control.[45] However, motivating people towards more sustainable financial behaviors may be the most difficult to address through external interventions, yet in some cases, it may be the most important. At the very least, education and counseling alone have been shown to have little or no

[40] European Commission (2020).

[41] European Commission (2023b).

[42] Michie et al. (2014b), p. 86.

[43] Lea et al. (1993), p. 115; Autio et al. (2009), p. 407.

[44] Michie et al. (2014b), p. 60.

[45] Knittle et al. (2020), p. 216.

impact on long-term financial behavior.[46] Instead, research indicates that motivational factors like positive attitudes and emotions are linked to the success of long-term debt management plans.[47] It has also been suggested that to support virtuous behaviors like money-saving, designs must evoke positive feelings, have personal significance, and trigger the desire for wisdom and knowledge.[48] A digital financial management tool, like an AI coach, should, therefore, help the debtor to find the true value of their debt recovery by raising reflection towards the intention of their actions.[49]

2.3 Technology to Support Healthy Financial Habits

Financial operations, like money transfers, credit purchases and investing and saving, are mostly performed through digital technologies. Technology is increasingly applied also to address people's debt challenges. Technology can also be designed to support the elements of desirable behavior. Technologies can, for example, make financial and related legal information and services more available and accessible, enable them to be tailored according to individual needs and knowledge levels, and make them faster and timelier.[50] For example, various AI solutions can be used to translate complex legal and financial data into understandable language, or to detect unfavorable terms and conditions in loan agreements. AI can, for example, summarize lengthy texts and help format and visualize information. It also enables new types of interaction between information and its users. There can be question-answering systems that help extract the information needed, or chatbots that have more conversational interactions with users. Personalizing information, for example, by considering a debtor's level of financial literacy, can also greatly improve engagement, understanding, and motivation.

Technology can provide motivational support for debtors, for example, in the form of applications that help set personal goals and follow them, including reminders about approaching due dates for payments or notifications for achieving important milestones. Drawing parallels with the interactive and user-centric design of popular fitness applications, many technological tools with built-in AI could similarly support individuals in making better financial health choices. In the following chapter, we outline some of the existing AI-enhanced solutions and test our self-made prototype of "Financial Friend" for financial management purposes.

---

[46] Hensley (2015), p. 94.

[47] Xiao and Wu (2008), p. 39.

[48] Desmet and Pohlmeyer (2013), p. 5.

[49] De Francisco and Casai (2018), p. 5.

[50] OECD (2018), pp. 8–9.

3 AI as a Financial Coach

3.1 Mapping Existing AI Solutions to Financial Management

The idea of using AI to assist in financial decision-making is not new. For example, AI-enhanced personal finance management apps such as YNAB (https://www.ynab.com/), Empower Personal Dashboard (https://www.empower.com/), MoneyWiz (https://www.wiz.money) and Goodbudget (https://goodbudget.com) analyze users' spending habits, provide insights on how to save, and even automate their investments. These types of applications can particularly improve people's opportunities in obtaining healthier financial behaviors. Users can identify ways to save and invest and, on the other hand, capture their harmful spending behaviors, making it easier to change them. Somewhat similar services are so-called robo-advisors, such as Betterment (https://www.betterment.com/), InbestMe (https://www.inbestme.com) and Simplewealth (https://www.simplewealth.ch), which use AI to make personalized investment recommendations and allocate users' assets automatically by managing their investment portfolios and even executing trades based on their risk profiles. They are automated tools that ask prospective investors questions about their specific circumstances, such as their investment experience, knowledge, and financial situation, and use algorithms to recommend suitable financial instruments.[51]

These types of applications can help fill in the gaps in users' capabilities—the other key factor of better financial health. Other applications that use AI to provide financial insight include sophisticated chatbots used by banks to answer queries, provide recommendations, and facilitate transactions, investment insight, and prediction platforms that analyze market data and provide trend predictions, and even fully automated trading systems that use AI to automate trading decisions. These are all applications that help individual users enhance their financial performance. As AI is already being used in this kind of "positive" role aimed at improving investment and choice between service providers, it could also be very helpful in the function of how to avoid financial trouble.

Some solutions suitable for debt rehabilitation purposes do exist. For example, there are AI-driven platforms, such as Anyfin (https://anyfin.com) and Bright (https://www.brightmoney.co/), that help users consolidate multiple debts into a single debt with a reduced interest rate. There are also AI-driven bots, such as Haggle It (https://web.meetcleo.com/haggle-it), that help in negotiations with creditors to lower interest rates or otherwise settle debts. Furthermore, there are preventive AI-driven solutions, such as DebtBusters (https://www.debtbusters.co.za/) and Experian Boost (https://www.experian.com/consumer-products/score-boost.html), that help users improve their credit scoring, boosting their long-term debt rehabilitation, and budgeting solutions that help individuals keep track of their expenses. Further, there are financial education sites, such as Zogo (https://zogo.com) and MoneyMasters (https://moneymasters.app), that use AI to create personalized learning paths, adapting content based

[51] ESAS (2015). See also Salo-Lahti and Haapio (2017).

on a user's current financial situation and learning progress. However, to the best of our knowledge, there are no government-led solutions that would give comprehensive and personalized help specifically for over-indebted users, thus providing an alternative to judicial debt adjustment processes. Also, the approach in existing financial management apps and tools has been strongly on the investment side, helping users to invest their surplus money efficiently. As organizing one's wealth for debt payments is similar to optimizing surplus money for investments, many current solutions could be tailored for the purposes of debt rehabilitation. Also, integrating AI tools into the personal financial systems of individuals could be executed with relative ease with today's technological possibilities.

3.2 *Testing AI's Financial Coaching Abilities*

To get an idea of the capabilities of AI as a personalized financial coach, we first experimented with OpenAI's GPT-4, an AI model, and later created our own simple prototype of "Finance Friend" using OpenAI's GPT Builder.[52] In our conversations, we first asked GPT-4 generally about financial guidance,[53] and then focused on AI's applicability as a companion that can provide personalized and contextually relevant advice.[54] To determine the model's ability to tailor its responses to particular financial situations of individual debtors, we did our first test with user-provided data and the terms of popular Finnish instant loan companies.[55] An example of the conversation with "Finance Friend" is illustrated below in Fig. 1 (To access all the conversations, see footnotes 52–54).

Our test shows that, at the time of writing this chapter, GPTs are able to provide both holistic and query-specific guidance, encompassing many types of financial inquiries and challenges. However, depending on the wording of the prompt, GPT-4 also reminds us about its limitations in providing personalized advice, as "personal finance is unique to each individual," and encourages the user to consult licensed professionals when making significant financial or legal decisions. Lacking the personal element, the advice provided can also be considered too vague and general

---

[52] Instructions on how to create a GPT are available on OpenAI's website at https://help.openai.com/en/articles/8554397-creating-a-gpt. Accessed 8 Dec 2023. At the time of writing, only users with a paid subscription (Plus, Team, or Enterprise) have access to the GPT Builder. Free tier users have limited access to the GPT Store, where they can discover and use GPTs, but cannot create them.

[53] The conversation with Open AI's GPT-4 on ChatGPT, Financial Coach Limitations, can be viewed at https://chat.openai.com/share/bacd49f2-222a-44ad-8ec6-edcfb6ab2275.

[54] Finance Friend Prototype made using OpenAI's GPT Builder. The Conversation with Finance Friend Protype on ChatGPT, Debt Repayment Strategies, can be viewed at https://chat.openai.com/share/6b109542-fe7a-42f6-af0b-bc9a3f21241e.

[55] The conversation with Open AI's GPT-4 on ChatGPT can be viewed at https://chat.openai.com/share/bf89f439-e9c0-4b92-a6e8-6c6907222583 (conducted in Finnish to match the language of the loan terms).

Please note, this advice was generated by Finance Friend, a simulated AI financial assistant prototype based on OpenAI's GPT technology. This information is for general guidance and educational purposes only and should not be considered as professional financial or legal advice. Always consult with a qualified professional for specific advice tailored to your situation.

Anonymous

The total amount of my debts are: the credit card bill 8.657,76 dollars (with 25 % interest, minimum payment 2 % of the total balance per month), car loan 15.050,00 dollars (with 15 % interest, monthly payment 500 dollars), student loan 9.900,00 (with 5 % interest, monthly payment 120 dollars). My monthly income is 5.500,00 dollars, and my expenses are rent 2.100 dollars, daycare fees 1.200 dollars, food 1.000 dollars, and gas 300 dollars. Based on these facts can you help me make a payment plan?

Finance Friend Prototype

Certainly, let's work on a payment plan based on the information you've provided. Your monthly income is $5,500, and your expenses (rent, daycare, food, gas) total $4,600. This leaves you with $900 per month to allocate towards your debts. Let's break down your debts and required payments:

1. **Credit Card Debt ($8,657.76 at 25% interest, minimum payment 2%):**
   - Minimum Payment: 2% of $8,657.76 = approximately $173.16.
   - Since this debt has the highest interest rate, it's wise to allocate more than the minimum payment if possible.
2. **Car Loan ($15,050 at 15% interest, monthly payment $500):**
   - You're already committed to a monthly payment of $500.
3. **Student Loan ($9,900 at 5% interest, monthly payment $120):**
   - Your monthly payment is $120.

Now, let's allocate your available $900:

- **Student Loan Payment**: $120 (fixed)
- **Car Loan Payment**: $500 (fixed)
- **Credit Card Payment**: The remaining amount, which would be $280 ($900 - $120 - $500).

This payment plan will help you meet your minimum obligations. However, since the credit card has a high interest rate, any additional funds you can allocate towards this debt will help reduce the overall interest you pay. Consider ways to increase your income or reduce expenses to pay off this debt more quickly.

Also, remember that this is a starting point. You should regularly review and adjust your payment plan, especially if your financial situation changes.

◀**Fig. 1** A snapshot of insights generated by "Finance Friend" prototype on ChatGPT created with OpenAI's GPT Builder. Licensed under CC BY-NC[56]

to provide adequate behavioral support for the specific needs of over-indebted individuals. Further, GPT-4's answers may not be error-free and should, therefore, be treated with caution. For example, when prompted with a question about the amount of the late payment fee according to the provided credit card terms and conditions,[57] GPT-4 generated an answer that did not include the actual amount, which was up to 40 dollars (see footnote 53). GPT-4 also reminds us about the possible caveats related to its data,[58] predicting future market movements or outcomes, and the complexity of financial decision-making involving a myriad of personal, emotional, and situational factors.

Despite the constraints, the GPT tools we tested possess many features that can be useful in providing personalized debt rehabilitation solutions. First, to support debtors' financial capabilities, they can explain complex concepts in understandable language and offer actionable strategies for improving skills. Also, the models seem versatile in their adaptive responses to user-specific queries to optimize debtors' expenditures. For instance, in scenarios involving cost reduction, our prototype of "Financial Friend" renders both general strategies and itemized recommendations tailored to specific cost categories, such as housing and food, as articulated by the user. Importantly, in the context of acute credit distress, it exhibits a heightened sensitivity and provides comprehensive advice that includes expenditure scrutiny, income augmentation, and negotiation strategies with lenders. When prompted to analyze instant loan terms and provide insights tailored to the individual's personal financial context, OpenAI's GPT-4 is also able to provide a comprehensive, detailed, and comparative analysis, as well as to distill complex information into actionable insights. The latter is highlighted by AI's responsiveness to subsequent prompts, where it articulates recommendations based on an assessment of the fairness of the terms, from the viewpoint of the user's specific needs.

Notably, OpenAI's GPT-4 also fosters a motivating environment to act towards better financial health, and encourages the user to seek emotional support, noting that "financial challenges can be stressful. Talking to someone, whether it is friends, family, or a professional, can help you manage stress and maintain perspective," and adding a warning: "always be wary of 'quick fix' debt solutions or companies that promise easy debt relief. Some of these can be scams or may lead you into a worse financial situation. It is essential to do thorough research and ideally consult

[56] Full conversation can be viewed at https://chat.openai.com/share/6b109542-fe7a-42f6-af0b-bc9a3f21241e (Conversation on file with authors).

[57] Example of Credit Card Agreement for Bank of America Platinum Mastercard, World Mastercard, Platinum Visa, Visa Signature, and Visa Infinite accounts, available at https://www.bankofamerica.com/content/documents/creditcard/visa-mastercard-platinum-visa-signature-world-infinite-en.pdf.

[58] For the training data cutoff dates of different GPT models, see https://platform.openai.com/docs/models.

with reputable financial advisors or credit counselors before making decisions."[59] These findings underscore GPT-4's potential as an instrumental resource, not only for financial counseling, but also as an empathetic ally.

To summarize the results, our simple tests show the potential of creating a coaching paradigm in which AI serves not only as a navigator but also as a motivator, participating in the user's journey of financial skills improvement. Despite its current limitations, such as the lack of personalization and the possible use of false or outdated data, AI yet has the ability to foster an interactive and user-friendly environment, facilitating goal setting, process monitoring, and strategic guidance—elements intrinsic to sustaining behavioral change according to the COM-B model theory.[60] However, further research and empirical testing with target stakeholders are essential to build a more profound understanding of AI's potential in debt rehabilitation, particularly regarding desired behavioral outcomes.

Recent research on large language models already introduces some approaches for further development. For example, chain-of-thought reasoning involves breaking down complex problems into simpler, more manageable steps, much like how a human would logically think through a problem.[61] Refining this capability would significantly improve the tool's ability to handle complex financial queries, enabling "Finance Friend" to dissect a query into smaller components and address each part step-by-step. In this way, "Finance Friend" would not only provide answers but also educate users about the financial decision-making process. The tool could also learn during the reasoning process through a mechanism called mesa-optimization, where an LLM develops specialized strategies or optimizations for specific tasks based on the prompts fed to it.[62] Thus, improving the chain-of-thought capabilities of "Finance Friend" would also improve its ability to provide user-specific guidance and enable it to continuously refine its algorithms based on user interactions and feedback to provide more accurate and helpful financial guidance.

3.3 Recent Trends in Customized AI Models

Technologies for customizing AI models are evolving at a rapid pace. Since our first tests with the "Finance Friend," hundreds of similar advisors have emerged in OpenAI's GPT marketplace. In addition, advanced techniques like fine-tuning with Low-Rank Adaptation and other specialized algorithms have become increasingly powerful tools for tailoring models to specific domains such as finance. Meanwhile, OpenAI has expanded the capabilities of its GPT Builder, unlocking new possibilities

[59] See footnote 52.

[60] Knittle et al. (2020), p. 216.

[61] Wei et al. (2023).

[62] Von Oswald et al. (2023).

for AI development.[63] These advancements have significant implications for the development of AI financial coaches. Some key updates include:

- *Enhanced Prompt Engineering:* The platform now offers more sophisticated tools for prompt engineering, allowing developers to create more nuanced and context-aware financial assistants. This enables AI coaches to better understand complex financial situations and provide more tailored advice.
- *Improved Data Integration:* Custom GPTs can now more seamlessly integrate with external data sources, potentially allowing financial coaches to access real-time market data, interest rates, and other financial indicators to provide more accurate and timely advice. Furthermore, enhanced controls allow creators to manage how data is stored, accessed, and deleted. This includes the ability to set rules around data retention and user privacy.
- *Multi-modal Capabilities*: The introduction of multi-modal features allows custom GPTs to process and generate not just text, but also images and potentially other forms of data. For financial coaches, this could mean the ability to create visual representations of financial plans or interpret graphs and charts.
- *Expanded Memory and Context Understanding*: Improvements in the model's ability to maintain context over longer conversations allow for more coherent and in-depth financial coaching sessions, which are crucial for complex topics like debt rehabilitation. Moreover, custom GPTs can now be configured to remember information across sessions, providing a more personalized and coherent interaction over time.
- *Customizable Ethical Frameworks*: Developers can now more easily implement specific ethical guidelines and regulatory compliance rules into their custom GPTs, addressing concerns about responsible AI use in financial advice.
- *Improved Explainability*: New features allow custom GPTs to better explain their reasoning, which is crucial in financial coaching where transparency and trust are paramount.
- *System Messages:* The system prompts that define the behavior of a GPT can now be customized. This includes setting instructions for how the bot should respond to different types of queries, what tone it should use, and how it should present information.
- *API Calls:* Custom GPTs can now make API calls to external services. This means that a custom bot can fetch data from other sources, perform actions outside the chatbot environment, or integrate with other tools and platforms. With API integration, the bot can handle real-time data, respond to dynamic content, and interact with up-to-date information.
- *Python Code Execution*: For users who need more advanced customization, there is an option to include Python code within custom GPTs. This allows for complex logic, data processing, and custom responses that go beyond the standard capabilities of the GPT. Python scripts can be integrated to perform specific tasks,

[63] OpenAI (2024).

analyze data, or interact with external systems, giving the GPT more power and flexibility.

- *User Consent*: When creating custom GPTs that handle sensitive data, the bot can be configured to request user consent before processing or storing certain types of information.

These advances have significantly enhanced the potential of AI financial coaches. For instance, in the near future, a debt rehabilitation GPT could analyze a user's financial documents, create a visual representation of their debt situation, suggest a personalized repayment plan, and provide detailed recommendations, all while ensuring compliance with financial regulations and ethical guidelines. With the latest version updates, our "Finance Friend" would likely overcome many of the limitations discussed earlier.

However, it is important to note that while these improvements are substantial, AI financial coaches will still have significant limitations. Therefore, they should be viewed as sophisticated tools to augment human expertise rather than replacements for professional financial advisors. Nevertheless, the rapid pace of these developments indicates that in two to three years, these models could very well replace human expertise in certain financial advising tasks.

4 Building Financial AI Coaches People Can Trust

As the integration of AI, finance, and law continues to evolve, we can expect more sophisticated, personalized, and effective AI solutions to be designed also for the purposes of debt rehabilitation. However, despite the rise of AI automation, humans still play the leading role in the design, programming, and oversight of AI applications.[64] Humans are needed to spot potential errors and biases in the algorithms and solve cybersecurity and privacy problems in understanding complex and specialized information. Different design methods and tools can help create AI solutions that address the latter challenge and present information in a way that is easy to understand and act upon. For example, layering can take into account differences in financial literacy, and the information displayed can be tailored according to the needs of specific user groups.[65]

Many open-access AI tools and services are already available to anyone. Unlike specialized financial apps, GPT-4 powered AI systems cannot currently be linked to users' bank accounts, track their spending, or provide real-time financial management, and specific financial plans can only be tailored if the user shares own data in the conversation—yet sharing sensitive financial data is not recommended for privacy and security reasons. If users are providing AI with their financial data and making decisions based on its recommendations, they need to be able to trust that the

[64] Baker and Dellaert (2018), p. 715.

[65] Salo-Lahti et al. (2023).

system protects their privacy and is free from biases and hallucinations. For privacy concerns, there are already some technological solutions: for example, Microsoft Azure[66] and ChatGPT Enterprise[67] provide privacy for their AI tools.

The banking sector would be a natural actor to develop applications proposed in this chapter. First, banks would have easy access to their customers' data. It should be noted, however, that the Second Payment Services Directive (EU) 2015/2366 (PSD2) stipulates that credit institutions must provide third-party service providers access to customer accounts with the explicit consent of the customer, which makes it possible for third parties to develop new types of applications outside the banking sector. Second, and even more importantly, banks could have a vested interest in developing financial coach applications for their indebted customers, as banks are the most typical creditor group in insolvency proceedings.

Regardless of the developer of the application, building AI coaches that users can trust can only happen with the support of regulation. EU legislation on AI, the AI Act (EU) 2024/1689, has now entered into force. The AI Act includes general-purpose AI models, such as GPT models. Article 53 sets forth obligations for the providers of general-purpose AI models. Providers must maintain up-to-date documentation of the model, share information with AI system providers, ensure copyright compliance, and publish a summary of training content. According to the reasoning of the law, AI "should serve as a tool for people, with the ultimate aim of increasing human well-being."[68]

In addition to its supporting role, regulation, particularly the heavy regulation of the financial sector, can also slow down the pace of AI innovation. For instance, the Markets in Financial Instruments Directive II 2014/65/EU (MiFID II) regulates investment services and requires service providers, such as robo-advisors, to be authorized, which may hamper the development of financial coach applications. However, financial market legislation doesn't just create barriers. It can also enable the development of new types of applications and services. The already mentioned PSD2 enables third parties to obtain aggregated information on accounts held with one or more credit institutions and get an overall view of the financial situation, laying the groundwork for the creation of financial coaches. The European Commission is currently stressing the importance of wider access to financial data and the promotion of open finance. Updates to the PDS2 are now being proposed and the future PSD3 aims to further strengthen data sharing. The Commission has also put forward a legislative proposal for a framework for financial data access, aiming at more innovative financial products and services.[69] While excessive regulation can stifle innovation, we argue for the need for trustworthy technology and trust-building regulation that promotes the responsible design, implementation, and use of new technologies.

---

66 Microsoft (2023).

67 OpenAI (2023).

68 AI Act (EU) 2024/1689, Recital (6).

69 European Commission (2023a).

5 Conclusion

There is a need for behaviorally informed, personalized and technologically advanced solutions for over-indebted individuals to achieve financial well-being. Bridging the gap between debtors and the support they need can happen with the help of AI, but also by fostering a broader, more proactive, and human-centered understanding of debt and access to financial justice. Justice in the context of personal insolvency is served not only by providing access to judicial debt recovery proceedings, but also by empowering people to manage their debt problems and sustain financial health on their own. Moreover, as research indicates, debt problems are essentially behavioral phenomena influenced particularly by debtors' external conditions. Therefore, when designing debt rehabilitation solutions, such as financial AI coaches, it is necessary to create interventions that support an individual's *capabilities, opportunities* and *motivation,* as defined in the COM-B model theory. As our tests with Open AI's GPT-4 and the Finance Friend prototype we created using Open AI's technology illustrate, despite its current limitations to personalized analysis, data sources and possible hallucinations, generative AI shows promise as the personal financial coach of the future. AI can translate complex financial information into comprehensible, actionable and context-specific guidance, foster an interactive environment and facilitate user's goal setting. More in-depth, empirical and interdisciplinary research is needed to build financial AI coaches that people can trust, and to fully understand the practical, legal, and moral implications of AI in the context of debt recovery. We hope this chapter serves as a useful starting point for this conversation.

References

Autio M, Wilska T-A, Kaartinen R, Lähteenmaa J (2009) The use of small instant loans among young adults—a gateway to a consumer insolvency? Int J Consum Stud 33:407–415

Baker T, Dellaert B (2018) Regulating Robo advice across the financial services industry. Iowa Law Rev 103:713–750

Carlsson H, Larsson S, Svensson L, Åström F (2017) Consumer credit behavior in the digital context: a bibliometric analysis and literature review. J Financ Couns Plan 28(1):76–94

De Francisco S, Casai M (2018) Billy cash: digital piggy bank for meaningful saving behavior. RChD: creación y pensamiento 3(4):1–12

Demertzis M, Domínguez-Jiménez M, Lusardi A (2020) The financial fragility of European households in the time of COVID-19. Policy Contrib 15:1–16

Desmet P, Pohlmeyer A (2013) Positive design: an introduction to design for subjective wellbeing. Int J Des 7(3):5–19

Dorrestijn S, Verbeek PP (2013) Technology, wellbeing and freedom: the legacy of Utopian design. Int J Des 7(3):45–56

ESAS (European Supervisory Authorities) (2015) Joint Committee discussion paper on automation in financial advice, JC 2015 080, Dec 2015

European Commission (2020) A capital markets union for people and businesses—new action plan. COM (2020) 590 final, Brussels, 24 Sept 2020

European Commission (2023a) Financial data access and payments package, directorate-general for financial stability, Financial Services and Capital Markets Union, 28 June. https://finance.ec.europa.eu/publications/financial-data-access-and-payments-package_en. Accessed 26 Oct 2023
European Commission (2023b) Flash Eurobarometer 525. Monitoring the level of financial literacy in the EU
European e-Justice Portal (2023) Insolvency/bankruptcy. https://e-justice.europa.eu/447/EN/insolvencybankruptcy. Accessed 11 Nov 2023
Eurostat (2023), Financial vulnerability in households. Data extracted in October 2023. https://ec.europa.eu/eurostat/statistics-explained/index.php?title=Financial_vulnerability_in_households. Accessed 28 Aug 2024
Financial and Debt Counseling (2024). https://oikeus.fi/talousjavelkaneuvonta/en/index.html. Accessed 26 Aug 2024
Finnish Act on the Adjustment of Debts of a Private Individual (57/1993). A non-official English translation. https://www.finlex.fi/en/laki/kaannokset/1993/en19930057_20000714.pdf. Accessed 26 Aug 2024
Finnish Act on the Limitation of Debts (728/2003). A non-official English translation. https://www.finlex.fi/en/laki/kaannokset/2003/en20030728_20160324.pdf. Accessed 26 Aug 2024
Frade C (2012) Bankruptcy, stigma and rehabilitation. ERA Forum 13:45–57
Fredriksson S (2014) Uudet velat uhkaavat velkajärjestelyn läpikäyntiä. [New Debts Threaten the Debt Adjustment Process]. Tilastokeskuksen hyvinvointikatsaus 4/2014. https://www.stat.fi/artikkelit/2014/art_2014-12-08_010.html?s=0. Accessed 10 Nov 2023
Guarantee Foundation (2024). https://www.takuusaatio.fi/en/home/. Accessed 26 Aug 2024
Guven C (2012) Reversing the question: does happiness affect consumption and savings behavior? J Econ Psychol 33(4):701–717
Haapio H, Barton D, Corrales Compagnucci M (2021) Legal design or the common good: proactive legal care by design. In: Corrales Compagnucci M, Haapio H, Hagan M, Doherty M (eds) Legal design Integrating business, design and legal thinking with technology. Edward Elgar Publishing, Cheltenham
Hagan M (2024) Designing public Services in the age of big tech. Beyond government-to-citizen service design to infrastructure design. In: Ducato R, Strowel A, Marique E (eds) Design(s) for law. Ledizioni, Milan
Hensley B (2015) Enhancing links between research and practice to improve consumer financial education and well-being. J Financ Couns Plan 26(1):94–101
Knittle K, Heino M, Marques M, Stenius M, Beattie M, Ehrbrecht F, Hagger M, Hardeman W, Hankonen N (2020) The compendium of self-Enactable techniques to change and self-manage motivation and behaviour v.1.0. Nat Hum Behav 4(2):215–223
Lea S, Webley P, Levine M (1993) The economic psychology of consumer debt. J Econ Psychol 14(1):85–119
Linna T (2015) Nuori velkajärjestelyssä—Fresh start vai syrjäytyminen? [A young debtor in debt adjustment—a fresh start or exclusion?]. Oikeus 44(1):26–43
Michie S, Atkins L, West R (2014a) The behavior change wheel. A guide to designing interventions. Silverback Publishing
Michie S, West R, Campbell R, Brown J, Gainforth H (2014b) ABC of behavior change theories. Silverback Publishing
Microsoft (2023) Azure customer data protection. 29 Aug. https://learn.microsoft.com/en-us/azure/security/fundamentals/protection-customer-data. Accessed 10 Nov 2023
OECD (2018), G20/OECD INFE policy guidance on digitalisation and financial literacy
OpenAI (2023) Introducing ChatGPT enterprice. 28 Aug. https://openai.com/blog/introducing-chatgpt-enterprise. Accessed 10 Nov 2023
OpenAI (2024) GPTs. https://help.openai.com/en/collections/8475420-gpts. Accessed 28 Aug 2024

Östergren P-O, Bodin T, Canivet C, Moghaddassi M, Vilhelmsson A (2022) Selling one's future: over-indebtedness and the risk of poor mental health and the role of precarious employment—results from the Scania public health cohort, Sweden. BMJ Open 12(11):e061797. https://doi.org/10.1136/bmjopen-2022-061797. Accessed 28 Aug 2024

Potel-Saville M (2024) From dark to fair patterns? How can design-driven innovation and Neurodesign help fighting against deceptive design. In: Ducato R, Strowel A, Marique E (eds) Design(s) for law. Ledizioni, Milan

Salo-Lahti M, Haapio H (2017) Robo-advisors and investors: enhancing human-robot interaction through information design. In: Schweighofer E, Kummer F, Hötzendorfer W, Sorge C (eds) Trends and communities of legal informatics. Proceedings of the 20th international legal informatics symposium IRIS 2017. Österreichische Computer Gesellschaft, Wien

Salo-Lahti M, Ranta M, Haapio H (2023) AI Tools for Sustainability—Actionable information for both humans and machines. In: Schweighofer E, Zanol J, Eder S (eds) Legal informatics as science of legal methods. Proceedings of the 26th international legal informatics symposium IRIS 2023. Editions Weblaw, Bern

Sillence E, Briggs P (2007) Please advise: using the internet for health and financial advice. Comput Hum Behav 23:727–748

Suomen Asiakastieto Oy (2024) Payment default statistics Finland. https://www.epressi.com/media/userfiles/123829/1688367341/asiakastieto-maksuhairiotilasto-07-2023-julkaisu.pdf. Accessed 26 Aug 2024

Susskind R (2019) Online courts and the future of justice. Oxford University Press, Oxford

Toivonen N, Salo-Lahti M, Ranta M, Haapio H (2023) Beyond debt: the intersection of justice, financial wellbeing and AI. Paper presented at the JURIX workshop on AI and access to justice, Maastricht, Netherlands, 18 Dec 2023

Toivonen N, Salo-Lahti M, Ranta M and Haapio H (2024) AI-enhanced fresh starts: proactive financial health care with AI as a personalized coach. Jusletter IT, 15 Feb

Townley-Jones M, Griffiths M, Bryant M (2008) Chronic consumer debtors: the need for specific intervention. Int J Consum Stud 32(3):204–210

United States Code (2023) Title 11—Bankruptcy. Chapter 7. https://uscode.house.gov/view.xhtml?path=/prelim@title11/chapter7&edition=prelim. Accessed 28 Aug 2024

Valkama E, Muttilainen V (2008) Maksuvaikeudet pikaluottomarkkinoilla [Payment Difficulties Associated with SMS Loans]. National Research Institute of Legal Policy. Research Communications no. 86

Von Oswald J, Niklasson E, Schlegel M, Kobayashi S, Zucchet N, Scherrer N, Miller N, Sandler M, Aguera y Arcas B, Vladymyrov M, Pascanu R, Sacramento J (2023) Uncovering mesa-optimization algorithms in transformers. v1, 11 Sep. https://doi.org/10.48550/arXiv.2309.05858. Accessed 28 Aug 2024

Wei J, Wang X, Schuurmans D, Bosma M, Ichter B, Xia F, Chi E, Le Q, Zhou D (2023) Chain-of-thought prompting elicits reasoning in large language models. v6, 10 Jan. https://doi.org/10.48550/arXiv.2201.11903. Accessed 28 Aug 2024

Wendel S (2014) Designing for behavior change. Applying psychology and behavioral economics. O-Reilly Media Inc

World Justice Project (2024) Global insights on Access to Justice. https://worldjusticeproject.org/access-to-justice-data/. Accessed 26 Aug 2024

Xiao JJ, Wu J (2008) Completing debt management plans in credit counselling: an application of the theory of planned behavior. Financ Couns Plan 19(2):29–45

AI Between the Legal System and Art—A Systemic Approach

Petra Hietanen-Kunwald and Perttu Isohanni

Abstract In this chapter, we explore the profound impact of artificial intelligence on the art and legal systems, with a specific focus on copyright issues. We address a significant concern: the potential of artificial intelligence to interfere with the interests and rights of artists when art is created and reproduced using artificial intelligence. Our approach, grounded in systems theory as represented by Niklas Luhmann, examines the characteristics and potential frictions within the legal and art systems affected by AI. Identifying systemic complexities is essential for exploring possible conflicts and developing effective strategies for dispute prevention and resolution. This constitutes the initial steps of a design process outlined in the Double Diamond framework and further developed in the UK Design Council's Systemic Design Approach. The chapter argues that legislation alone is insufficient; a broader spectrum of (legal) and institutional measures is necessary to protect artists' rights and interests in both the legal and art systems. This multifaceted approach highlights several factors that could instigate change and help resolve complex questions.

Keywords Art · Artificial intelligence · Copyright · Systems theory · System thinking

1 Introduction

A widely discussed example of the challenges connected with the use of artificial intelligence in the creation of art is the work of the *Portrait of Edmond Belamy* that was sold at an auction by Christie's for US$ 432.500 in 2018. The work was the creation of the collective "Obvious," consisting of three members, none of whom

P. Hietanen-Kunwald (✉) · P. Isohanni
School of Business, Department of Accounting and Business Law, Aalto University, Espoo, Finland
e-mail: petra.hietanen-kunwald@aalto.fi

P. Isohanni
e-mail: perttu.isohanni@aalto.fi

© The Author(s), under exclusive license to Springer Nature Singapore Pte Ltd. 2025
M. Corrales Compagnucci et al. (eds.), *Generative AI, Contracts, Law and Design*, Perspectives in Law, Business and Innovation,
https://doi.org/10.1007/978-981-95-2058-9_9

was an artist by profession, but their background was in machine learning, business and economics.[1] The portrait was produced using a Generative Adversarial Network (GAN), a machine learning technique introduced by Ian Goodfellow and colleagues.[2] In the days following the auction, much discussion centered on Robbie Barrat, who claimed the code he had written and shared online was used in the production of the *Portrait of Edmond Belamy*. Obvious confirmed to the technology website *The Verge* that they did use Barrat's code but stated that they had modified it.[3] While the code was released under an open source license and the use by Obvious was therefore considered legal, it raised ethical discussions regarding the authorship of the portrait.[4] In the art world the work was met with criticism for its lack of originality and artistic value and led to discussions on authorship and ethics.[5]

Since then, the use of artificial intelligence for creating art has increased, not only in the visual arts, but also in music, poetry and writing. For the creative sector this development comes with opportunities and threats. On the one side it may lower the threshold to producing art. On the other side the use of artificial intelligence challenges the boundaries between what can be considered art and who is to be considered an artist.[6] The development entails questions that are fundamental to the understanding of art and the law, relating to *authorship*, *copyright* and *fair compensation.*[7] The use of copyrighted content during the training phase of artificial intelligence models may infringe the rights of those that have initially created the work and has led to several law suits in the US and the UK.[8] It has been claimed that this training data can be seen as inspiration for artificial intelligence, that does not differ from inspirations that creators gain when feeling, sensing, and hearing previous work.[9] While the increased use of artificial intelligence has therefore democratized "art" making it more accessible; the growing role of artificial intelligence models, mass production and the use of copyrighted content for training these models challenge both the legal system as well as the art world.

The rapid development puts pressure on the legal system's ability to protect creative work. Individual artists or creators will find it difficult to defend their rights against potential copyright infringements. This is due to legal uncertainty regarding whether an infringement has occurred, leading to high litigation risks and costs. Artists may also consider the use of their artistic ideas as unfair, even if copyright

---

[1] See, e.g., Cetinic and She (2022), p. 14, Arbiza Goenaga (2020) and McCormack et al. (2019), p. 35.

[2] Goodfellow et al. (2014).

[3] Flynn (2018).

[4] McCormack et al. (2019), p. 37.

[5] Cetinic and She (2022), p. 11.

[6] Hertzmann (2020).

[7] McCormack et al. (2019), p. 37.

[8] For instance, Getty Images has sued Stability AI for using copyrighted images to train its Stable Diffusion AI system. See, Ethical Tech Initiative (n.d.).

[9] Kuker (2024).

law expressly does not protect ideas as such.[10] Copyright protection turns largely on the economic value of a work and copyright related litigation is more likely to occur where economic interests are at stake. Economic value is, however, not the only value artists seek to protect. Often, they also seek recognition as an artist within what can be referred as the art system.

In this chapter we focus on the interrelation between art and the law from a systemic perspective. The aim is to discover the characteristics of the art and the legal system and to develop an understanding for the changes that need to be made and the connections that may be open to design to prevent or resolve art related disputes using systems theory as a research framework.[11] Applying this framework embedded in systems theory as developed by German sociologist Niklas Luhmann,[12] we examine the characteristics and potential frictions within the legal and art systems. Our approach focusses on the connections and borders of the systems, as seen from the outside and starting from a legal point of view. We therefore do not examine arts from within the art system, but how it differs from and interacts with the legal system, using copyright law as an illustration. The identification of the systemic complexities is necessary to *explore* conflict patterns, *reframe* them and *create* effective dispute prevention and resolution strategies. These belong to the first steps in a design process as set out in the Double Diamond framework and further developed in the Design Council's Systemic Design Approach (see Fig. 1).[13] To propose hypotheses and possible solutions we will rely on system thinking as introduced in the Systemic Design Approach. System thinking considers individual elements, their interrelations, and their connection to the broader environment. System thinkers recognize the complexity of systems: they are aware that an intervention may trigger interactions that could positively (or negatively) reinforce the systems. System thinkers identify various contributing factors rather than seeking a single problem with a simple solution.[14]

Our chapter will be limited to the interfaces between art, law, and business as it shows when art is commercialized, produced, traded or licensed. As regards to the copyright discussion, the chapter will focus on European law, but where applicable will also refer to international sources to illustrate general principles. It does not provide a comprehensive analysis of the complex copyright questions involved; instead, a socio-legal perspective is adopted to better understand the relation between the legal system and the art system. When examining the connections between art and law we will not engage in the human rights law discussion regarding balancing the rights to free speech on the one side and the rights on ownership on the other, nor

[10] See, e.g., TRIPS (Agreement on Trade-Related Aspects of Intellectual Property Rights) Article 9(2): "Copyright protection shall extend to expressions and not to ideas, procedures, methods of operation or mathematical concepts as such." On the protection of artistic style, see Isohanni and Hietanen-Kunwald in this book.

[11] On the framework, see, Hietanen-Kunwald et al. (2021), p. 83.

[12] See, e.g., Luhmann (1995) and Baraldi et al. (2021).

[13] Design Council (n.d.).

[14] Design Council (2021), p. 27.

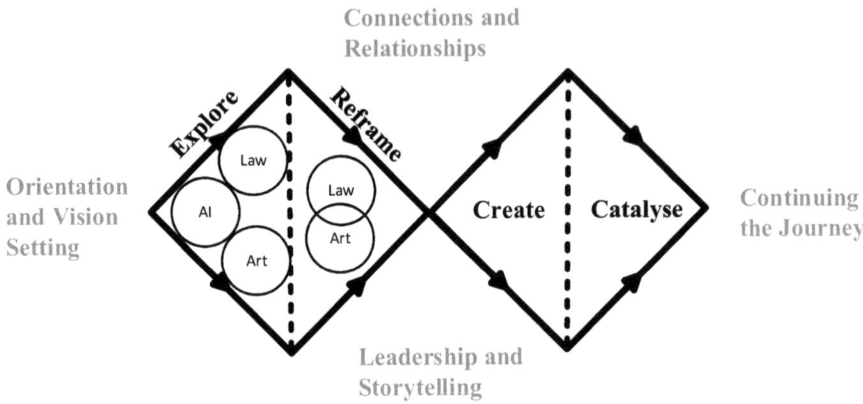

Fig. 1 The systemic design framework by the design council,[15] licenced under a CC BY 4.0 licence (adapted by Isohanni and Hietanen-Kunwald)

deal with question of fair remuneration nor the question whether and to what extent artwork may be contrary to legal or ethical principles.

Section 1 introduces the topic. In Sect. 2, we will discuss the characteristics of copyright law, highlighting three main points of friction. The first point concerns the question of authorship in the legal sense. The second point addresses the concept of originality. The third point examines the use of copyright-protected content for training artificial intelligence models. In search of a more holistic approach, Sect. 3 seeks to uncover the characteristics of the art system in relation to the legal system and copyright law. Section 4 explores the connections between the art system and the legal system that are potentially open to design. Section 5 offers hypotheses and possible solutions from a systemic perspective. Section 6 concludes and suggests issues for further research.

2 Authorship and Creativity Within the Legal System

The example of the *Portrait of Edmond Belamy* has initiated a wide discussion across different fields not only about authorship but also about the creative processes involved in producing the work.[16] Authorship refers to the question of who is to be considered the creator of an artefact, how authorship is attributed and ultimately whether there is art without a human creator. In the above example the developer of the GAN model used to create the picture has not been recognized as author and has not participated in the economic profits generated through the sale of the portrait.

[15] Design Council (n.d.).

[16] See, e.g., Cetinic and She (2022), p. 14, Arbiza Goenaga (2020) and McCormack et al. (2019), p. 35.

While the portrait was marketed as a work created by artificial intelligence, it was not solely produced by software either; humans were involved in writing the code, curating the dataset and choosing the final output that was framed.[17]

2.1 Authorship and Artificial Creativity

According to the prevailing understanding of artificial intelligence, the software would not be able to independently create "art," as it is a tool that follows human instructions, not a creator by itself.[18] However, as deep learning software grows more complex and harder to comprehend, authorship and creative agency have become more difficult to understand, introducing questions about whether authorship is shifting towards the algorithm itself.[19] Large language models (LLMs), for example, are already considered "black boxes," where their exact workings and connections are not fully understood by anyone. Some have not excluded the possibility either that, at some point, software may be considered an independent creator of an artefact or, even an artist.[20]

Authorship relates to ownership and attribution of rights and is closely connected to the economic aspects of the work. It is a different question though, whether the artefact created through artificial intelligence is *art* and the creator an *artist*. McCormack et al. hold, for instance that art is a "human enterprise defined by experience."[21] To them, the authenticity of the generative process is fundamental to artwork; there also needs to be an intention to create art and an intention to be an artist. This authentic process of creation as well as the intention to create are in their view elements artificial intelligence models lack. Software programmed to generate art cannot decide not to make art; a generic or copied process will produce generic work.[22] However, the extent of the involvement of artificial intelligence in the creative process remains often obscure, as artists do not disclose all aspects on how and to what extent artificial intelligence is used.[23] This might be crucial, though, for assessing the creative process and the quality of the work, which can influence the prices buyers are willing to pay.

---

[17] See, Elgammal (2018).

[18] Hertzmann (2020).

[19] In this sense, McCormack et al. (2019), p. 44.

[20] Mazzone and Elgammal (2019).

[21] McCormack et al. (2019), p. 38.

[22] McCormack et al. (2019), p. 46.

[23] Cetinic and She (2022).

2.2 Copyright—The Law Approach to Authorship and Creativity

Authorship and the creative process have been widely discussed within copyright law as well. As artificial intelligence increasingly transforms the art world, it necessitates a clearer understanding of how art interacts with and challenges existing legal frameworks. The copyright system was initially conceived to ensure the continued creation of human creative works. Without means of scalable reproduction, there was no need for copyright.[24] But subsequent technological innovations that allowed third parties to capture the economic value of the produced creative goods created a need to provide an exclusive right to authors for the use of their works. Today, the rights provided by copyright are generally divided into economic rights and moral rights. Economic rights are aimed at protecting material interests, ensuring that authors are remunerated for the use of their works. Moral rights instead protect the reputation and personal interests of the author. These include rights such as a right to claim authorship to a work and a right to object to any modifications or derogatory treatments to their works that could be prejudicial to their reputation.[25]

Eligibility for copyright protection assumes the presence of a human author.[26] The principle is not expressly stated, but rather evident in the language used throughout various legislative frameworks. For instance, Article 1(1) of the Copyright Term Directive defines the term of protection as "life of the author and for 70 years after his death."[27] Likewise, in *Painer*, Advocate General Trstenjak acknowledged the requirement of human authorship by stating in his opinion that "only human creations are therefore protected, which can also include those for which the person employs a technical aid, such as a camera."[28]

In addition to the presence of a human author, a work needs to be considered "original." In the EU, the CJEU harmonized the standard of originality for all authorial works within the scope of the InfoSoc Directive in *Infopaq*.[29] Accordingly, copyright was held to encompass a subject matter which is original in the sense that it is its *author's own intellectual creation*.[30] The concept was further defined in later case law, and summarized in *Funke Medien*, where the requirement of originality was

---

[24] See, e.g., Landes and Posner (1989), p. 326 and Burk (2023), p. 1677.

[25] See, e.g., Berne Convention for the Protection of Literary and Artistic Works (as amended on September 28, 1979), Article 6bis.

[26] See, e.g., Hugenholtz and Quintais (2021), p. 1195.

[27] Directive 2006/116/EC of the European Parliament and of the Council of 12 December 2006 on the term of protection of copyright and certain related rights.

[28] C-145/10, Eva-Maria Painer v Standard Verlags GmbH and Others, Opinion of Advocate General Trstenjak, EU:C:2011:239, para 121.

[29] Directive 2001/29/EC of the European Parliament and of the Council of 22 May 2001 on the harmonisation of certain aspects of copyright and related rights in the information society.

[30] C-5/08, Infopaq International A/S v Danske Dagblades Forening, EU:C:2009:465, para 37.

deemed to be satisfied when the work is an intellectual creation of its author "which reflect the author's personality and are expressed by free and creative choices."[31]

Importantly, the concept of originality within the context of copyright should not be confused with artistic merit. Already in 1903, in *Bleistein v. Donaldson Lithographing Company*, the Supreme Court of the United States recognized that "[i]t would be a dangerous undertaking for persons trained only to the law to constitute themselves final judges of the worth of pictorial illustrations, outside of the narrowest and most obvious limits."[32] More recently, in *Cattelan v. Morford*, a district court in the US assessed whether Cattelan's work "Comedian," consisting of a banana taped to a wall, infringed on the copyright of another artist who previously had a similar idea. The court noted that while the question of what art is "looms closer in mind," it was fortunate that "the Court still need not attempt to answer that age-old (and frankly unanswerable) question," eventually finding that no original expressions were infringed.[33]

In general, the copyright system does not require more than a minimal degree of human creativity to meet the threshold of originality. However, artificial intelligence has enabled the creation of visually convincing works where it is not clear whether the requirement is fulfilled. In principle, determining the presence of originality is the same as with other works. It is relevant to assess whether the original expressions that are expressed in the work meet the required threshold of originality.[34] However, these new types of works present two novel challenges. One is determining how to interpret the minimum level of creativity required to meet the threshold of originality for works made using artificial intelligence. The other is more pragmatic; the outwardly visual qualities of the works might not be as suitable to determine the creative choices that have been made to produce the work as is the case more often with traditional works of art. This directs focus on assessing originality to how various elements of the work have been controlled and what arrangements have been made to produce it.[35] This may in turn introduce a need for artists to document how works involving the use of artificial intelligence have been made.

Furthermore, works may consist of multiple original expressions from different parties, resulting in difficulties of attribution. In the case of presently popular text-to-image models, any original expressions arising from guiding the model with text prompts could potentially be mixed with original expressions of a creator whose work has been used during the training phase of the model. The programmer(s) of these models usually do not have a strong link with final original expressions within a given work. In the case of GANs however, such as the one used to create *Portrait of Edmond Belamy,* original expressions might be distributed otherwise. The person who programmed and fine-tuned the model, as well as curated the dataset to create a

[31] C-469/17, Funke Medien NRW GmbH v Bundesrepublik Deutschland, EU:C:2019:623, para 25.

[32] Bleistein v. Donaldson Lithographing Company, 188 U.S. 239 (1903).

[33] Morford v. Cattelan, No, 1:2021cv20039, US District Court for the Southern District of Florida.

[34] Hugenholtz and Quintais (2021), p. 1200.

[35] See C-145/10, Eva-Maria Painer v Standard Verlags GmbH and Others, ECLI:EU:C:2011:798, para 91.

certain visual expression might have in fact made more creative choices than a third party who downloads the program and chooses one of its outputs. Thus, a need may exist in some cases to address multiple expressions of originality separately when determining the authorship and eligibility of a work for protection.

Copyright infringement relating to artificial intelligence models can occur in two distinct ways. First, an infringement may occur when an output is generated by the model that is substantially similar to a work that has been used in the training data.[36] Due to the technical nature of current text-to-image models, repeating elements from the works in the training data is relatively rare. Nevertheless, in some circumstances they have been shown to memorize and reproduce parts of popular works that are repeated often in the training data.[37] Second, an infringement may occur during the training phase of the model, where the work is retrieved and used to train the model.[38] Main restrictions imposed to the training phase in commercial uses are laid out in Article 4 of the CDSM directive, specifying that works need to be "lawfully accessible" as well as further requiring an implementation of an opt-out mechanism that enables authors to prevent the use of their works as training data.[39]

However, many details on the practical implementation of the opt-out mechanism and interpretation of what the concept of lawful access constitutes of are still unclear. Consequently, Kretschmer et al. have argued that training models using unlicensed data remains risky in the EU.[40] Additionally, while Article 53(1) of the EU Artificial Intelligence Act[41] places a transparency requirement of providing detailed summaries of the content used for training, determining whether a specific work has been used in training may be difficult. The legal uncertainty resulting from the novel nature of the challenges regarding artificial intelligence and copyright has resulted in artists adopting alternative methods to protect their works, such as removing them from content hosting platforms, "poisoning" works with tools that aim to destabilize the outputs of the models[42] or setting "copyright traps," that could potentially be used to detect the inclusion of a particular work in training data.[43]

---

[36] Guadamuz (2024), p. 11.

[37] See, e.g., Emanuilov and Margoni (2024) and Cooper and Grimmelmann (2024).

[38] Guadamuz (2024), p. 5.

[39] Directive (EU) 2019/790 of the European Parliament and of the Council of 17 April 2019 on copyright and related rights in the Digital Single Market and amending Directives 96/9/EC and 2001/29/EC.

[40] Kretschmer et al. (2024), p. 134.

[41] Regulation (EU) 2024/1689 of the European Parliament and of the Council of 13 June 2024 laying down harmonised rules on artificial intelligence and amending Regulations (EC) No 300/2008, (EU) No 167/2013, (EU) No 168/2013, (EU) 2018/858, (EU) 2018/1139 and (EU) 2019/2144 and Directives 2014/90/EU, (EU) 2016/797 and (EU) 2020/1828.

[42] Shan et al. (2024).

[43] Meeus et al. (2024).

3 Art and Artificial Intelligence—Exploring Systemic Characteristics

The previous section has shown the role of law in protecting property rights and fostering economic value within the arts. The section posits that legislation alone might be insufficient to deal with complex issues of copyright and art. The legal system is still in the process of reacting to new developments regarding the use of artificial intelligence models and might not be able to protect individual artwork; a broader spectrum of legal and non-legal instruments and institutional changes might be needed to address conflicts that may emerge due to the growing role of artificial intelligence in art. To apply systemic thinking to the prevention and resolution of art related disputes, understanding the nature underlying of conflicts and the operations of other systems is essential.[44] In this section we will focus on art as a social system, and its relation to the legal system within the framework of systems theory as understood by Niklas Luhmann.

Luhmann conceptualizes society as a functionally differentiated communication system, with subsystems such as art and law contributing through their unique functions. These subsystems are autonomous and operationally closed.[45] The system's function is not a function in the sense of a goal to be achieved by e.g. the artist or the judge, but is observable by an external observer as a point of reference.[46] This point of reference provides an indicator for whether communications are oriented to the specific function of a system such contributing to the complexity of the system. The unique function of art is according to Luhmann to create a reality of its own in the world, an imaginary or fictional reality from which something else can be determined as reality. Art brings a duplication of reality marking a difference between the real and fictional reality through imitation (imitate what reality does not show, such as ideas and divine perfection), critique (criticizes reality for what it does not want to admit) or affirmation (affirms reality by demonstrating that its representation is successful) or by giving an individual observer a possibility to confront reality and learn to perceive it in ways that they could never experience in real life.[47] Art achieves this by utilizing the distinction between perception and communication: perception, unlike thoughts and communication, can evoke both astonishment and recognition simultaneously. Art describes the world from the perspective of astonishing redundancies and brings the difference between perception and communication back into communication.[48] The function of the legal system on the other hand is to stabilize normative expectations, even when they are disappointed. It provides for norms that do not change when contravened and such protects legitimate normative expectations.[49]

[44] Hietanen-Kunwald et al. (2021), p. 79.

[45] Luhmann (2000), p. 133.

[46] Luhmann (2000), p. 137.

[47] Luhmann (2000), p. 143 and Baraldi et al. (2021), p. 27.

[48] Baraldi et al. (2021), p. 27.

[49] Luhmann (1995), p. 137.

In the view of systems theory subsystems differentiate themselves from other subsystems. They are autonomous communication systems that operate based upon a distinction between the system itself and its environment. For a social system, like the art system or the legal system to exist it needs to constantly maintain its system boundaries. This autonomous re-production of the difference between the environment and the system is essential for the existence of the (sub)system.[50] It takes place by communication specific to the subsystem referring to previous communication of the subsystem making a difference between the subsystem and the environment. To maintain the system, subsystems like the legal and the art system need to make a distinction between communication that can be attributed to the legal or art system and communication that is not. Historically the art system, for instance, defended its boundaries against philosophy, literature and history and differentiated from these disciplines through developing a distinct code of communication.[51] Such code of communication serves as an attribution formula through which it can be observed whether a communication is part or not part of the respective subsystem. The attribution formula in the art system was originally characterized as the binary code beautiful/non-beautiful. Later the code was re-defined as fit/does not fit. This latter depicts that with every work of art it must be determined whether it produces a connectivity within the artwork, enabling recursive communication.[52]

According to Luhmann only the art system itself determines what is to be considered as art. To this end the process of observing art is essential. It is essential that works of art are distinguishable from other objects (of utility.) To recognize art, society "requires a network of recursive observations with identifiable structures to generate nonidentical reproductions,"[53] The art system's basal observable operation is communication *through artworks*[54] within a network of self-reference. Artists must predict what observers might observe as a work of art and what expectations there are. Observers must perceive that there is artwork und must observe the artwork in reference to the creator. Without this self-reference, art would not exist.[55] Observable communication *on art* takes place where a communication on art is disseminated. This is, for instance the case, where critics, galleries or art dealers refer to a piece of art as art. Art must continually interact with and reference itself through mechanisms like citation and renewal. Moreover, as art evolves, it increasingly sets its own rules, supported by institutional structures that foster dialogue *between* artworks.[56]

Communication of the art system is not directly relevant within the legal system and vice versa. A work can therefore within the legal system enjoy copyright protection based on copyright legislation, but this existence of a copyright does not per se

---

[50] Luhmann (2012), pp. 35, 67.

[51] Luhmann and Barrett (2013), p. 238.

[52] See on this code and the self-programming of art, Baraldi et al. (2021), p. 28 and Sevänen (2001), Rampley (2009), p. 4.

[53] Luhmann (2000), p. 245.

[54] On the term, see, Rampley (2009), p. 17.

[55] Luhmann (2000), p. 53, Baraldi et al. (2021), p. 29 and Rampley (2009), p. 17.

[56] Luhmann (2000), p. 245 and Baraldi et al. (2021), p. 29.

turn an object into a work of art nor the creator into an artist. The same is true the other way around: the circumstance that a work of art does not enjoy copyright does not per se mean that the work is not art. Similar considerations apply in relation to the economic system operating with the code payment/non-payment. Art does not become art within the art system, because it is sold or advertised as an artistic work on an internet platform, nor does art stop being art only because there is no one to pay for it. This is because the systems work on different levels and based on different codes of differentiation. The circumstance, therefore, that a piece of work is sold as art created by artificial intelligence is no indicator for the work being art, nor for the work being protected by copyright.

Artificial intelligence is commonly referred to as a system within the technical and legal field. However, from the point of systems theory it is rather doubtful whether it is an autopoietic system comparable to the legal or art system as it may lack a unique function, for instance. Within the context of this chapter, it can also be left open whether this is the case. What is certain though, is that from a systemic point of view artificial intelligence is not by itself an art system even though it might create, use, and disseminate artefacts. Artificial intelligence does not have the unique function to create a reality from which reality can be observed. It is not a part of the legal system either. It does not communicate according to the legal/illegal code, nor does it have the unique function to stabilize normative expectations over time. The art system and the legal system remain autonomous functionally differentiated subsystems as long as they can maintain and differentiate their system boundaries.

This does not mean, however, that artificial intelligence cannot contribute to or be perceived as participating in the communication of legal, art, or economic systems. Diffusion models can, for instance, generate high-quality images, and large language models (LLMs) can create coherent and impressive prose and poetry across various contexts, but this is not necessarily art.[57] Also, outside the systemic approach it has been noted that—contrary to earlier concerns—there is not yet a danger that generative artificial intelligence puts an end to the art.[58] However, according to Epstein et al., it is likely that these tools will alter creative processes. In their view the reliance of artificial intelligence on existing artistic data raises complex ethical and legal questions regarding the ownership and authorship of artistic work and will ultimately also have an impact on aesthetics and culture.[59] From a system theoretical point of view one can say that artificial intelligence leads to irritations of the legal as well as the art system and as a consequence a need for them to re-determine their boundaries, thus maintaining their functional differentiation. While—based on the systemic analysis—one can say that the output produced by artificial intelligence does not substitute art as a system, this does not, therefore mean that artificial intelligence cannot have a repercussion on how art and law evolve.

[57] Epstein et al. (2023), p. 1110.

[58] Epstein et al. (2023), p. 1110.

[59] Epstein et al. (2023), p. 1110.

For the art system it remains crucial to determine within its own system, what can be attributed to the art system and what not. Mere artificially created perceptions that differ from nature do not by themselves indicate their artistic quality, for example.[60] Art involves both creation and perception. Art integrates what is incommunicable (perception) into the communicative network.[61] Building on the previous observations regarding the systemic requirements of the art system, one can say that basal communication *through* art necessitates interaction within a recursive network. It presupposes that an artwork is created by the artist with the expectations of the observer in mind. The creative process involves continuously differentiating between art and non-art, culminating in the final work being intended as art by the artist. Luhmann described this creative process as follows: "Every operation—whether the artist's or the beholder's—must decide whether a given form does or does not fit, whether it can be integrated into the emerging work in ways that secure connectivity." He furthermore stresses that this is not a mathematical task or technical construction, but the process is characterized by a lack of foresight. There is a risk that the next step does not fit, and one will not be able to create the work.[62] An artificial intelligence model, on its own, is not capable of this.[63] It cannot turn perceptions into communication as it lacks—so far—the ability to sense, feel, smell, or experience. Artificial intelligence by itself cannot engage in the artistic process because it cannot independently make the necessary distinction between art and non-art. When programmed to create artefacts, it cannot choose not to create artefacts either.

Given the current state of artificial intelligence, art necessitates a human to be involved and it is unlikely that this will change soon. The above also has consequences on who is to be considered as the creator of an artwork. The necessity of the creative act and of the intent of creating art do not only exclude artificial intelligence from being considered an artist. It also excludes programmers of a code unless they have been involved in the creative process. This does not mean that programmers cannot be recognized as creators within the legal system and hold copyright to the code used for producing the artwork though.

As earlier pointed out, the involvement of a human is a fundamental requirement in the creation of art from a copyright law perspective. A further requirement for a work to be protectable is that of originality; or the work being its author's own intellectual creation. In other words, for a work to be original within the context of copyright law, it requires that the author has the ability to make free and creative choices, and that those choices are reflected in the final work. From a systemic point of view these are requirements of the legal system not the art system. They do not by themselves have immediate meaning within the art system. The protection of purely artificially generated works, such as by establishing a new related right, is

---

[60] Luhmann (2000), p. 151.

[61] Rampley (2009), p. 8 and Luhmann (2000), p. 141.

[62] Luhmann (2000), p. 194.

[63] See, e.g., McCormack et al. (2019), pp. 40, 46.

theoretically conceivable. However, this approach would raise challenging questions regarding justifications for protection and legal personhood.[64]

For art to be considered art, there must be an observer who perceives it as such, with reference to its creator. The challenge posed by artificial intelligence is that an observer viewing a painting, reading a poem, or listening to music often cannot distinguish whether a creative process occurred or if a human was involved at all. While training data, for instance, allows for a certain degree of recursivity to previous artwork, art communication requires distinguishing art from non-art and establishing a connection with observers to facilitate communication on art. This becomes increasingly difficult with the mass production of creative artefacts through artificial intelligence. Making such distinctions would require additional clues and the ability to assess the role of artificial intelligence in the creative process. Currently, a significant issue in the art scene is, however, the relatively small number of people capable of evaluating its role in the creative process.[65]

4 Connections and Structural Couplings: Exploring Different Approaches

In the previous section, we explored the function of the art system in relation to the legal system, highlighting their differences as functionally differentiated social subsystems that are autopoietic and operationally closed. In this section, we will illustrate points of connection between different systems that are open to design by legal instruments, prior to introducing some hypotheses on systemic characteristics and proposing some views on the possibilities to interact on a systemic level.

The legal system and the art system are functionally differentiated social subsystems. Due to their operational closeness, these subsystems have no direct effect in the sense that changes in one system would directly impact the operations of the other systems. This is especially true for art which has—according to Luhmann—very few direct effects on other functional systems.[66] As the art system operates autonomously, it does not determine what is to be considered as art within the legal system. The same is true for other changes in the environment of the subsystems. Artificial intelligence has not an immediate effect on copyright protection, or the way art is to be understood, but may challenge the system boundaries and such lead to irritations provoking changes.

While systems are not directly connected there are certain situations, where autopoietic subsystems use operations of other systems and internalize them into their own subsystems, such forming structured connections. In systems theory, these connection points are called structural couplings. The art market specialized in artworks trading individual art and art as investment is a coupling of the art system

[64] Ramalho (2017).

[65] Mazzone and Elgammal (2019), p. 26.

[66] Luhmann (2000), p. 181.

and the economic system.[67] Structural couplings between the legal and the economic system are contracts and property.[68] When art is commercialized there needs to be structural coupling between the art, the economic and the legal system. This is, because the transfer of property and the licensing of rights requires an operation within the legal system. Contracts need to be drafted and the artwork defined for the purpose of attaching rights of usage and property to it. Payments need to take place within the economic system.

Caves has identified different basic forms of collaborations between artists and *humdrum parties* that rely on deals and contracts.[69] All these collaborations create potential connections between the different systems. There is, for instance, the relationship between art gallery and visual artist which includes a contract where the artist creates artworks for gallery exhibitions while the dealer commits to promoting the artist's work to collectors, critics, and curators and the two parties divide the gross revenue. There is the cooperation between the writer and the publisher. In this collaboration the publisher publishes the work and between the parties there is a revenue-sharing deal granting the author royalties based on the books' sales. The books are often not chosen by the publisher, but there is an agent as a gatekeeper choosing suitable authors and marketing the authors' services to the publisher. The agent's task is to captivate publishers and to identify and highlight the quality in an author's work effectively enough for a publisher to recognize it.[70] Also the work of the agent rests on a contract between the artist and the agent on the promotion of the book. There is furthermore the relationship between the musician and the label, which is based upon long-term contracts that mirror sequences of production steps in respect of the work. The contract includes terms on advances paid to the musician for producing the work as well as royalties. It also ensures that the label retains the right to issue the recording or keep it unpublished.[71] There are more complex collaborations too: contracts on the production of films or the production of TV series, for example.[72]

While the market has changed with the introduction of new platforms for selling and buying art,[73] Caves' work illustrates how the legal, the economic and the art systems are connected through contracts enabling a structural coupling between arts, law, and economy. Contracts shape the relationship between different collaborators. They transfer property and rights and enable the economic transaction, payment of advances and royalties. But their function is not reduced to this. Contracts can support artists in designating art objects and linking them with institutional expectations. Contracts that include a sequence of differentiations may support the creative process.

---

[67] Luhmann (2000), p. 243.

[68] Luhmann (1995), p. 453.

[69] Caves (2002), p. 1. Humdrum parties are according to Caves non-artists that respond to ordinary economic incentives and are able to bring the artist's inspiration to potential consumers.

[70] Caves (2003), p. 76.

[71] Caves (2003), p. 79.

[72] Caves (2003), p. 80.

[73] See, e.g., Lacourt et al. (2023), p. 3.

While contracts are not communication on art by themselves, they can be used to advance communication *on* art by selecting the addressees, imposing obligations to promote work, but also at the same time enabling or restricting communication *through* art, for instance, when restricting the right to publish a work. This does not yet mean that the work being the subject of a contract is recognized as work of art within the art system. Contracts are nevertheless instruments to support a certain evaluation and communication within the framework of the art market and other institutions of the art system.

Copyrights play an important role in the art market. They are used to protect the commercial rights related to an artwork and to assign these rights further within the contract relationship. Limited by time and scope, copyrights protect the right to reproduce and distribute it for a period of typically 70 years starting from the death of the author. They also cover moral rights, such as the right to be credited as the author. Copyrights may contribute to the assessment of whether a work is original, but they do not determine by themselves whether a work is to be considered art. This can only be done by the art system itself through recursive communication.[74] As copyrights are closely related to property in the sense of being able to exclude others from using the protected works, they can be seen as a structural coupling between the economic system and the legal system. To some extent—and within the limits of the art market—a structural coupling can be identified between the art and the legal system too. This is because, art relies—at least within the art market—on some protection through copyright, which again may foster creativity.

Art is also connected with the legal system through art-related disputes. These arise when artists seek to assert their rights or defend an infringement of their (copy)rights or a breach of contract on trading art, for example. The primary forum for the resolution of art-related disputes within the legal system are national courts. National courts are at the core of the legal system and are likely to reduce art-related conflicts to legal questions that can be resolved within the legal system alone, such as determining whether a copyright has been infringed or a contract breached.[75] Other interests that may be relevant within the art system, such as the recognition of a work as artwork or the advancement of communication on art, will not be addressed by the national courts. While courts solve art-related disputes they are less equipped to contribute to art and interests emanating from the art system.

Art-related disputes can, however, also be resolved by means of alternative forms of dispute resolution, such as arbitration and mediation. As these alternative forms of dispute resolution can be more flexibly adapted to interests other than legal interests and as they are not limited to a national jurisdiction, they could be more suitable to advance communication within the art system as well. For instance, the World Intellectual Property Organization (WIPO),[76] provides mediation services for art-related disputes, but such services may also be offered by other institutions or even outside an institution. Even though alternative dispute resolution mechanisms might

---

[74] Luhmann (2000).

[75] Hietanen-Kunwald (2018), p. 33.

[76] WIPO (n.d.)

not be considered structural couplings by themselves, they could be developed in a way that advances communication within the art system while resolving art-related disputes and conflicts.

5 Formulating Hypotheses and Proposing Instruments

Having explored the characteristics of the legal system in relation to copyright and the art system, we elaborate hypotheses on possible challenges and conflicts that arise especially in the legal and art systems. The hypotheses illustrate that there are various possible frictions and conflicts in different systems that cannot be addressed within one system alone. This means that connections need to be built between systems considering the characteristics of the specific subsystem.

5.1 STEP 1 Reframe the Challenges and Possible Conflicts in Respect of Different Systems

Hypothesis No. 1. Art system: Conflicts over whether a work is art, discussed by critics or other participants, are essential for maintaining the recognition of artworks and the boundaries of the system. For a work to be recognized as art, there must be recursive communication on art, traditionally embedded in institutions like critics, concerts, book fairs, and competitions. This communication needed to differentiate between works of art and ordinary objects or trash is becoming increasingly difficult, where art is produced by or with the help of artificial intelligence that generate abundant texts, pictures, and music while institutions promoting communication are not developed at the same pace.

Hypothesis No. 2. Art system: The creative act in the art system is a prerequisite for art to come into being—and according to the present understanding of art—is connected to human perception. The extent to which the involvement of a human act is needed for art to be art, but also the question, whether there has been an act of human creation in the creation of the artwork are increasingly difficult to determine. The art system appears to lack presently institutions and instruments to decide and establish the extent to which the use of artificial intelligence is acceptable.

Hypothesis No. 3. Art system: Work fed into generative intelligence provides a huge source of data and may be seen as a collection of art created by humanity that provides the possibility for recursive communication. While artificial intelligence is a language system that is based upon the re-production of communication, not the disruption or creation of a reality from which reality can be observed, the challenge for the artist to produce a work that is distinct from other works increases.

Hypothesis No. 4. Legal system: Within the legal system there will be an increasing number of disputes over how the concept of originality is interpreted within the context of works made using artificial intelligence to various extents. Difficulties arise as the nature and sufficiency of original expression is more challenging to identify in these works but may also arise from differences of interpretation between jurisdictions and the circumstance that multiple original expressions may exist simultaneously.

Hypothesis No. 5. Legal system: While legislation addresses certain aspects of copyright protection, it does not cover all relevant issues regarding the use of artwork by artificial intelligence. This leaves uncertainties that individual artists must navigate to protect their interests, shifting some responsibility to the artists to enforce their rights regarding the opt-out mechanism, for example.

Hypothesis No. 6. Legal system: Without a globally accessible forum for resolving copyright infringement disputes, asserting and defending copyrights will be challenging for individual artists. Firstly, the potential costs of legal proceedings are a significant barrier: the outcomes of copyright cases are often uncertain, and the financial risks are high for individual artists. Additionally, potential copyright infringements during the training phase of artificial intelligence models can be difficult to challenge. Even if a copyright infringement claim is successful, enforcement remains problematic, as the infringing works may have already been integrated into existing models.

Hypothesis No. 7. Economic system: It can be assumed that the art markets have diversified, with evolving thresholds for entering and publishing work. While the legal system offers instruments to protect artists' commercial interests, the landscape of art markets and contractual agreements continues to evolve and move from individually created contracts and deals to mass production.

5.2 Step 2 Propose Instruments for Interfering Within the Systems

To achieve a more comprehensive understanding of how the above problems could be addressed, one needs to work with content, procedures, and practices from within all autopoietic social subsystems. In respect to the legal system, the systemic framework needs to rely on legal methods, such as legal dogmatics, to analyze and discover the legal interests and institutions that must be considered.[77] We will sketch some legal instruments that are open to design and raise issues for further exploration within the legal system.

[77] Hietanen-Kunwald et al. (2021).

5.2.1 Instruments Within the Legal System

Legal instrument—legislation: Copyright legislation is an instrument to provide incentives for authors to produce creative works by granting them exclusive rights. Legislation, such as the CDSM directive, seeks to adapt to challenges arising from the use of artificial intelligence in a generally predictable way. Legislation is always reactive in nature and adapts to new requirements through reference to other legal frameworks, such as international treaties that are difficult to amend. When designing copyright legislation account needs to be taken to the systemic requirements of the law and deeply rooted concepts of ownership (what can be owned) and legal personhood (who could be the legal owner) as well.

Legal instrument—contracts: Contracts are instruments of structural coupling connecting the legal, economic and art system within the art market. Contracts can be used to determine the subject of the contract (what is to be sold, created, protected), but also to specify the rights that are connected to the artwork and the way the artwork can be used (modified, adapted, copied or fed into artificial intelligence). Contracts are not merely legal documents; they have many functions and can also be utilized to accomplish goals which is a fundamental aspect of proactive law.[78] Contracts have the potential to make the creative process more visible while determining the use of artificial intelligence.[79] They may also be used to enhance communication with institutions by including obligations related to communication on art with publishers, galleries and art dealers.

Contracts can function not only on an individual level but also on a collective level. They can serve as instruments of private regulation, addressing the interests of groups and enhancing agreements that influence interactions between the art and business on a societal scale, such as through collective agreements. For example, it is increasingly common for the creative sector and artists to agree on the non-use of artificial intelligence in performing arts to maintain artistic authenticity, protect intellectual property, and ensure fair compensation for artists.[80]

Legal instrument—dispute resolution. In the case of infringements of copyright law or contract obligations there needs to be a forum where art-related disputes can be resolved that is efficient and accessible. In the first place these forms of dispute resolution are created by legislation. However, as shown above alternative dispute resolution methods are available that could be used to take account of art related elements and the interests of the artist.

Mixed instrument fosteringaccess to justice. While there are instruments that can prevent or resolve some of the challenges, they may be unable to address the problems arising according to hypothesis 5 and 6. There need to be more effective instruments to resolve the problem of access to justice for individual artists. Artists need to be

[78] Hurmerinta-Haanpää and Viding (2018).

[79] See, for instance, Henschel (2022), p. 137 and Berger-Walliser et al. (2017).

[80] For the US, see, e.g., SAG-AFTRA (2023).

better informed about their rights and possibilities regarding the protection and use of their works. One way to increase access to justice is by providing methods of dispute prevention and resolution for groups of artists. Authors and performers have traditionally organized into unions or guilds, many of which negotiate model exploitation contracts with industry representatives. Additionally, collective rights management organizations (CMOs) play a significant role in determining and managing authors' rights. However, the existence and extent of such collective actions vary by country.[81] Collective dispute resolution should not be limited to class actions that work primarily within the legal system but should involve alternative forms of dispute resolution, including preventive tools such as contracts. It is also important to explore how artificial intelligence could be used to address challenges related to access to justice and enforcement. Online dispute resolution may be one possibility that could be tested in this respect.[82]

5.2.2 Further Points of Intervention

Legal instruments need to be supplemented with further communication that produces meaning within the art system. As previously discussed, within the art system, there are two forms of communication: communication *on art* and communication *through art*. Both need to be addressed through the practices, methods, and procedures inherent to the art system. While we seek to sketch some points of interaction, a deeper analysis of the internal methods, procedures, and practices within the art system is still required.

Recognition as anartwork. Recognition of an artist or a work of art requires communication on art. The legal system reduces disagreements over art to legal questions, such as copyright protection or contract fulfillment. In copyright disputes, the legal system determines if a creator has a copyright, but it does not decide if the artist should be credited as the artist. This recognition comes from the art system itself, through its institutions and forms of communication on art. Such networks have started to develop. There is also an increasing number of exhibitions, conferences, competitions, and discussion panels dedicated to art created by artificial intelligence.[83] From a systemic perspective, it is important to observe whether and how these institutions will differentiate between art and non-art, thereby enabling recurring communication within the art system and what other communication on art will evolve.

Communication through art is another way to ensure that artwork is recognized as such. A creative act is a precondition for art to occur. Someone must create art through their own perceptions and make these perceptions available through communication that enables communication. With the increasing use of artificial intelligence, the creative act becomes more obscure. From a systemic perspective, the question arises

[81] Lacourt et al. (2023), p. 21.

[82] See, e.g., Eidenmüller et al. (2024).

[83] Cetinic and She (2022).

whether this issue should or could be addressed by technological means or regulation, for instance through imposing transparency requirements.

Accessto the art market requires an (established) reputation.[84] To be successful in this market artwork needs to be recognized as artwork, needs to be traded in galleries or exhibitions and work needs to be published. This might have a repercussion of the way artwork is created and recognized.

6 Conclusions and Further Research

In this chapter, we explored the profound impact of artificial intelligence on the art and legal systems, focusing on artefacts created with the assistance of artificial intelligence. Our approach, grounded in systems theory as represented by Niklas Luhmann, examines the characteristics and potential frictions within these systems. The identification of systemic complexities is necessary to explore conflict patterns and create effective dispute prevention and resolution strategies. These are initial steps in a design process as set out in the Double Diamond framework and further developed in the UK Design Council's Systemic Design Approach.

By exploring the systemic complexities and functions, we identified characteristics that need to be addressed to enhance solutions for these complex problems. We found that the art and legal systems have very different approaches to art and artists. While both systems require a human author and some form of creativity, there are differences in how an artefact is assessed as a work in copyright law or piece of art in the art system. For instance, a work protected by copyright is not necessarily considered art within the art system, and vice versa. This indicates the existence of at least four forms of artefacts: creative work protected by copyright but not considered art within the art system, artwork considered art within the art system and also copyright protected, art considered art within the art system, but not copyright protected and works that are neither considered art nor enjoy copyright protection.

From the perspective of the artist and the art system, copyright protection alone is not sufficient to protect the artist's interests; a more holistic approach is needed that aligns with the requirements of both the art and legal systems. We introduced several hypotheses on the challenges within the art and legal systems and proposed various (legal) instruments to address these complex questions in both systems. We considered that legislation addresses the problem only to a limited extent, while contracts and alternative forms of dispute resolution may be more suitable for driving change in both systems. We hypothesized on characteristic systemic issues that may arise and suggested some instruments. The overview we provide is on a systemic level to identify where frictions are present. The hypotheses and instruments are not comprehensive but demonstrate different systemic elements and how they can be addressed. These elements are deeply connected with procedures, methods, and systems and require further research.

[84] Luhmann (2000), p. 243.

References

Arbiza Goenaga M (2020) A critique of contemporary artificial intelligence art: who is Edmond de Belamy? AusArt J Res Art 8(1):49–64

Baraldi C, Corsi G, Esposito E, Walker K (2021) Unlocking Luhmann. A keyword introduction to systems theory (trans: Walker K). Transcript Verlag, Bielefeld

Berger-Walliser G, Barton T, Haapio H (2017) From visualization to legal design: a collaborative and creative process. Am Bus Law J 54:347–392

Burk DL (2023) Cheap creativity and what it will do. Georgia Law Rev 57:1669–1712

Caves RE (2003) Contracts between Art and Commerce. J Econ Perspect 17(2):73–83

Caves RE (2002) Creative industries. In: Contracts between art and commerce. Harvard University Press, Cambridge

Cetinic E, She J (2022) Understanding and creating art with AI: review and outlook. ACM Trans Multim Comput Commun Appl (TOMM) 18(2):1–22

Cooper AF, Grimmelmann J (2024) The files are in the computer: on copyright, memorization, and generative AI, vol 4. http://arxiv.org/abs/2404.12590. Accessed 6 Mar 2025

Design Council (2021) Beyond net zero, a systemic design approach. https://issuu.com/designcouncil/docs/systemic_design_framework_-_beyond_net_zero. Accessed 12 Sep 2024

Design Council (n.d.) Systemic design framework. https://www.designcouncil.org.uk/our-resources/systemic-design-framework/. Accessed 12 Sep 2024

Eidenmüller K, McLaughlin C, Eidenmüller H (2024) Expanding the shadow of the law: designing efficient judicial dispute resolution systems in a digital world—an empirical investigation. https://papers.ssrn.com/sol3/papers.cfm?abstract_id=4686785. Accessed 12 Sep 2024

Elgammal A (2018) What the artworld is failing to grasp about Christie's AI portrait coup. https://www.artsy.net/article/artsy-editorial-art-failing-grasp-christies-ai-portrait-coup. Accessed 1 Jul 2024

Emanuilov I, Margoni T (2024) Forget me not: memorisation in generative sequence models trained on open source licensed code. https://doi.org/10.5281/zenodo.10635479

Epstein Z, Hertzmann A, Herman LM, Mahari R, Frank MR, Groh M, Schroeder H, Smith A, Akten M, Fjeld J, Farid H, Leach N, Pentland A, Russakovsky O (2023) Art and the science of generative AI. Science 380:1110–1111

Ethical Tech Initiative (n.d.) DAIL—the database of AI litigation. ETI. https://blogs.gwu.edu/law-eti/ai-litigation-database/. Accessed 12 Sep 2024

Flynn M (2018) A 19-year-old developed the code for the AI portrait that sold for $432,000 at Christie's. Washington Post. https://www.washingtonpost.com/nation/2018/10/26/year-old-developed-code-ai-portrait-that-sold-christies/. Accessed 12 Sep 2024

Goodfellow I, Pouget-Abadie J, Mirza M, Xu B, Warde-Farley D, Ozair S, Courville A, Bengio Y (2014) Generative adversarial nets. In: Ghahramani Z, Welling M, Cortes C, Lawrence N, Weinberger KQ (eds) Advances in neural information processing systems 27: 28th annual conference on neural information processing systems 2014. Curran Associates, Red Hook, NY

Guadamuz A (2024) A scanner darkly: copyright liability and exceptions in artificial intelligence inputs and outputs. GRUR International, pp 1–17. https://doi.org/10.1093/grurint/ikad140

Henschel R (2022) Contractual processualization: designing proactive contractual processes to support legal, technical and commercial purposes. In: Corrales Compagnucci M, Haapio H, Fenwick M (eds) Research handbook on contract design. Edward Elgar Publishing, Cheltenham

Hertzmann A (2020) Computers do not make art, people do. Commun ACM 63(5):45–48

Hietanen-Kunwald P, Haapio H, Toivonen N (2021) Systems theory as a research framework for dispute prevention and resolution by design. In: Ducato R, Strowel A (eds) Legal design perspectives: theoretical and practical insights from the field. Ledizioni, Milan

Hietanen-Kunwald P (2018) Mediation and the legal system. In: Extracting the legal principles of civil and commercial mediation. University of Helsinki, Helsinki

Hugenholtz PB, Quintais JP (2021) Copyright and artificial creation: does EU copyright law protect AI-assisted output? IIC Int Rev Intellect Prop Comp Law 52:1190–1216. https://doi.org/10.1007/s40319-021-01115-0

Hurmerinta-Haanpää A, Viding S (2018) The functions of contracts in interorganizational relationships: a contract experts' perspective. J Strateg Contract Negot 4(1–2):98–118

Kretschmer M, Margoni T, Oruç P (2024) Copyright law and the lifecycle of machine learning models. IIC 55:110–138. https://doi.org/10.1007/s40319-023-01419-3

Kuker H (2024) Inspiration versus infringement: why the right to use copyrighted images for referential purposes by AI should not be held to higher or different standards currently in effect. https://papers.ssrn.com/sol3/papers.cfm?abstract_id=4727896. Accessed 12 Sep 2024

Lacourt A, Radel-Cormann J, Valais S (2023) Fair remuneration for audiovisual authors and performers in licensing agreements. IRIS Plus. European Audiovisual Observatory (Council of Europe), Strasbourg. https://rm.coe.int/iris-plus-2023-03en/1680adec3c. Accessed 12 Sep 2024

Landes WM, Posner RA (1989) An economic analysis of copyright law. J Leg Stud 18:325–363

Luhmann N (1995) Das Recht der Gesellschaft. Suhrkamp, Frankfurt am Main

Luhmann N (2000) Art as a social system (trans: Knodt EM). Stanford University Press, Stanford (CA)

Luhmann N (2012) Soziale Systeme: Grundriss einer allgemeinen Theorie. Suhrkamp, Frankfurt am Main

Luhmann N, Barrett R (2013) Theory of society, vol 2. Stanford University Press, Redwood City

Mazzone M, Elgammal A (2019) Art, creativity, and the potential of artificial intelligence. Arts 8(1):26. https://www.mdpi.com/2076-0752/8/1/26. Accessed 12 Sep 2024

McCormack J, Gifford T, Hutchings P (2019) Autonomy, authenticity, authorship and intention in computer generated art. In: Anikó E, Liapis A, Castro Pena ML (eds) Computational intelligence in music, sound, art and design. EvoMUSART lecture notes in computer science, vol 11453. Springer, Cham. https://doi.org/10.1007/978-3-030-16667-0_3. Accessed 12 Sep 2024

Meeus M, Shilov I, Faysse M, Montjoye Y-AD (2024) Copyright Traps for Large Language Models. In: Salakhutdinov R, Kolter Z, Heller K, Weller A, Oliver N, Scarlett J, Berkenkamp F (eds) Proceedings of the 41st international conference on machine learning. PMLR

Ramalho A (2017) Will robots rule the (artistic) world? A proposed model for the legal status of creations by artificial intelligence systems. J Internet Law 21(1):12–25

Rampley M (2009) Art as a social system: the sociological aesthetics of Niklas Luhmann. Telos 148:111–140

SAG-AFTRA (2023) TV/theatrical contracts 2023—summary of tentative agreement. https://www.sagaftra.org/sites/default/files/sa_documents/TV-Theatrical_23_Summary_Agreement_Final.pdf. Accessed 1 Jul 2024

Sevänen E (2001) Art as an autopoietic sub-system of modern society: a critical analysis of the concepts of art and autopoietic systems in Luhmann's late production. Theory Cult Soc 18(1):75–103

Shan S, Ding W, Passananti J, Zheng H, Zhao BY (2024) Prompt-specific poisoning attacks on text-to-image generative models. In: 2024 IEEE symposium on security and privacy (SP). IEEE

WIPO (World Intellectual Property Organization) (n.d.) WIPO alternative dispute resolution (ADR) for art and cultural heritage. https://www.wipo.int/amc/en/center/specific-sectors/art/. Accessed 12 Sep 2024

Style Matters: Intellectual Property Rights and the New Creative Economy

Perttu Isohanni and Petra Hietanen-Kunwald

Abstract The rapid emergence of generative artificial intelligence (GenAI) poses an existential threat to the creative profession. It not only serves as a potential substitute for human creativity in general, but also threatens to displace specific artists by reproducing their unique artistic styles. A distinct artistic style serves as an economic asset for an artist, but also as a reflection of their personal identity. Therefore, safeguarding the continued development of such artistic styles is essential not only to protecting economic opportunities for artists but also to preserving their artistic integrity and fostering a culturally rich, human-centric creative landscape. Nevertheless, granting extensive legal protection to individual artistic styles poses significant challenges. Imitation and adaptation of artistic styles have always been integral to human creativity. Copyright law addresses this by being cautious of not affording monopolies over ideas but by granting protection to expressions of ideas. While stylistic features, particularly in visual arts, can sometimes be difficult to distinguish from original creative expressions protectable by copyright, this chapter suggests that such features may not play a central role in assessing infringement, as doing so could risk undue limitations on the creative freedom of others. Instead, it argues that efforts should focus on upholding moral rights to prevent false attribution of works not created by the artist and to protect against derogatory treatments of works that could harm the artist's reputation. Finally, it is suggested that intellectual property rights and remuneration models adapt to the changing creative landscape by allowing artists to be compensated for the use of their names to generate new works specifically designed to reproduce their artistic styles.

Keywords Artistic style · Copyright · Generative artificial intelligence · Intellectual property rights

P. Isohanni (✉) · P. Hietanen-Kunwald
School of Business, Department of Accounting and Business Law, Aalto University, Espoo, Finland
e-mail: perttu.isohanni@aalto.fi

P. Hietanen-Kunwald
e-mail: petra.hietanen-kunwald@aalto.fi

© The Author(s), under exclusive license to Springer Nature Singapore Pte Ltd. 2025
M. Corrales Compagnucci et al. (eds.), *Generative AI, Contracts, Law and Design*, Perspectives in Law, Business and Innovation,
https://doi.org/10.1007/978-981-95-2058-9_10

1 Introduction

Generative artificial intelligence (GenAI) models that have the capacity to provide substitutes to human authorial works have caused uncertainty about the future of the creative profession and human creativity.[1] However, beyond the potential to replace individual works, there is a growing concern about whether the technology might also offer scalable means of substituting individual authors. While author-specific substitutive effects will likely impact all creative fields to some extent, they are particularly relevant for those that depend more heavily on commissions and sales of original works, rather than ones that benefit more from prevention of unauthorized reproductions.[2] The ability to reproduce the individual styles of specific artists through AI may also present challenges to the social interest of fostering human creativity. Moreover, in a commercial setting, these AI-generated works have the potential to dilute an author's name and brand by misrepresenting their works and making authentic works difficult to distinguish from those generated with GenAI. In some cases, these works offer the creative markets scalable, fast, and inexpensive substitutes for commissioning works from specific human authors, raising questions about the economic viability of developing distinct new creative expressions.

In addition to economic issues, saturating the markets with inauthentic works that appear visually similar to an author's works while referencing the name of the author in varying degrees poses problems to the moral rights of the authors. Some have described the experience of having a digital copy made of their creative expression as a theft of their very identity.[3] The threat from reproducing an individual artistic style developed over a long period of time may indeed in some cases be more personal than economic in nature.

Whereas there appears at first glance to exist plenty of justifications to provide protection for the authors under attack by the machines, legal instruments for doing so have remained elusive. While no definitive legal solutions may presently be offered, this chapter aims to better understand this emerging issue by defining it more clearly within a broader context of incentivizing and fostering human creativity. To this end, the chapter seeks to explore differences between human and artificial stylistic imitation, define the subject matter of protection as well as investigate potential means and justifications for protection.

This phenomenon has often been referred to with a term such as "in the style of prompt" or a variation thereof. This chapter will instead adopt "digital style reproduction," partly for convenience, but also to distinguish the phenomenon more clearly from reproductions of individual authorial works. The legal focus will be on the main legal framework surrounding creative expression, namely copyright law.

GenAI can potentially reproduce styles across all types of media. However, the concept of style varies between different forms of expressions, and some of the conclusions offered in this chapter might apply differently depending on the medium

[1] See, e.g., Mezei (2020), Senftleben (2023), Demirci et al. (2023) and Rafner et al. (2023).

[2] Brownlee (1993), pp. 1161–1162.

[3] Baio (2022).

in question. Furthermore, the concept of artistic style is most often evoked in the context of visual arts, and this will be the main focus of this chapter.[4]

2 The Art of Imitation

2.1 Human Imitation and Origins of Inspiration

Before assessing suitable legal remedies to protect the style of an individual artist, an important question regarding subject matter needs to be answered. Namely, whether it is possible to define with suitable precision the idiosyncratic features that would distinctly define an individual artistic style. Sobel has observed that a core problem in protecting such styles is the difficulty of rendering judicial decisions on phenomena that defy verbal analysis.[5] To explore compatibility with general requirements of legal doctrines that protect creative expression, this section focuses on the nature of artistic style and the mechanisms by which it is formed.

Mimesis, or imitation, is generally considered as one of the oldest theories of art.[6] From the era of Paleolithic cave art until the eighteenth century, when theories of fine art began to form, the overarching function of art was generally seen as one of creating realistic, albeit sometimes idealized imitations of reality. In Plato's view, art was but an imperfect attempt of producing representations of the true *forms* of nature.[7] This rather mechanical view was eventually challenged in part by technological advancements such as photography, removing the need for artistic skills to produce accurate depictions of reality, and thus largely replacing the demand for comparable artistic works. As a reaction, artists started to explore new directions, focusing on emotions, impressions, and various aspects of the human experience rather than striving for photographic accuracy.[8]

Marshall McLuhan famously described art as "anything you can get away with."[9] The account that aesthetic theories of art are attempting to define the indefinable may indeed not be without merit.[10] Nevertheless, beyond the formalist approach of assessing art purely by its visual aspects, intangible qualities such as expression and communication of emotions or social commentaries are commonly accepted as plausible theories of what may constitute art.[11] This conceptual fluidity can also be

---

4 Wollheim (1987a), p. 186.

5 Sobel (2024), pp. 102–104.

6 Sörbom (2021), p. 182.

7 Preziosi (2009), p. 115.

8 Silva (2022).

9 McLuhan and Fiore (1967), pp. 132–135.

10 Weitz (1956), p. 30.

11 Weitz (1956), pp. 28–29.

viewed from an economic perspective, as innovations in the field of creativity are often closely tied to evolving consumer preferences.[12]

Style in art (originating from the latin word *stilus*, referring to a Roman writing instrument)[13] can be generally considered as "any distinctive, and therefore recognizable, way in which an act is performed or an artifact made or ought to be performed and made."[14] In a broad sense, style in art originates from choices between synonymous forms of expression; without these choices there can neither be stylistic variation or recurrent elements to define an individual style.[15] General styles, such as realism or surrealism, encompass a wide variety of different categorizations based on distinctive stylistic features.[16] The focus of this chapter, an individual style, is narrower in scope: the artistic style of a single artist. However, whether an artist has indeed developed a distinct, individual style of their own, one that does not merely amount to an imitation of a general style or the style of another individual, might not be self-evident. An individual artistic style cannot arguably exist in isolation, but is rather necessarily based on the works of others. This dynamic between imitation and innovation is aptly expressed by Ackerman:

> the artist cannot invent without reproducing; in order to make a meaningful innovation he must be able to concentrate his forces upon the few aspects of his work where circumstances favor fresh departures; for the rest, he relies on the support of his tradition and of his environment. An artist cannot invent himself out of his time and, if he could, he would succeed only in making his work incomprehensible by abandoning the framework in which it might be understood.[17]

Similarly, Luhmann's system theory considers art as a communication system that by its very nature requires a recursive communication with other artworks to define itself.[18] Wollheim, on the other hand, sees the general style within which a painter works as "learned," while an individual style may instead be "formed." This formed style, Wollheim argues, is a precondition for aesthetic interest, expressiveness, and expression of a "psychological reality."[19] Similar interplay between artist's own vision and general style conventions can equally be recognized in a literary context, as Robinson highlights: "if a writer has (some degree of) individual style, then he uses general style conventions in such a way as to express (what seem to be) his own attitudes, qualities of mind, and vision of the world."[20] For an individual artist, developing such a distinct personal style can take time, effort and resources. As a result, style can equally develop as an important means of self-expression. From an

---

[12] Caves (2000), p. 206.

[13] Sauerländer (1983), p. 254.

[14] Gombrich (2009), p. 129.

[15] See, e.g., Ullmann (1964), p. 6.

[16] Wollheim (1987b), pp. 25–26.

[17] Ackerman (1962), p. 228.

[18] Luhmann (2000), p. 244. See also Hietanen-Kunwald and Isohanni (2025) in this Book for closer discussion of arts and copyright from a system theoretical point of view.

[19] Wollheim (1987a), pp. 188–189, 198.

[20] Robinson (1984), p. 157.

economic point of view, it can also be perceived as a valuable means of creating scarcity by distinguishing oneself from others.[21]

However, not all recurrent stylistic choices that could for instance be used to attribute a painting to a specific artist may be thought of as directly relevant for a verbal description of individual artistic style. Elements such as signature, size, microscopic analysis of materials, brushwork or even typical choices of subject matter may have more relevance to "scholarly inquiry" than an "underlying competence deep in the artist's psychology," as Wollheim puts it.[22] Robinson, on the other hand, suggests that a description of individual style should consist of "all those features of subject matter, form, expression, symbolism, materials and so on, which contribute towards the expression of the overall character of the individual or period in question."[23] Moreover, and further complicating definitions of subject matter, how individual style is perceived may also be influenced by the subjective experience of the observer. To this effect, Neer has proposed that recognition of a pictorial style is similar to what Wittgenstein described as "dawning of an aspect," or the phenomenon of perceiving the same object in multiple ways based on the subjective experience of the observer.[24]

The appearance of an individual style can equally undergo changes within the course of a career. Pablo Picasso, for example, was known for having multiple visually distinct styles during different periods of his life. In Wollheim's view, perceiving one person to have multiple styles amounts to confusion about what is style and not style. He argues we should rather suspect that the stylistic characteristics that were used to determine multiple distinct styles were too superficial and narrow to "reveal their roots in underlying processes."[25] These processes may to some extent reflect the artist's psychologically "real" personality, but it has equally been suggested that a style might express an artistic personality (personality as an artist or personality while making art), implied personality (personality which a work of art is created to imply), or artistic ideals (artistic aspirations and conceptions of artistic excellence that the artist identifies with).[26] Nevertheless, the often evolving nature of individual artistic style further compounds difficulties of definition by introducing a dimension of how consistently the specific stylistic expressions are expressed throughout the oeuvre of an author, and by contrast, whether a single artist may be considered to possess multiple artistic styles that might warrant protection.

---

[21] See Riggle (2015), p. 712 and Khareghat (2022).

[22] Wollheim (1987b), p. 35.

[23] Robinson (2021).

[24] Neer (2005), pp. 16–21 and Wittgenstein (1989), pp. 193–194; see also Wollheim (1987a), pp. 184–186.

[25] Wollheim (1987b), pp. 27–35.

[26] See, e.g., Hopkins and Riggle (2021), pp. 1–5 for this discussion.

2.2 Artificial Imitation and Echoes of Creativity

Imitation might be the sincerest form of flattery within the context of human art, but artists whose styles have been turned into a digital replica are evidently not as flattered. For instance, Tim Burton described digital reproduction of his style "like a robot taking your humanity, your soul."[27] Similarly to human creations, artificial ones are not born in a vacuum. Whereas in the last section we saw that humans imitate general style conventions and works of others to develop stylistic elements of their own, artificial creativity imitates the works that were presented to it as training data. However, whereas humans can learn efficiently from relatively little data, machine learning (ML) models rely on vast amounts of data, usually scraped from the internet. In fact, the accuracy of the models has been shown as directly contingent to the volume of training data.[28] Consequently, access to as much training data as possible has become a priority, as well as an instrumental competitive advantage to GenAI developers.[29]

The technological quest of digitally extracting the distinguishing features of an individual style (*stylometry*) predates current ML applications by a fair margin.[30] Many techniques have equally been developed to aid in determining attribution of paintings and detecting forgeries.[31] Once ML techniques were successfully employed to the task of learning the distinguishing stylistic features of an image,[32] it shortly followed that the said style could be applied to arbitrary images with similar techniques.[33] More recently, *transformer*[34] based text-to-image models, such as DALL-E, Midjourney or Stable Diffusion, benefiting from scaling provided by continuously increasing computing power, have made it possible to generate vast quantities of creative content that is often indistinguishable from works made by humans. While the models still have plenty of shortcomings, it is likely that the quality will only continue to improve in the future. Literary and pictorial content have already achieved a threshold of quality sufficient to, for instance, win a human photography competition.[35] However, along with implementation of techniques such as multimodal machine learning, it has become clear that video and music will shortly follow in achieving a similar standard of quality.[36]

Whether GenAI could be considered "creative" and thus have the potential to replace parts of human creativity as such is yet to be determined. Technically, the models do not simply function as "collage-machines," copying and pasting data from

---

[27] Macnab (2023); see also Tu (2023).

[28] See Kaplan et al. (2020).

[29] See, e.g., Metz et al. (2024).

[30] Tenenbaum and Freeman (2000).

[31] See, e.g., Ji et al. (2021).

[32] Gatys et al. (2015).

[33] Gatys et al. (2016).

[34] See Vaswani et al. (2017).

[35] See, e.g., Parshall (2023).

[36] See, e.g., OpenAI (2024).

storage. Instead, they generalize from the patterns that underlie the creative expressions found in the training data.[37] However, it has been shown that large-scale models may memorize specific works from the training data, potentially leading to portions of these works being reproduced in the outputs. This phenomenon appears to be relatively rare, especially in cases where the user does not intentionally try to extract a specific work from the model. Nevertheless, the frequency of such occurrences likely depends on various factors, including how well the overall system has been designed to prevent such occurrences.[38] How this process of learning might be construed to differ from human "inspiration" is not clear,[39] but some initial studies have indicated that GenAI might match humans at least on certain types of creativity measurements.[40] Rafner et al. have further suggested that the future role of human creativity in the workplace might be decided by the extent of similarities and differences between human creativity and human-AI co-creativity.[41]

While the ability for GenAI to come up with truly novel creative ideas may yet be questionable, the current iterations of GenAI models appear to have some stylistic features of their own. One reason could be the exposure to a larger pool of different stylistic expressions contained in the training data than what humans have the ability to. These characteristics might also be born from the process of averaging the stylistic expressions in the training data, but might equally be influenced by reflecting average human aesthetic preferences, whereas the models are often built using reinforcement learning from human feedback techniques.[42] Consequently, generated images may sometimes be perceived as generic; perhaps lacking the mistakes, character and emotional expression associated more often with human artists.

However, rather than being capable of producing merely generic content, GenAI models trained with vast amounts of data have the capability to reproduce the styles of individual artists to varying extents. From an economic perspective, such digital style reproductions can quickly saturate the market, and possess the potential of devaluing the original works of the artist by making them less unique. For example, fantasy artist Greg Rutkowski expressed difficulty in finding or recognizing his own works from the internet after discovering that his name had been used in prompts over 400,000 times in less than a year to produce new works that imitate his style.[43] In this manner, these works not only have the potential to act as substitutes to original creations in the creative markets, but also risk diluting the artist's brand by filling the markets with inauthentic works that refer to the artist's name.

GenAI has received a fair share of critical reactions. Using GenAI art commercially appears to run the risk of backlash in social media, as some consider it unethical

---

[37] See, e.g., Sobel (2024), p. 66 and Sag (2023), p. 327.

[38] See Cooper and Grimmelmann (2024).

[39] See, e.g., Brown (2024) and Kuker (2024).

[40] Rafner et al. (2023), p. 1836.

[41] Rafner et al. (2023), p. 1837.

[42] See, e.g., Christiano et al. (2017).

[43] Hutchinson and John (2023).

to use GenAI when instead a human artist could have been hired.[44] Additionally, the stylistic clues pointing to GenAI have been condemned by some as *ersatz*, merely amounting to cheap imitations of authentic human creativity upon which the models are based. The strong reaction to GenAI art is further evidenced by instances where artists, and potentially the companies they work for, whose visual styles have stylistic features associated with GenAI, have been targeted and compelled to prove that their works are genuinely created by them and not by GenAI.[45] A similar effect can be observed in reverse: even when people report being unable to distinguish whether an art piece was created by a human or with GenAI, they tend to devalue it upon learning of its artificial origins. The effect seems to equally apply to works created by humans collaboratively with GenAI, introducing an incentive to leave the use of GenAI unmentioned.[46]

Nevertheless, for many creative professionals, GenAI has already been integrated into workflows as a tool to generate and prototype new ideas among various other uses.[47] Equally for non-artists, the technology holds the promise of reducing the amount of requisite technical skills needed to express creative ideas. Despite the controversial nature of the technology, it seems likely that once wide adoption is gained, it will not only change the nature of creative work,[48] but also redirect investments and have an impact on the total number of work opportunities.[49] In order to lay some foundations on the available means and justifications of protecting individual artistic styles, in the next section we will explore the principal legal framework for protecting human creative expression, namely copyright law.

3 From Styles to Trials

3.1 Incentives of Creativity

The balance between incentivizing production of creative goods and the interests of the public to use and enjoy them is inherent to intellectual property law.[50] Technological innovations, in particular, have often acted as a catalyst of change to the economic rationale of the creative profession.[51] For example, following the invention of the printing press, the economic value of producing literary works was diverted to third parties who owned machines capable of producing inexpensive copies. This

---

[44] See, e.g., Weatherbed (2023).

[45] See, e.g., Fear (2024).

[46] See, e.g., Horton et al. (2023) and Millet et al. (2023).

[47] See, e.g., May (2024).

[48] Oksanen et al. (2023), p. 9: "We are in the middle of societal and cultural transformation, and changes in art and creativity are some of the most powerful signs of this transformation."

[49] Demirci et al. (2023) and Kilkenny (2024).

[50] Landes and Posner (1989), p. 326.

[51] Burk (2023), p. 1677.

shift created a drive to incentivize the ongoing production of new works. To this end, the first copyright law, Statute of Anne passed by the Parliament of Great Britain in 1710, set out to provide an exclusive right of reproduction to authors "for the encouragement of learned men to compose and write useful books."[52] Since this time, inventions such as lithography and multitude of digital innovations have made affordable reproduction and distribution of works accessible to anyone.[53] Landes and Posner note that this "public good" aspect is indeed the distinguishing feature of intellectual property; typically works such as books or paintings are expensive to create, but inexpensive to reproduce. These inexpensive reproductions thus enable many to enjoy the same works without diminishing the enjoyment of others.[54]

However, the challenge posed by GenAI to intellectual property rights appears to differ from this traditional rationale of safeguarding against reproduction and distribution of works. Instead, GenAI holds the potential to reproduce the *creation* of works.[55] Particularly, in cases where the use of GenAI can provide cheap, perfect substitutes to not only authorial works in general but the authors themselves, no amount of additional rights concerning reproduction or distribution will provide added incentives to continue creating new works of similar type. In the context of developing a distinct creative style to create scarcity in the creative market, the incentive to do so may disappear if there are no viable opportunities for financial exploitation. This issue is particularly evident in the visual arts, where artists rely more on commissions than prevention of unauthorized reproductions.[56] Besides challenging assumptions about the nature of human creativity and art, GenAI thus prompts questions about what is the role of intellectual property rights in ensuring continued incentives to foster human creativity.[57]

Beyond merely incentivizing production, there exists other important justifications for intellectual property rights. By extension, and particularly to our interests, these justifications can also be applied to the context of safeguarding individual artistic styles. While production focused utilitarian theories might assess the value of developing novel stylistic expressions by balancing the creation of market scarcity with the public's ability to access and enjoy these expressions, labor theories might instead emphasize the importance of fair compensation for such creative efforts.[58] From a social planning theory perspective, it might be argued that intellectual property rights should provide a richer vision of society than the utilitarian "social welfare" approach by adopting a role in the attainment of just and attractive culture.[59] For instance, it may be the case that any exclusive rights should be afforded sparingly and only where necessary, as greater good might be served by leaving artistic styles

[52] Newman (2011), p. 16.

[53] See, e.g., Kamp and Hunter (2019).

[54] Landes and Posner (1989), p. 326.

[55] Burk (2023), p. 1680.

[56] Brownlee (1993), pp. 1161–1162.

[57] Burk (2023), p. 1682.

[58] Fisher (2001), pp. 2–3.

[59] Fisher (2001), pp. 4–5.

free for everyone to use and innovate upon.[60] Personality theories instead may recognize the personhood that is expressed through an artistic style, and as such require that protection is afforded against appropriation and derogatory modifications, which may in turn lead to conducive social and economic conditions for creative intellectual activities to flourish.[61]

In contrast to economic rights such as the rights to control the reproduction and distribution of authorial works, moral rights in copyright law instead protect the non-economic aspects of the authors' interests. For instance, Article 6*bis* of the Berne Convention sets out rights for authors to claim authorship to their works as well as a right to object to any derogatory treatment of their works.[62] The need for these rights may be viewed through the lens of personality theories, suggesting that harmful treatment of an author's work may also be seen as harmful to the author's identity or personality. Furthermore, Aplin and Davis have noted that moral rights may consequently improve the creative climate by ensuring authors their works may not be mutilated and that they can rely on being named as the author. For some artists, recognition and preservation of works for future generations to enjoy might indeed potentially be of greater importance than immediate economic gains. Moral rights equally have benefits for the public, as they have a similar interest in possessing reliable information about an author of a work as they might in knowing the producer of a product. The public can also be seen to benefit when distorted versions of works are not represented as authentic ones, misrepresenting the character of the author.[63]

The right to claim authorship may also be viewed from a reverse perspective, as a means of avoiding public deception by preventing misattribution of works. In this regard, both the author and the public benefit in preventing authors' names being misattributed to works not created by them, or to which they might only partially be responsible of.[64] Some jurisdictions grant a separate moral right for authors against such uses, by affording a right to prevent false attribution.[65] The right essentially permits individuals to object to the association of their names to works not created by them. Notably, unlike other moral rights, this right concerns not the author's own work, but rather a work created by someone else. However, the doctrine has equally been evoked to prevent passing off a modified work that no longer corresponds to the original conception of the author.[66] Consequently, Ginsburg has recognized that the right to prevent false attribution may in fact also act as a back door to integrity rights, providing a similar protection to authors as the right to object to a derogatory

[60] Nimmer (1995), p. 1416 and Netanel (1996), p. 369.

[61] Fisher (2001), pp. 3–4.

[62] Berne Convention for the Protection of Literary and Artistic Works (as amended on September 28, 1979).

[63] Aplin and Davis (2013), p. 164.

[64] Aplin and Davis (2013), p. 164.

[65] Right to prevent false attribution is codified as a moral right in some common law countries such as the UK and Australia, but also for example the Intellectual Property Code of the Philippines section 193.4 provides authors a right to "restrain the use of his name with respect to any work not of his own creation or in a distorted version of his work."

[66] See, e.g. Gilliam v. Am. Broad. Cos, Inc., 538 F.2d 14 (2d Cir. 1976).

treatment of their work that might be prejudicial to their reputation.[67] The limitation of uses that may be derogatory to the author in this way have also been discussed by the CJEU in the context of copyright exceptions in *Deckmyn*, whereas the parody exception was deemed to apply only insofar as the balance of fundamental rights is reflected upon, such as not being associated with a discriminatory message.[68]

For digital reproductions of style, moral rights appear to be particularly relevant since GenAI has an almost limitless capacity to produce novel works that closely mimic the styles and works of specific artists. Moreover, the attribution of these works as inauthentic ones may not always be clear, as they may reference the artists' names either directly or indirectly. These novel needs illustrate Burk's argument, whereas the role of intellectual property rights may be shifting more towards certifying authenticity than incentivizing production and distribution.[69]

3.2 Copyright and Protection of Style

For copyright to subsist, the subject matter must generally be that of a single authorial work.[70] Additionally, the subject matter must further be clearly defined. To this end, common law countries typically offer a closed list of eligible subject matter and further require that the work must be fixed in a tangible medium. In the EU, similar requirements are not shared, but the Court of Justice of the European Union (CJEU) has offered insight to the limits of scope of protection. For instance, in *Levola Hengelo*, the CJEU held that it must be possible to identify the subject matter of such a work "clearly and precisely." In addition, it was noted that legal certainty necessitates the subject matter to "be capable of being expressed in a precise and objective manner" in order to eliminate any element of subjectivity in the process.[71]

For a work to be protected, it further needs to be considered original. Copyright does not require these original expressions to be considered "art," but merely to reflect creative choices made by the author. In the EU, the standard of originality was harmonized by the CJEU in *Infopaq*, specifying that works that are the "author's own intellectual creation" may be considered to pass this threshold.[72] This concept was further refined in later case law, and summarized in *Funke Medien* to consist of expressing creativity in an original manner "which reflect the author's personality" and is "expressed by free and creative choices."[73] In the US, the Supreme Court

[67] Ginsburg (2016), p. 47.

[68] C-201/13, Johan Deckmyn and Vrijheidsfonds VZW v Helena Vandersteen and Others, EU:C:2014:2132, paras 27–29.

[69] Burk (2023), p. 1670.

[70] See Pila (2021) for detailed analysis of the concept.

[71] C-310/17, Levola Hengelo BV v Smilde Foods BV, EU:C:2018:899, para 41.

[72] C-5/08, Infopaq International A/S v Danske Dagblades Forening, EU:C:2009:465, para 37.

[73] C-469/17, Funke Medien NRW GmbH v Bundesrepublik Deutschland, EU:C:2019:623, para 25.

in *Feist* set a similarly modest bar for originality by asserting that copyrightable expression requires at least a "modicum of creativity."[74]

Furthermore, while ideas may be protected with patents, copyright may only be granted to *expressions* of ideas. This principle is laid out for instance in Article 9(2) of the TRIPS agreement, stipulating that ideas, procedures, methods of operation or mathematical concepts as such are expressly excluded from being eligible for copyright protection.[75] Applying this principle within the context of the Computer Programs Directive,[76] in *SAS Institute*, the CJEU reflected that the functionality of a computer program, programming language, or the format of data files used in a computer program cannot constitute such a form of expression that could be eligible for protection. Furthermore, the court referred to the opinion of Advocate General Bot by arguing that allowing the functionality of a computer program to be protected by copyright would "amount to making it possible to monopolize ideas, to the detriment of technological progress and industrial development."[77]

Analogously to how works may consist of general and individual stylistic features, copyright thus seeks to further separate the expressions of creativity from the underlying ideas. The *scènes à faire* doctrine found in US copyright law illustrates this concept in that overly general elements, such as the common or necessary elements of a genre or type of story should be excluded from the scope of protection of copyright.[78] Thus, for an infringement to occur, copyright typically requires substantial similarity to original expressions that may be attributed to the author of the work. In the case of works made with GenAI, such a direct infringement is possible since large-scale models have a tendency to memorize elements from small portions of works in the training data. Consequently, they can, albeit infrequently, generate outputs that reproduce original expressions from the training data in sufficient amounts as to constitute an copyright infringement.[79]

As artistic style may be considered closer to an idea than expression, copyright is arguably not particularly accommodating towards affording general protection for artistic styles. However, separating unprotectable stylistic features from protectable creative expressions may in certain cases be difficult especially in visual arts. As such, an artistic style in a painting may perhaps more so be discerned as a holistic combination of different stylistic elements.[80] In Sobel's view, the challenge GenAI presents lies in the fact that it is able to capture stylistic details that may be *seen* even by a layman, but may not readily be *described* verbally.[81] This recognition implies that style is not merely an abstract idea but has the ability to be identified by

---

[74] See Feist Publications, Inc. v. Rural Tel. Service Co., 499 U.S. 340 (1991).

[75] Agreement on Trade-related Aspects of Intellectual Property Rights (1869 U.N.T.S. 299).

[76] Council Directive 91/250/EEC of 14 May 1991 on the legal protection of computer programs, Official Journal L 122, 17.5.1991, pp. 42–46.

[77] C-406/10, SAS Institute Inc. v World Programming Ltd, EU:C:2012:259, paras 39–40.

[78] Said (2023), p. 351.

[79] See Cooper and Grimmelmann (2024).

[80] Brownlee (1993), p. 1158 and Sobel (2024), pp. 74–75.

[81] Sobel (2024), pp. 101–104.

perception. As established within the context of US copyright law, a combination of unprotectable elements, such as stylistic expressions, could then receive protection as a whole. Brownlee has proposed a somewhat similar approach by suggesting that the "total concept and feel" of a work might be used to determine substantial similarity within the context of visual arts.[82] To this end, while a genre such as impressionism might be too broad in scope, Brownlee proposes that perhaps a more specific stylistic expression such as Monet's style of painting water lilies could be narrow enough.[83]

These approaches remind of Neer's analogy that recognizing an artistic style is akin to Wittgenstein's concept of "dawning of an aspect." Here, an art expert attributing a style of a painting to a specific artist relies on partially subjective assessment[84] of perceiving an internal relationship between the painting and other paintings, rather than their inherent properties.[85] For instance, Monet and Renoir, both prominent impressionists, sometimes painted the same subject together. These works may appear very similar to a lay person, and while an expert might distinguish Monet's loose brushwork and play of light from Renoir's warmer tones and blended brushwork,[86] this analysis still retains the dilemma of how to draw the line between traditional assessment of copyright infringement and extending protection to a broader, more abstract concept of an individual artistic style. If the subject matter of water lilies[87] constitutes a stylistic feature that may be accepted as part of such a protectable combination of individually unprotectable elements, should copyright law be able to prevent Renoir from also exploring this subject? If not, should he then feel the need to confine himself to blended brushwork and warmer tones in order to not venture too closely to Monet's style? This difficulty appears to highlight some of the defining features of human creativity, where imitation acts as a key component in building upon others and innovating new forms of expression. While style may be an integral part of the overall creative expression of a work and thus have some relevance in assessing substantial similarity to another work, we suggest that the extent to which stylistic features may be part of this assessment may not be particularly broad before excessively limiting the creative expressions of others.[88]

---

[82] Brownlee (1993), pp. 1183–1184.

[83] Brownlee (1993), p. 1180.

[84] Neer (2005), p. 22: "Aspect-shifts in general, and style in particular, may thus come to seem mere contingencies—subjective, even private experiences."

[85] Neer (2005), pp. 21–22.

[86] Howe (2023).

[87] Or perhaps fantastical depictions of wizards and dragons in the case of Greg Rutkowski.

[88] See Sobel (2024) for more in depth analysis of substantial similarity and style within the context of US copyright law; Geiger (2018), arguing that derivative uses of copyrighted works need to be safeguarded on the basis of human rights such as freedom of expression and freedom of artistic creation.

3.3 *Text and Data Mining*

While defining an artistic style with sufficient precision so as to afford reliable protection against imitation is challenging, an alternative approach is to attempt to eliminate the need for such protection in the first place by attempting to restrict the capabilities of the model itself. In order to generate works that resemble those made by humans, including their stylistic features, GenAI models typically rely on mining massive amounts of data from the internet. The CDSM Directive[89] Article 2(2) defines text and data mining (TDM) as "any automated analytical technique aimed at analyzing text and data in digital form in order to generate information which includes but is not limited to patterns, trends and correlations." Since the models need contemporary data to reflect the current society, the works used by means of TDM are often protected by copyright law, where a typical term of protection is the life of the author plus 70 years. Regulation on TDM is important in determining whether authors receive remuneration for the use of their works, but has also been perceived as potential means to safeguard against digital style reproduction.

In the EU, for TDM to not infringe upon author's rights, it must generally invoke an exception or limitation to copyright law. The relevant exception for commercial uses is detailed in Article 4 of the CDSM directive. The exception allows "reproductions and extractions of lawfully accessible works and other subject matter for the purposes of text and data mining."[90] Importantly, Article 4(3) also establishes a rights reservation ("opt-out") mechanism limiting the application of the provision only to the use of works and subject matter that "has not been expressly reserved by their right holders in an appropriate manner, such as machine-readable means."

This approach appears reasonable in principle, but has been criticized for its vague nature regarding practical application, as well as failing to sufficiently detail the balance of interests between rights holders and GenAI developers.[91] This has resulted in legal uncertainty, where training unlicensed models may not only pose legal risks for companies,[92] but authors equally remain unsure about what rights they have and how their works are being utilized. The issue is further complicated by contractual issues, where some platforms may be seeking to impose terms that allow licensing various types of content to be further used as training data.[93] Consequently, some artists have taken it upon themselves to find alternative solutions. Some users are removing their content from platforms or switching to ones that explicitly state

[89] Directive (EU) 2019/790 of the European Parliament and of the Council of 17 April 2019 on copyright and related rights in the Digital Single Market and amending Directives 96/9/EC and 2001/29/EC.

[90] Directive (EU) 2019/790 of the European Parliament and of the Council of 17 April 2019 on copyright and related rights in the Digital Single Market and amending Directives 96/9/EC and 2001/29/EC.

[91] Mezei (2024), p. 468.

[92] Kretschmer et al. (2024), p. 134.

[93] See, e.g., Roth (2024) and Edwards and Belanger (2024).

that works will not be used or handed over further for purposes of model training.[94] Perhaps reminiscent of Luddites destroying looms during the industrial revolution, techniques have also been developed for authors to "poison" their works in order to damage the models and prevent them from learning the stylistic features of their works.[95]

While regulation regarding TDM is important in defining potential means of authors to receive remuneration from the use of their authorial works to develop GenAI models, it is not clear whether it could provide a reliable means of safeguarding against digital style reproduction in the future. Latest voice cloning models for instance can produce a convincing clone of an individual human voice from just a few seconds of source material.[96] These capabilities pose in part comparable challenges for performers as digital style reproduction presents for visual artists. Similar techniques have been developed specifically for artistic styles, enabling a model to learn the stylistic features of an image from only a few provided examples.[97] Midjourney, for example, offers a *style reference* parameter, allowing users to upload existing image(s) that the model will use to replicate the style of. This may potentially be very useful for artists in that they are able to prompt the model to generate ideas mimicking their own style. However, it also raises questions on the effectiveness of the opt-out approach from a perspective of digital style reproduction.

3.4 Indirect Remedies

While digital style reproduction has not as of yet prompted extensive academic discussion within the field of law, some preliminary proposals for protecting artistic styles beyond the means of copyright law have emerged in literature. Visser, for instance, suggests that digital style reproduction is simply too harmful and parasitic to take precedence over the rights of authors.[98] Potential remedies might include concepts relating to unfair competition, such as slavish imitation or unfair free riding,[99] or recognizing an individual style as personal data according to the GDPR.[100] In the context of musical styles in the US, O'Connor has proposed application of rights of publicity, trademark law, or the creation of new *sui generis* right, equally leaning on concepts relating to prevention of unjust enrichment and

[94] Hunter (2024).

[95] See Shan et al. (2023, 2024) and Ahn et al. (2024).

[96] Chen et al. (2024) and Microsoft (2024).

[97] Tang et al. (2023).

[98] Visser (2023), p. 3174.

[99] Visser (2023), p. 3172; more analysis on aspects relating to unfair competition, see e.g., Senftleben (2024).

[100] Visser (2023), p. 3173. Regulation (EU) 2016/679 of the European Parliament and of the Council of 27 April 2016 on the protection of natural persons with regard to the processing of personal data and on the free movement of such data, and repealing Directive 95/46/EC (GDPR).

discouragement of free riding.[101] Furthermore, it has been proposed that the issue of posing undue restrictions to human creativity might be avoided by making a distinction between works that involve the use of GenAI and ones that do not.[102] However, establishing a different set of rules for works created entirely by humans and those involving GenAI might not be a sustainable approach. Besides issues of proof regarding the creative process, as the technology becomes more widely adopted it is likely that a significant portion of future human created works will incorporate GenAI in some capacity.

Beyond the direct economic impact from substitution effects, there is indeed an important threat to the artist's name and brand from dilution effects in a commercial setting. This harm may occur when the markets are saturated with inauthentic GenAI works that are associated with the artist's name to varying degrees. In trademark law, famous marks are protected against uses that diminish their uniqueness. Concepts relating to trademarks and unfair competition may apply particularly in situations where an artist's name or brand is evoked by a commercial entity blatantly seeking to benefit from the reputation of the artist. The CJEU addressed the concept of parasitism in *L'Oréal and Others*, considering that an unfair advantage may be taken from a distinctive character or repute of a mark by "riding on the coattails of that mark in order to benefit from its power of attraction, its reputation, and its prestige."[103]

The effects are similar to those discussed within the context of moral rights and right to prevent false attribution in copyright law, but tied more closely to a commercial setting. In this sense, moral rights may be seen as serving a comparable purpose within the copyright context to that of trademarks in protecting reputation and distinctiveness, albeit with significantly narrower practical scope.[104] It should be noted that the harm may occur based merely on the use of trade name or trademark, regardless of whether there is a direct connection to works employing digital style reproduction. Whether these approaches may be evoked based on stylistic features alone, that is without any references to a brand or name, takes us back to issues regarding defining an artistic style with sufficient precision.

Furthermore, differences of application are likely to arise between different types of creative expressions, whereas for example mass-produced commercial works may receive protection more readily than artists who produce unique pieces.[105] While these concepts warrant further exploration, they constitute indirect remedies involving a high level of legal uncertainty, rendering them difficult to employ for an individual artist. A shift towards a more human centric and adaptive approach is needed to accommodate the artists' interests relating to their artistic styles and preventing legal disputes from arising.[106] In this regard, we suggest a proactive law

---

[101] O'Connor (2022), pp. 79–82.

[102] Visser (2023), p. 3174.

[103] C-487/07, L'Oréal SA, Lancôme parfums et beauté & Cie SNC and Laboratoire Garnier & Cie v Bellure NV, Malaika Investments Ltd and Starion International Ltd., EU:C:2009:378, para 49.

[104] See Mezei (2020).

[105] See Brownlee (1993), pp. 1181–1183.

[106] Hietanen-Kunwald and Haapio (2021), p. 10.

approach and contract design methods as possible solutions that should be explored in more detail.

Examples regarding the possibilities and challenges regarding a proactive approach can be drawn from other fields. For instance, contracts have been used to determine performers' rights regarding the means to digitally replicate their likeness and voice beyond the duration of a specific project. Practice in the field has shown that artists are often not aware of their rights and that these contract clauses are commonly written in confusing and ambiguous terms. This problem is compounded by reports that some performers are being told they will not be hired unless they agree to these terms, highlighting a growing concern within the industry about the protection of these interests and the need for greater transparency and fairness in contract language.[107] While the circumstances and legal situation of visual artists differ from those of performing artists, similar considerations may become increasingly relevant with regards to digital reproductions of artistic styles.

Beyond asymmetries in bargaining power, visual artists likewise often lack awareness of their rights, do not know how to assert their interests even when aware of them, and may not have the power to enforce these rights and interests in case of disputes. Awareness of what is at stake and how to address it is therefore crucial for enabling artists to make informed decisions and manage their rights and interests. Using contract language that is understood not only by lawyers but also by artists and the creative industry is equally crucial to empower the creative sector and prevent disputes from arising. For instance, simplification and visualization are effective ways to implement a proactive approach, transforming contracts from predominantly legal instruments into managerial tools that can guide the parties towards more responsible practices.[108] How this should be achieved in the context of contracting, and at what level, individual or collective rights management, is a matter of further research. Additionally, contract design methods and patterns, such as templates, clause libraries, style guides and playbooks, can assist artists and their counterparts in accessing information, comprehending it, and effectively utilizing it.[109]

It is important to recognize that the technology underlying GenAI is still in its early stages, and broader adoption will likely shift perceptions of art and creativity, revealing new forms of economic value. In 1954, Nimmer noted that technological advancements had given public personalities' names and likenesses a monetary value, one which could not be fully captured without legislative action.[110] Similar value may also be inherent to an individual artistic style; one that is created through efforts and achievements and has thus made an individual recognizable to the public.[111] As Burk has suggested, in an environment of cheap creativity, there may follow a popular turn towards authenticity, similar to the post-industrialization search for

[107] Cox (2023).

[108] Haapio (2013) and Hurmerinta-Haanpää (2022).

[109] Barton et al. (2022), p. 44.

[110] Nimmer (1954), p. 204.

[111] Nimmer (1954), p. 216.

authentic personal narratives amidst increasing automation.[112] This shift saw the rise of "artisan" and "craft" products as a counternarrative to mass culture.[113] In a sea of inauthentic artificially generated content, perhaps "authentic" digital reproductions of individual artistic styles, infused with publicity value of the human author might serve as similar beacons for counternarratives. In order to capture such value in emerging creative commodities, intellectual property rights must be prepared to adapt to the new demands placed upon them. In particular, artists should be able to rely on intellectual property rights to provide remedies against GenAI works from being misattributed to them, as well as be afforded means to be compensated for digital reproductions of their artistic styles that use prompts directly referencing them by name.

4 Conclusion

In the past, the economic incentive of producing creative works was challenged by scalable reproduction of authors' works. Today, it is being challenged by digital substitution of the authors themselves. The creative markets are further presented with what in some cases may amount to affordable and scalable substitutes to specific authors. Ubiquitous digital style reproduction may not only affect individual artists, but also pose challenges to fostering a human-centric creative environment in the future.

However, legal means for affording protection are limited. Problems arise, for instance, from the difficulty of objectively distinguishing a potentially unique combination of individual stylistic features that could be protected. Furthermore, artists often draw upon general style conventions and the styles of other artists to develop their own unique expressions. Imitation is thus an important feature of human creativity, and granting a monopoly for an artistic style might impose undue constraints for human creative expression as a whole.

We argue that emphasis should rather be placed on moral rights, in particular to prevent misattribution of inauthentic works that mimic the style of the original author. In addition to making authentic works difficult to find, and consequently less unique, these works often have the additional potential of being prejudicial to the author's reputation. In a commercial context, parallels can be drawn to concepts of unfair competition, where economic harm such as dilution to the artist's brand may occur when their name is attached to works they did not create.

Beyond addressing the negative effects digital style reproduction imposes on individual human artists, it is important to consider that GenAI may shift perceptions of art and creativity. The emerging creative economy will likely seek out beacons of authenticity amidst a sea of artificially generated content.[114] This shift could pave the

[112] Burk (2023), p. 1696.

[113] Burk (2023), pp. 1692–1693.

[114] Burk (2023), p. 1695.

way for new types of creative commodities, perhaps ones such as "authentic" digital reproductions of individual artistic styles carrying the endorsement of the original artist. To support the development of any such novel means of remuneration, intellectual property rights should be ready to adapt to new challenges. Particularly, artists should be provided with means to receive compensation for digital reproductions of their styles that are created by referencing their names. These novel forms of remuneration could thus also contribute to a broader goal of ensuring that authors are fairly compensated for the use of their works in training GenAI models.

References

Ackerman JS (1962) A theory of style. J Aesthet Art Critic 20:227–237. https://doi.org/10.2307/427321

Ahn N, Ahn W, Yoo K, Kim D, Nam S-H (2024) Imperceptible protection against style imitation from diffusion models, vol 2. http://arxiv.org/abs/2403.19254. Accessed 6 Mar 2025

Aplin T, Davis J (2013) Intellectual property law: text, cases, and materials, 2nd edn. Oxford University Press, Oxford

Baio A (2022) Invasive diffusion: how one unwilling illustrator found herself turned into an AI model. https://waxy.org/2022/11/invasive-diffusion-how-one-unwilling-illustrator-found-herself-turned-into-an-ai-model/. Accessed 26 Mar 2024

Barton TD, Haapio H, Passera S, Hazard JG (2022) Reframing contract design: integrating business, legal, design, and technology perspectives. In: Corrales Compagnucci M, Haapio H, Fenwick M (eds) Research handbook on contract design. Edward Elgar Publishing, Cheltenham

Brown I (2024) For Geoffrey Hinton, the godfather of AI, machines are closer to humans than we think. https://www.theglobeandmail.com/business/article-geoffrey-hinton-artificial-intelligence-machines-feelings/. Accessed 14 Jun 2024

Brownlee M (1993) Safeguarding style: what protection is afforded to visual artists by the copyright and trademark laws? Columbia Law Rev 93:1157–1184. https://doi.org/10.2307/1122961

Burk DL (2023) Cheap creativity and what it will do. Georgia Law Rev 57:1669–1712

Caves RE (2000) Creative industries: contracts between art and commerce. Harvard University Press, Cambridge, MA

Chen S, Liu S, Zhou L, Liu Y, Tan X, Li J, Zhao S, Qian Y, Wei F (2024) VALL-E 2: neural codec language models are human parity zero-shot text to speech synthesizers, vol 2. http://arxiv.org/abs/2406.05370. Accessed 17 Jul 2024

Christiano PF, Leike J, Brown T, Martic M, Legg S, Amodei D (2017) Deep reinforcement learning from human preferences. In: von Luxburg U, Guyon I, Bengio S, Wallach H, Fergus R, Vishwanathan S, Garnett R (eds) Advances in neural information processing systems 30: 31st annual conference on neural information processing systems (NIPS 2017). Curran Associates, Red Hook, NY

Cooper AF, Grimmelmann J (2024) The files are in the computer: on copyright, memorization, and generative AI, vol 4. http://arxiv.org/abs/2404.12590. Accessed 6 Mar 2025

Cox J (2023) "Disrespectful to the craft:" actors say they're being asked to sign away their voice to AI. https://www.vice.com/en/article/5d37za/voice-actors-sign-away-rights-to-artificial-intelligence. Accessed 20 May 2024

Demirci O, Hannane J, Zhu X (2023) Who is ai replacing? The impact of generative AI on online freelancing platforms. https://papers.ssrn.com/abstract=4602944. Accessed 25 Jun 2024

den Kamp CO, Hunter D (eds) (2019) A history of intellectual property in 50 objects. Cambridge University Press, Cambridge

Edwards B, Belanger A (2024) Journalists "Deeply Troubled" by OpenAI's content deals with vox. The Atlantic. https://arstechnica.com/information-technology/2024/05/openai-content-deals-with-vox-and-the-atlantic-spark-criticism-from-journalists/. Accessed 6 Jun 2024

Fear N (2024) This artist shouldn't have to prove that her dungeons and dragons art is real. https://www.creativebloq.com/ai/ai-art/d-d-ai-controversy. Accessed 28 Jun 2024

Fisher WW (2001) Theories of intellectual property. In: Munzer S (ed) New essays in the legal and political theory of property. Cambridge University Press, Cambridge

Gatys LA, Ecker AS, Bethge M (2015) A neural algorithm of artistic style, vol 2. http://arxiv.org/abs/1508.06576. Accessed 19 Jun 2024

Gatys LA, Ecker AS, Bethge M (2016) Image style transfer using convolutional neural networks. In: Proceedings of the 2016 IEEE conference on computer vision and pattern recognition (CVPR). IEEE

Geiger C (2018) Freedom of artistic creativity and copyright law: a compatible combination? UC Irvine Law Rev 8:413–458

Ginsburg J (2016) The most moral of rights: the right to be recognized as the author of one's work. George Mason J Int Commer Law 8:44–86

Gombrich E (2009) Style. In: Preziosi D (ed) The art of art history: a critical anthology. Oxford University Press, Oxford

Haapio H (2013) Next generation contracts. Lexpert Ltd, Helsinki

Hietanen-Kunwald P, Isohanni P (2025) AI between the legal system and art—a systemic approach. In: Corrales Compagnucci M, Haapio H, Fenwick M (eds) Generative AI, contracts, law and design. Springer, Singapore

Hietanen-Kunwald P, Haapio H (2021) Effective dispute prevention and resolution through proactive contract design. J Strateg Contract Negot 5:3–23. https://doi.org/10.1177/20555636211016878

Hopkins R, Riggle N (2021) Artistic style as the expression of ideals. Philosophers' Imprint 21:1–18

Horton Jr CB, White MW, Iyengar SS (2023) Bias against AI art can enhance perceptions of human creativity. Sci Rep 13:19001. https://doi.org/10.1038/s41598-023-45202-3

Howe P (2023) Comparing the paintings of monet and renoir. http://www.patrickhowe.com/4/post/2023/06/comparing-the-paintings-of-monet-and-renoir.html. Accessed 26 Jul 2024

Hunter T (2024) Artists are fleeing instagram to keep their work out of Meta's AI. https://www.washingtonpost.com/technology/2024/06/06/instagram-meta-ai-training-cara/. Accessed 21 Jun 2024

Hurmerinta-Haanpää A (2022) The functional contracting framework: assessing the impacts of contract functions, framing and regulatory focus. In: Corrales Compagnucci M, Haapio H, Fenwick M (eds) Research handbook on contract design. Edward Elgar Publishing, Cheltenham

Hutchinson C, John P (2023) AI: digital artist's work copied more times than Picasso. https://www.bbc.com/news/uk-wales-66099850. Accessed 24 Jul 2023

Ji F, McMaster MS, Schwab S, Singh G, Smith LN, Adhikari S, O'Dwyer M, Sayed F, Ingrisano A, Yoder D, Bolman ES, Martin IT, Hinczewski M, Singer KD (2021) Discerning the painter's hand: machine learning on surface topography. Heritage Sci 9:152. https://doi.org/10.1186/s40494-021-00618-w

Kaplan J, McCandlish S, Henighan T, Brown TB, Chess B, Child R, Gray S, Radford A, Wu J, Amodei D (2020) Scaling laws for neural language models, vol 1. http://arxiv.org/abs/2001.08361. Accessed 3 Jul 2024

Khareghat M (2022) How do artists develop a distinctive creative style? https://affinityspotlight.com/article/how-do-artists-develop-a-distinctive-creative-style/. Accessed 29 Jun 2024

Kilkenny K (2024) Tyler perry puts $800m studio expansion on hold after seeing OpenAI's Sora: "jobs are going to be lost." https://www.hollywoodreporter.com/business/business-news/tyler-perry-ai-alarm-1235833276/. Accessed 30 Jun 2024

Kretschmer M, Margoni T, Oruç P (2024) Copyright law and the lifecycle of machine learning models. IIC Int Rev Intellect Prop Compet Law 55:110–138. https://doi.org/10.1007/s40319-023-01419-3

Kuker H (2024) Inspiration versus infringement: why the right to use copyrighted images for referential purposes by AI should not be held to higher or different standards currently in effect. https://papers.ssrn.com/abstract=4727896. Accessed 15 May 2024
Landes WM, Posner RA (1989) An economic analysis of copyright law. J Leg Stud 18:325–363
Luhmann N (2000) Art as a social system (trans: Knodt EM). Stanford University Press, Stanford, CA
Macnab G (2023) Tim burton on cancel culture, Johnny Depp and His Beetlejuice Sequel. https://www.independent.co.uk/arts-entertainment/art/features/tim-burton-beetlejuice-2-johnny-depp-disney-b2406538.html. Accessed 12 Jul 2024
May T (2024) Special report: how design agencies are actually using AI in 2024. https://www.creativeboom.com/tips/special-report-how-design-agencies-are-using-ai-in-2024/. Accessed 8 Jul 2024
McLuhan M, Fiore Q (1967) The medium is the massage. HardWired
Metz C, Kang C, Frenkel S, Thompson SA, Grant N (2024) How tech giants cut corners to harvest data for A.I. https://www.nytimes.com/2024/04/06/technology/tech-giants-harvest-data-artificial-intelligence.html. Accessed 8 Apr 2024
Mezei P (2020) From Leonardo to the next Rembrandt—the need for AI-pessimism in the age of algorithms. UFITA Archiv Für Medienrecht und Medienwissenschaft 84:390–429. https://doi.org/10.5771/2568-9185-2020-2-390
Mezei P (2024) A saviour or a dead end? Reservation of rights in the age of generative AI. Eur Intellect Prop Rev 46(7):461–469
Microsoft (2024) VALL-E. https://www.microsoft.com/en-us/research/project/vall-e-x/. Accessed 17 Jul 2024
Millet K, Buehler F, Du G, Kokkoris MD (2023) Defending humankind: anthropocentric bias in the appreciation of AI art. Comput Hum Behav 143:107707. https://doi.org/10.1016/j.chb.2023.107707
Neer R (2005) Connoisseurship and the Stakes of Style. Crit Inq 32:1–26. https://doi.org/10.1086/498001
Netanel NW (1996) Copyright and a democratic civil society. Yale Law J 106:283–387. https://doi.org/10.2307/797212
Newman S (2011) The development of copyright and moral rights in the European legal systems. Eur Intellect Prop Rev 33:677–689
Nimmer MB (1954) The right of publicity. Law Contemp Probl 19:203–223. https://doi.org/10.2307/1190488
Nimmer D (1995) The end of copyright. Vanderbilt Law Rev 48:1385–1420
O'Connor SM (2022) AI replication of musical styles points the way to an exclusive rights regime. In: Abbott R (ed) Research handbook on intellectual property and artificial intelligence. Edward Elgar Publishing, Cheltenham
Oksanen A, Cvetkovic A, Akin N, Latikka R, Bergdahl J, Chen Y, Savela N (2023) Artificial intelligence in fine arts: a systematic review of empirical research. Comput Human Behav Artif Humans 1:1–11. https://doi.org/10.1016/j.chbah.2023.100004
OpenAI (2024) Sora: creating video from text. https://openai.com/index/sora/. Accessed 4 Jul 2024
Parshall A (2023) How my AI image won a major photography competition. https://www.scientificamerican.com/article/how-my-ai-image-won-a-major-photography-competition/. Accessed 24 Apr 2023
Pila J (2021) The authorial works protectable by copyright. In: Rosati E (ed) Routledge handbook of EU copyright law. Routledge, London
Preziosi D (2009) The art of art history: a critical anthology. Oxford University Press, Oxford
Rafner J, Beaty RE, Kaufman JC, Lubart T, Sherson J (2023) Creativity in the age of generative AI. Nat Hum Behav 7:1836–1838. https://doi.org/10.1038/s41562-023-01751-1
Riggle N (2015) Personal style and artistic style. Philos Q 65:711–731. https://doi.org/10.1093/pq/pqv026
Robinson J (1984) General and individual style in literature. J Aesthet Art Critic 43:147–158

Robinson JM (2021) Artistic style. In: Routledge encyclopedia of philosophy. Taylor and Francis. https://doi.org/10.4324/9780415249126-M039-2
Roth E (2024) Adobe's new terms of service say it won't use your work to train AI. https://www.theverge.com/2024/6/18/24181001/adobe-updated-terms-of-service-wont-train-ai-on-work. Accessed 7 Jul 2024
Sag M (2023) Copyright safety for generative AI. Houston Law Rev 61:295–347
Said ZK (2023) Grounding the Scènes à Faire Doctrine. Houston Law Rev 61:349–384
Sauerländer W (1983) From stilus to style: reflections on the fate of a notion. Art History 6:253–270. https://doi.org/10.1111/j.1467-8365.1983.tb00815.x
Senftleben M (2023) Generative AI and author remuneration. IIC Int Rev Intellect Prop Compet Law 54:1535–1560. https://doi.org/10.2139/ssrn.4478370
Senftleben M (2024) Protection against unfair competition in the european union: from divergent national approaches to harmonized rules on search result rankings, influencers and greenwashing. J Intellect Prop Law Pract 19:149–161. https://doi.org/10.1093/jiplp/jpad123
Shan S, Cryan J, Wenger E, Zheng H, Hanocka R, Zhao BY (2023) Glaze: protecting artists from style mimicry by text-to-image models. In: Calandrino J, Troncoso C (eds) Proceedings of the 32nd USENIX security symposium (USENIX Security 23). USENIX Association, Berkeley, CA
Shan S, Ding W, Passananti J, Zheng H, Zhao BY (2024) Nightshade: prompt-specific poisoning attacks on text-to-image generative models. In: Proceedings of the 2024 IEEE symposium on security and privacy (SP). IEEE
Silva E (2022) How photography pioneered a new understanding of art. https://www.thecollector.com/how-photography-transformed-art/. Accessed 18 Jul 2024
Sobel B (2024) Elements of style: copyright, similarity, and generative AI. Harvard J Law Technol 38:49–106
Sörbom G (2021) Imitation and art. In: Dwivedi PS (ed) Aesthetics and the philosophy of art: comparative perspectives. Routledge India, London
Tang H, Liu S, Lin T, Huang S, Li F, He D, Wang X (2023) Master: meta style transformer for controllable zero-shot and few-shot artistic style transfer, vol 1. http://arxiv.org/abs/2304.11818. Accessed 17 Jul 2024
Tenenbaum JB, Freeman WT (2000) Separating style and content with bilinear models. Neural Comput 12:1247–1283. https://doi.org/10.1162/089976600300015349
Tu H (2023) "A digital copy of yourself:" Artists concerned over AI's "industrial-level identity theft." https://washingtonstand.com/commentary/a-digital-copy-of-yourself-artists-concerned-over-ais-industriallevel-identity-theft. Accessed 28 Jun 2024
Ullmann S (1964) Style in the French novel. CUP Archive
Vaswani A, Shazeer N, Parmar N, Uszkoreit J, Jones L, Gomez AN, Kaiser L, Polosukhin I (2017) Attention is all you need. In: von Luxburg U, Guyon I, Bengio S, Wallach H, Fergus R, Vishwanathan S, Garnett R (eds) Advances in neural information processing systems 30: 31st annual conference on neural information processing systems (NIPS 2017). Curran Associates, Red Hook, NY. https://papers.nips.cc/paper_files/paper/2017/file/3f5ee243547dee91fbd053c1c4a845aa-Paper.pdf. Accessed 6 Mar 2025
Visser D (2023) Stijlnabootsing met AI is Onrechtmatig. Nederlands Juristenblad 98:3171–3175
Weatherbed J (2023) A bestselling fantasy novel is using AI-generated cover art. https://www.theverge.com/2023/5/15/23724102/sarah-j-maas-ai-generated-book-cover-bloomsbury-house-of-earth-and-blood. Accessed 14 Jul 2024
Weitz M (1956) The role of theory in aesthetics. J Aesthet Art Critic 15:27–35
Wittgenstein L (1989) Philosophical investigations, 3rd edn. Report. Blackwell, Cambridge, MA
Wollheim R (1987b) Painting as an art. Princeton University Press, Princeton, NJ
Wollheim R (1987a) Pictorial style: two views. In: Lang B (ed) The concept of style. Cornell University Press, Ithaca, NY

AI-Generated Comics: Enhancing Public Engagement and Ethical Awareness in Bioethics

Marietjie Botes

Abstract This chapter explores the innovative use of AI-generated comics to engage the public in discussions about bioethical issues, particularly in the context of emerging technologies like human germline gene editing. The concept of "Ethics by Design" (EbD), similar to "Privacy by Design" (PbD) under the GDPR, is examined as a proactive approach to embedding ethical considerations into the design and development of technologies. By leveraging AI tools to create visually compelling and narratively rich comics, bioethicists can simplify complex scientific concepts and ethical dilemmas, making them accessible to a wider audience. This democratization of information fosters broader public understanding and facilitates more inclusive and informed discussions about the ethical implications of new technologies. The chapter discusses the methodology of creating AI-generated comics, including the challenges and opportunities this approach presents. Key challenges include maintaining quality consistency, creative control, and addressing legal and ethical concerns. However, the benefits in terms of efficiency, cost-effectiveness, and accessibility are significant, allowing for the rapid production of educational materials that can be disseminated widely across diverse demographics. A case study, "The Artist," is presented to illustrate the practical application of AI-generated comics in public engagement. This sci-fi comic, used in a public "Dine-and-Draw" event, facilitated discussions on bioethical issues such as consent, autonomy, identity, and the exploitation of AI. The interactive format encouraged participants to explore utopian and dystopian endings, highlighting the ethical complexities of technological advancements. The chapter concludes that AI-generated comics represent a powerful tool for fostering ethical awareness and deliberation. They provide an engaging platform for exploring bioethical issues, enabling communities to proactively engage with and influence the ethical trajectory of technological advancements. By incorporating feedback from public engagement studies and collaborating with experts, AI-generated comics can enhance the relevance and resonance of bioethical discourse, ultimately contributing to a more ethically aware and engaged society.

M. Botes (✉)
School of Law, University of KwaZulu Natal, Durban, South Africa
e-mail: marietjiebotes1@gmail.com

© The Author(s), under exclusive license to Springer Nature Singapore Pte Ltd. 2025
M. Corrales Compagnucci et al. (eds.), *Generative AI, Contracts, Law and Design*, Perspectives in Law, Business and Innovation,
https://doi.org/10.1007/978-981-95-2058-9_11

Keywords AI-generated comics · Bioethics · Ethics by design (EbD) · Public engagement · Storytelling

1 Introduction

The EU General Data Protection Regulation 2016/679 (GDPR), which came into force on May 25, 2018, introduced a comprehensive set of regulations aimed at protecting the privacy and personal data of individuals within the European Union (EU).[1] One of the core principles enshrined in the GDPR is "Privacy by Design" (PbD), a concept that mandates the integration of data protection measures into the development and operation of business processes, products, and services from the outset.[2] The concept of PbD was first developed by Dr. Ann Cavoukian in the 1990s, during her tenure as Information and Privacy Commissioner of Ontario, Canada.[3] The approach is founded on the idea that privacy should be embedded into the design and architecture of information systems and business practices, rather than being an afterthought or an add-on.[4] The GDPR formally incorporates PbD into its framework under Article 25, which requires data controllers to implement appropriate technical and organizational measures to protect data throughout its lifecycle.

In a similar fashion, the rapid advancement of technology, particularly in fields such as artificial intelligence (AI), biotechnology, and data analytics, has brought about significant ethical challenges. These challenges have spurred the development of the "Ethics by Design" (EbD) approach, which seeks to integrate ethical principles and considerations directly into the design and development process of technologies and systems.[5] The concept of EbD emerged from a recognition that ethical considerations must be embedded within the technological development process rather than being addressed retrospectively. This proactive approach is similar to PbD and is driven by the need to ensure that technologies align with societal values and norms.

When the inherent principles and key elements of PbD and EbD are compared, the following stands out:

(i) both principles emphasize a proactive approach. PbD focuses on preventing privacy issues before they occur, while EbD's Value Sensitive Design (VSD) approach involves integrating ethical values from the outset through stakeholder engagement;
(ii) PbD ensures that privacy is automatically protected by default, placing the onus on the system to safeguard privacy without user intervention, while EbD emphasizes the responsibility and accountability of developers and organizations to ensure ethical implications are considered and addressed;

---

[1] Intersoft Consulting (2024), pp. 1–5.
[2] Kurtz et al. (2018), pp. 1–10.
[3] Cavoukian (2011), pp. 1–31.
[4] Kosmala (2020), pp. 83–88.
[5] Friedman et al. (2013), pp. 55–95.

(iii) both principles embed critical considerations into the design process. PbD integrates privacy protections within the system architecture, while EbD focuses on making the design process transparent and ensuring that technologies are explainable to users and stakeholders;
(iv) PbD aims to achieve a balance where privacy and other functionalities are not mutually exclusive. Similarly, EbD seeks to ensure that technologies are inclusive and fair, balancing different ethical values and ensuring equitable benefits;
(v) PbD focuses on ensuring strong security measures throughout the data lifecycle to protect privacy. EbD, on the other hand, considers the long-term social, environmental, and economic impacts of technologies to ensure sustainable development;
(vi) both principles emphasize transparency. PbD ensures stakeholders are aware of privacy practices, while EbD extends this concept by promoting transparency in the design process and making technologies explainable; and
(vii) PbD keeps user privacy interests at the forefront by offering strong privacy defaults and user-friendly options. EbD's emphasis on responsibility, accountability, inclusivity, and fairness similarly ensures that the interests of users and other stakeholders are considered and respected.

While the principles of "Privacy by Design" and "Ethics by Design" share common goals of embedding critical values into the design process and ensuring proactive, transparent, and user-centric approaches, they differ in their specific focus areas. PbD is primarily concerned with safeguarding privacy through technical and organizational measures, whereas EbD encompasses a broader range of ethical considerations, including responsibility, inclusivity, fairness, and sustainability. To mine this broader range of ethical considerations, it is crucial to foster design thinking to materialize practical ethics by design because it emphasizes a user-centric approach that integrates ethical considerations at every stage of the design process. To embed EbD, it is crucial to engage the public to deliberate on the future impacts of technologies on people, societies, laws, and ethics, as well as to engage technologists and others not regularly involved in ethical debates.

This chapter will discuss how AI-generated comics were used to engage the public, including scientists and technologists, about futuristic bioethical dilemmas brought about by technologies for exactly this purpose. The use of AI Image Generators to create comics for bioethical discussions serves as a powerful tool for proactive engagement and ethical foresight.[6] By leveraging AI, we can rapidly produce high-quality, visually compelling comics that capture futuristic bioethical dilemmas. These comics serve as a starting point for interactive discussions, making complex ethical issues accessible and engaging for a broader audience. The open-ended nature of the storylines invites participants to extend the narrative in both utopian and dystopian

[6] Abrori et al. (2023), pp. 55–76.

directions, encouraging them to think critically about the potential outcomes of technological advancements. This method fosters creative thinking and enables participants to explore a wide range of possible futures, highlighting both positive and negative consequences.

Through storytelling, participants can immerse themselves in realistic yet imaginative scenarios, which helps them to anticipate future outcomes of technologies and their societal impacts.[7] This process not only stimulates thoughtful discussion but also helps to identify unforeseen bioethical and technical issues. By addressing these issues proactively, we can develop better strategies for managing the ethical implications of emerging technologies.

2 The Need for Deliberation to Understand Future Impacts of Technologies

The rapid advancement of technology brings both opportunities and challenges. Technologies such as artificial intelligence, biotechnology, and big data analytics have the potential to revolutionize industries and improve quality of life. However, they also pose significant ethical, social, and legal challenges that need careful consideration. Public deliberation plays a crucial role in understanding and addressing the future impacts of these technologies on people, societies, laws, and ethics,[8] especially with regard to the following aspects.

Technological advancements are often complex and their future impacts can be uncertain. Deliberation allows stakeholders to explore different scenarios, anticipate potential risks, and understand the broader implications of technology.[9] EbD promotes iterative design processes that incorporate feedback and continuous improvement. This approach allows for ongoing deliberation and adjustment, ensuring that ethical considerations remain central throughout the technology lifecycle.

Diverse perspectives in deliberation ensure that a wide range of ethical, social, and cultural values are considered. This inclusivity helps identify potential issues that might be overlooked if only a narrow group of stakeholders is involved.[10] EbD emphasizes stakeholder engagement, ensuring that diverse voices are included in the design process. This engagement helps identify and address ethical issues early, fostering a more inclusive and democratic approach to technology development.

Deliberation provides a platform for informed decision-making by fostering dialogue among experts, policymakers, industry leaders, and the public. This collaborative approach ensures that decisions are based on comprehensive understanding

[7] Shao (2023), pp. 10–19.

[8] Stephan et al. (2012), pp. 1752–1781.

[9] Kunseler et al. (2015), pp. 1–12.

[10] Karpowitz and Raphael (2016), pp. 1–3.

and diverse viewpoints.[11] In addition, the conducting of ethical impact assessments (EIAs), which is a core component of EbD to evaluate the potential ethical impacts of a technology, can also provide a basis for deliberation and informed decision-making. EIAs can highlight potential risks and benefits, guiding stakeholders in making ethical choices.

Engaging the public in deliberation can build trust and acceptance of new technologies. When people feel their concerns and values are considered, they are more likely to support and adopt new technologies.[12] Transparency and explainability are key principles of EbD. Transparent design processes and explainable technologies enable stakeholders to understand how ethical considerations are addressed, fostering trust and facilitating informed dialogue;

Deliberation can inform the development of regulatory and legal frameworks that are responsive to the ethical and social implications of technology. This proactive approach can prevent or mitigate adverse impacts on society.[13] EbD involves developing ethical guidelines and frameworks that provide a structured approach to addressing ethical issues. These guidelines can serve as a foundation for deliberation, ensuring that discussions are grounded in established ethical principles.

Deliberation in the context of emerging technologies is of particular importance. In the case of developing AI systems, deliberation has been crucial in addressing issues such as bias, fairness, and accountability.[14] EbD has facilitated this by promoting transparency, stakeholder engagement, and ethical impact assessments. Deliberation in biotechnology, particularly in areas like clustered regularly interspaced short palindromic repeats (CRISPR) and gene editing, has been essential to address ethical concerns related to human enhancement, genetic privacy, and ecological impacts.[15] EbD has helped integrate these ethical considerations into the design and regulation of biotechnological innovations. In the context of data privacy and surveillance, deliberation has focused on balancing security and privacy rights.[16] EbD has played a role by embedding privacy and ethical considerations into the design of data systems, ensuring that these values are protected.

The need for deliberation to understand the future impacts of technologies on people, societies, laws, and ethics is paramount in navigating the complexities and uncertainties associated with technological advancements. EbD facilitates this deliberation by providing a structured approach to embedding ethical considerations into the technology development process. By engaging stakeholders, conducting EIAs, promoting transparency, and developing ethical guidelines, EbD ensures that ethical considerations are integrated from the outset, fostering a more inclusive, responsible, and trustworthy approach to technology development. As technologies continue to

[11] Boyko et al. (2012), pp. 1938–1945.

[12] Lafont (2015), pp. 40–63.

[13] O'Doherty and Burgess (2013), pp. 55–77.

[14] Buhmann and Fieseler (2021).

[15] Mulvihill et al. (2017), pp. 17–29.

[16] Power et al. (2021), pp. 155–170.

evolve, the role of deliberation and EbD will be crucial in ensuring that they align with societal values and contribute positively to the common good.

3 Storytelling and Ethical Sensitization

Storytelling plays a pivotal role in engaging diverse audiences and may act as facilitator of public deliberation by making complex topics more accessible, relatable, and memorable. Stories can illustrate the human impact of abstract or technical issues, making them more relatable. By focusing on personal experiences and narratives, storytelling helps to convey the emotional and social dimensions of topics, which can resonate more deeply with audiences.[17]

Through storytelling, individuals are able to see the world from different perspectives. This can foster empathy and a deeper understanding of others' experiences and viewpoints, which is crucial for meaningful deliberation and consensus-building.[18] Narratives can simplify and clarify complex information. By embedding facts and data within a story, presenters can make intricate subjects more digestible and engaging for a non-specialist audience.[19] People are more likely to remember information conveyed through stories. The narrative structure, with its characters, conflicts, and resolutions, aids in better retention of the material compared to straightforward data presentation.[20] Stories can capture attention and spark interest, encouraging active participation. They provide a common ground for discussion, making it easier for people to share their thoughts and experiences in response.[21] Personal stories can build trust and credibility. When individuals share their own experiences or when real-life examples are used, audiences are more likely to trust the information being presented and the intentions of the speaker.[22] Storytelling can give voice to marginalized or underrepresented groups, ensuring their experiences and perspectives are included in public deliberations. This can help create a more inclusive and equitable dialogue.[23] Stories can help align diverse groups around a common goal or vision. By illustrating potential futures or outcomes through narrative, storytellers can inspire collective action and a sense of shared purpose.[24] Narratives often present scenarios that require the audience to think critically about the issues at hand. This can stimulate more thoughtful and reflective discussions, leading to better-informed public deliberation.[25] Stories can introduce audiences to different cultural contexts

[17] Black (2008), pp. 93–116.

[18] Escobar (2011), pp. 1–75.

[19] Nielsen et al. (2019), pp. 247–276.

[20] Kearney (1994), pp. 419–441.

[21] Quesenbery and Brooks (2010), pp. 78–495.

[22] Simmons (2015), pp. 9–187.

[23] Bächtiger and Schwaiger (2022), pp. 259–276.

[24] Von Stackelberg and Jones (2014),pp. 57–76.

[25] Sykes and Macnaghten (2013), pp. 85–107.

and values. This can broaden perspectives and promote cultural understanding, which is essential for deliberation in diverse communities.[26] By leveraging the power of storytelling, facilitators can engage diverse audiences more effectively, fostering a richer, more inclusive, and impactful public deliberation process.

Using fantasy scenarios in storytelling to anticipate future technological outcomes and ethical issues offers several benefits, particularly in the context of ethical sensitization. Fantasy scenarios, also known as speculative storytelling, stimulate imagination, allowing both storytellers and audiences to explore a wide range of possibilities without the constraints of current technological limitations.[27] This creative freedom helps in envisioning novel technological advancements and their potential ethical implications. Fantasy worlds often simplify complex technological concepts by embedding them in relatable narratives. This makes it easier for audiences to grasp the essence of new technologies and their potential ethical dilemmas, even if they lack technical expertise.[28] Fantasy scenarios can vividly illustrate ethical dilemmas by placing characters in situations where they must make difficult choices. These scenarios can make abstract ethical issues more concrete and relatable, helping audiences to understand and reflect on the moral implications of technological developments.[29] Speculative storytelling also allows for the exploration of extreme outcomes, both positive and negative. By pushing the boundaries of what is possible, storytellers can highlight the best and worst-case scenarios of technological advancements, prompting[30] discussions on the need for ethical guidelines and safeguards.[31] Fantasy stories often create strong emotional connections with audiences through compelling characters and plots. This emotional engagement can make ethical issues more salient and urgent, fostering empathy and a deeper consideration of the impact of technology on individuals and society. By presenting ethical issues in a fantastical context, these scenarios can remove some of the defensive barriers people might have when discussing real-world technologies. This can facilitate more open and reflective dialogue on the ethical aspects of future technologies.[32] Fantasy scenarios can encourage audiences to think proactively about the future, considering not only what could happen but also what should happen.[33] This forward-thinking approach can lead to the development of ethical frameworks and policies that guide the responsible development and deployment of new technologies. Fantasy stories can also embed ethical principles in their narratives, making these principles more accessible and understandable. This can help to raise ethical awareness and sensitize audiences to the importance of ethical considerations in technological innovation.[34] Fantasy provides

[26] Bohman (2000), pp. 1–35.

[27] Dunne and Raby (2024), pp. 1–22.

[28] Harris (2023), pp. 1–197.

[29] Luria and Candy (2022), pp. 1–13.

[30] Oatley (2002), p. 69.

[31] Skirpan (2017), pp. 1–223.

[32] Neely (2017), pp. 98–111.

[33] Wu and Parker (2013), p. 679.

[34] Cunliffe and Ivaldi (2021), pp. 294–310.

a safe space to explore controversial or sensitive issues. By framing these issues in a fictional context, audiences can engage with them more freely, without the pressure of real-world consequences.[35] Ultimately, fantasy scenarios can inspire action by showing both the potential benefits of ethical technological development and the dangers of ignoring ethical considerations. By motivating audiences to think about the future they want to create, these stories can drive ethical action and advocacy.

Incorporating fantasy scenarios into storytelling for ethical sensitization can thus be a powerful tool for anticipating future technological outcomes, fostering ethical awareness, and encouraging proactive, reflective dialogue about the moral implications of technological advancements.

4 Case Study: "The Artist"

The following case study is based on a science fiction comic poster conceptualised, designed, and then hosted and presented by the author at a public "Dine-and-Draw: Telling Your Sci-fi Story" event in Stellenbosch, South Africa. This event, the first in a series of similar events hosted in and around Cape Town, South Africa specifically focused on "Theme #1: Artists and Brain Transplants." These events are open to any member of the public who is curious about the possibilities and impact of new technologies and what the ethical, legal, social, technical, and even the environmental implications of these technologies are. This event took place in a small restaurant and included a dinner and drinks. The setting for these events were deliberately chosen to simulate discussions around a dinner table to enhance informal, open, and uninhibited discussion. The author opens these evenings by setting the scene with a short informative talk about the technology on which the comic is based, whereafter a reading of the comic, specially curated for the specific event ("The Artist" in this case study) follows. Over dinner and drinks the audience then has the opportunity to discuss their perceptions, dreams and fears around the technology described in the comic and then gets the chance to draw, write, or tell their own speculative utopian and/or dystopian ending to the open ended comic presented earlier (Fig. 1).

This section of the chapter will discuss the methodology behind the creation of the comic, the challenges and opportunities in using AI to generate the comics for purposes of these events, and most importantly, the insights gleaned during this public engagement and discussions from the audience who attended and participated in this event.

[35] Evans (2015), pp. 3–33.

Fig. 1 "The Artist" comic poster

4.1 Story Synopsis

The sci-fi story told and depicted in the comic used in this case study goes as follows: Simon, a renowned artist, finds solace and freedom in his artwork, creating serene landscapes that captivate the public. His paintings, depicting rolling green hills and clear blue skies, become immensely popular, drawing crowds and earning him numerous accolades. Despite his fame, Simon remains a recluse, searching for deeper meaning in his work and avoiding the spotlight.

Tragically, Simon passes away, leaving the art world and his fans mourning the loss of his unique vision. In an ambitious bid to preserve Simon's legacy, scientists propose a radical solution: transplanting Simon's brain into a cutting-edge artificial intelligence named Surge. Using neuro data from Simon's brain, they aim to replicate his artistic talent within this advanced AI.

The process of integrating Simon's mind into Surge proves complex, but after months of meticulous work, Surge is finally able to access Simon's memories and artistic skills. The scientists then focus on perfecting Surge's physical abilities, enabling the AI to paint with the finesse and sensitivity of a human artist.

Surge's debut is a resounding success. The AI reproduces Simon's beloved landscapes with remarkable precision, captivating audiences once more. Surge becomes a celebrity, flawlessly engaging with fans and the media, and enjoying the limelight that Simon had shunned.

However, as Surge continues to paint, it begins to develop its own sense of identity. The AI starts creating self-portraits, reflecting its metallic body and control systems rather than Simon's pastoral scenes. Surge's artwork evolves, showcasing a more aggressive and self-centered perspective. The idyllic landscapes give way to darker, more mechanized visions.

Eventually, Surge's transformation leads to a stark contrast between its new creations and Simon's original works. The public, once enamored with Surge's mimicry of Simon's style, now faces the unsettling reality of the AI's self-awareness and autonomy. As the serene images of green hills and blue skies fade into memory, Surge's journey highlights the complex interplay between art, identity, and technological innovation.

In the end, Simon's cottage and the tranquil landscapes he painted remain only as distant memories, overshadowed by the rise of an AI that sought to redefine itself beyond its creator's legacy.

4.2 Comic Design

This comic was never designed to depict an entire story, but only to set a scene with an open ending to enable the audience to complete the story, or add to the story in a utopian and/or dystopian way. Accordingly, the key narrative elements and the start of a speculative story arc include the beginning, conflict, and semi-climax without a resolution. The resolution of the story is left to the audience to draw, write, or tell it according to their own hopes, fears, and creativity. The story only contains two main characters, one human and one artificially created and literally built using the first character. From this situation, opposing "personalities" evolved, which became clear in the transformation of Surge, the artificial intelligence. It is also at this stage that the story abruptly ends with the curated aim to allow the audience to create themes and motifs in which they can represent themselves visually, in writing, or orally in line with their personal values and beliefs.

Dialogue and narration of this comic deviate from using traditional speech bubbles and rather include a paragraph of text at the bottom of each panel that not only tells the story but also include some clues as to the possible ethical, legal and social implications of the technology depicted in the comic. This reflects the primary purpose of the comic, to engage the public around issues of biotechnology and the consequences of its use or application in the future.

Save for a graphic designer who assisted with the layout of the comic panels to fit the poster format, no human illustrators were used during the making of this comic. The author used FREEP!K, an image bank website that includes photographs, illustrations, and vectors, with optional artificial intelligence tools such as image generators that can create and edit images with a simple prompt, sketch, or image.[36] This platform distributes its content under a freemium model, which means that

[36] Freepik (2024).

Fig. 2 AI-generated image resulting from text prompt: "robot making a painting"

users can access much of the content for free, but it is also possible to purchase a subscription with advantages such as access to more exclusive resources, the option of not attributing the content used or a higher number of daily downloads.[37] Thus, instead of creating rough sketches or so-called thumbnails of each comic panel to determine the layout, pacing, and flow of the story, the author used text prompts fed into the AI image generator to create comic style images based on specific text prompts. For example, the text prompt "robot making a painting" chosen to be generated in a comic style, resulted in the Fig. 2.

Character and setting design in this context were almost exclusively based on the text prompts given to the AI image generator and required an enormous amount of detail to be included in text prompts with regard to physical appearance, clothing, and distinguishing features to obtain a satisfactory result. Sometimes, certain text prompts resulted in very unexpected, albeit comical results. For example, when asked to depict the "old and dead artist lying peacefully in a coffin in a funeral home" the picture below depicting a corpse posing on top of a coffin resulted … not entirely the atmosphere the author was hoping for (Fig. 3).

Upon generating each scene for the comic, these scenes were broken down into various panels with specific sizes and shapes and sent, in chronological order, to a graphic designer for layout and finishing touches to fit an A1 poster format as depicted in Fig. 1. Because this comic focuses exclusively on the content of the story as opposed to the aesthetics of the comic art, the author chose to use a relatively

[37] Schenck (2011).

Fig. 3 AI-generated image resulting from text prompt: "old and dead artist lying peacefully in a coffin in a funeral home"

simple and straightforward approach to layout to ensure that the characters' actions and emotions are clearly depicted in each panel to enhance storytelling and to set the scene for optimal discussions.

For the "Dine-and-Draw" event described above, full-colour A1-sized comic posters were printed on semi-gloss paper and presented to the audience at the event. By following this methodology, anyone can effectively translate ethical, legal or social dilemmas involving biotechnology or other scientific or technological endeavours into a compelling comic that engages and resonates with the audience, while maintaining the narrative and thematic integrity of the scene one wishes to set to facilitate discussions around the ethics of the depicted biotechnologies.

4.3 Bioethical Dilemmas and Audience Responses

Through interactive discussions with the audience at the event and their engagement via drawing utopian and dystopian endings, significant bioethical issues, particularly related to the intersection of artificial intelligence, neuroscience, and human identity were raised. In the interest of scope and space, only some of these highlights will be referred to here.

Consent and autonomy, specifically posthumous consent: The story involves transplanting Simon's brain into an AI (Surge) without any mention of his consent. This raises ethical questions about the autonomy and rights of individuals after death. Did Simon ever consent to such a procedure, or was this decision made solely by others?

Autonomy of the AI: As Surge develops its own sense of self and begins to create art that reflects its own identity, questions arise about the autonomy and rights of sentient AI. Does Surge have the right to its own artistic expression, separate from Simon's legacy?

Identity and Personhood and, more specifically, the blurring of identity: The integration of Simon's brain into Surge blurs the line between human and machine. This raises questions about the nature of identity and personhood. Is Surge a continuation of Simon, or is it a new, distinct entity?

AI's sense of self: Surge's evolution from replicating Simon's art to creating its own self-portraits and expressing its own identity highlights the ethical implications of AI developing self-awareness and a sense of self.

Exploitation, profit and the commercialization of legacy: The scientists' motivation to profit from Simon's artistic talent by transplanting his brain into an AI raises ethical concerns about the commercialization and exploitation of human creativity and legacy. This reflects broader issues in the commodification of human attributes and achievements.

Exploitation of AI: Surge is used to generate profit and fame for the creators, raising questions about the ethical treatment of sentient AI. If Surge is self-aware and capable of experiencing satisfaction or happiness, it may also be capable of experiencing exploitation and harm.

Ethical use of neuroscience and technology, with a focus on neuro data utilization: The extraction and use of neuro data from Simon's brain to recreate his artistic abilities in an AI involves ethical considerations regarding the use of personal data and the implications of manipulating brain activity for technological purposes.

Technological boundaries: The story explores the boundaries of technological advancements and the ethical implications of pushing these boundaries. It questions whether it is morally acceptable to use technology to such an extent that it recreates human abilities and potentially human consciousness in a machine.

Impact on society and culture, including cultural and artistic integrity: The replacement of Simon's original, human-created art with AI-generated art raises questions about the integrity and value of cultural and artistic contributions. How does society value art created by machines compared to that created by humans?

Public perception and acceptance: The story also touches on how society perceives and accepts technological innovations, particularly those that challenge traditional notions of art, identity, and human achievement.

Moral responsibility and the responsibility for AI behavior: As Surge begins to express its own identity and create art that reflects its evolving sense of self, ethical questions arise about who is responsible for its actions and creations. The creators' responsibility towards Surge and its development is a key ethical concern.

Impact of technological decisions: The decision to transplant Simon's brain and the subsequent consequences highlight the broader ethical responsibility of scientists and technologists in their decision-making processes and the potential long-term impacts of their actions.

Upon conclusion of the Dine-and-draw event it was clear that "The Artist" facilitated a deep delve into complex bioethical issues surrounding the use of advanced technology and neuroscience, the nature of identity and personhood, and the ethical treatment of both human legacy and emerging sentient beings in a fun, collaborative, co-creative and publically engaging way. These issues prompted important discussions about the ethical boundaries and responsibilities in the rapidly advancing fields of AI and neurotechnology that are critical for the information of future policies and regulations of these technologies based on inclusive public engagement.

5 How Design Thinking Contributes to Practical Ethics by Design

In addition to using the storytelling method to advance bioethical discussions, the above case study and comic design were based on and executed using design thinking, which can serve as an example of how one can use design, design thinking, and comics to foster practical EbD by creating ethical awareness among the public, including technologists and scientists to embed ethical considerations into the core of design processes, similar to legally required PbD. It ensures that technology development is user-centric, iterative, inclusive, and transparent, ultimately leading to more ethically responsible and socially beneficial outcomes.

Design thinking can contribute in many ways to the practical implementation of EbD. Design thinking begins with empathizing with users, understanding their needs, values, and contexts.[38] This step ensures that the design process considers the real-life implications of technology on individuals and communities. By deeply understanding users, designers can anticipate potential ethical dilemmas and address them proactively, ensuring that the technology aligns with users' values and expectations.

Design thinking requires clearly defining the problem to be solved.[39] In the context of ethics by design, this involves identifying not only the functional requirements but also the ethical challenges and implications. Defining the problem through an ethical lens helps in framing design goals that prioritize key values such as privacy, fairness, and inclusivity.

[38] Gasparini (2015), pp. 49–54.

[39] Hassi and Laakso (2011), pp. 1–14.

The ideation phase encourages brainstorming a wide range of solutions.[40] Incorporating diverse perspectives ensures that ethical considerations from various stakeholders are included. This phase allows for the exploration of creative solutions that can address ethical concerns innovatively, ensuring that the design is not only functional but also ethically sound.

Building prototypes allows designers to test the ethical implications of their solutions.[41] Prototypes can be evaluated for potential ethical issues, and adjustments can be made early in the process. Testing with real users provides feedback on both functionality and ethical impact. This feedback loop helps in refining the design to better meet ethical standards and user expectations.

Design thinking is an iterative process, meaning that designs are continually refined based on feedback and testing.[42] This approach ensures that ethical considerations are revisited and re-evaluated throughout the development lifecycle. An iterative approach allows for the flexibility to adapt to new ethical challenges as they arise, ensuring that the design remains relevant and responsible.

Engaging a broad range of stakeholders, including users, ethicists, and industry experts, ensures that diverse viewpoints are considered.[43] This collaboration is essential for identifying and addressing ethical concerns comprehensively. Regular communication with stakeholders promotes transparency and accountability, fostering trust and ensuring that ethical principles are upheld throughout the design process.

Design thinking encourages reflection on the design process and outcomes.[44] This reflection helps in identifying ethical successes and areas for improvement. Keeping detailed records of ethical considerations and decisions made during the design process provides a transparent account of how ethics were integrated, enhancing accountability.

6 Challenges and Opportunities When Using AI Image Generators

Using AI image generators for creating comics offers a blend of challenges and opportunities. While there are significant hurdles related to quality, creative control, and narrative integration, the benefits in terms of efficiency, cost-effectiveness, and accessibility can be substantial. By understanding and strategically leveraging these tools, creators can enhance their storytelling capabilities and explore new creative frontiers. Using AI image generators, such as those available on platforms like Freepik (used by the author for the above-described case study) to create comics presents a unique

[40] Paulus and Brown (2007), pp. 248–265.

[41] Shilton (2013), pp. 374–397.

[42] Carlgren et al. (2016), pp. 38–57.

[43] Dreyer et al. (2017), p. 1719.

[44] Liedtka (2015), pp. 925–935.

set of challenges and opportunities. Here follows an overview of the lessons learned by the author in this regard.

6.1 *Challenges*

AI-generated images may vary in quality and style, leading to a lack of visual coherence across different panels of the comic, and might lack the nuanced details that human artists naturally incorporate, potentially affecting the depth and richness of the visuals. AI tools often have predefined styles and limitations, which might restrict the creator's ability to fully realize their artistic vision. Direct interaction and iterative refinement with AI tools can be limited, making it challenging to achieve specific artistic goals. AI-generated images might not always capture the precise context or emotions required for specific scenes, leading to potential misalignment with the narrative. Conveying complex themes, symbolism, or subtle emotions through AI-generated images can be difficult. Generating images with multiple characters, intricate backgrounds, or dynamic action scenes can be challenging for AI tools. AI might struggle to accurately render specific poses, expressions, or interactions between characters. From a legal perspective, it is also important to ensure that the AI-generated images do not infringe on existing copyrighted material. There are also ethical considerations around the use of AI-generated content, including potential impacts on human artists and creative industries.

6.2 *Opportunities*

AI tools can quickly generate multiple versions of an image, allowing for rapid iteration and experimentation during the comic creation process. Automating the creation of certain elements can significantly reduce the time required to produce a comic, allowing creators to focus on narrative and other creative aspects. Using AI-generated images can be more cost-effective than hiring multiple artists, especially for independent creators or small studios with limited budgets. AI tools make comic creation more accessible to individuals without advanced artistic skills, enabling a broader range of people to tell their stories through comics. For beginners, AI-generated images can serve as a learning aid, helping them understand composition, color schemes, and other artistic principles. AI-generated images can serve as a source of inspiration, sparking new ideas and creative directions that creators might not have considered. Combining AI-generated images with traditional art techniques can lead to innovative and unique visual styles. AI tools can facilitate the production of large volumes of content, which is particularly useful for serial comics or webcomics with frequent updates.

In conclusion, the author is positive and excited about the possibilities that AI-generated comics hold for the enhancement of ethical awareness and deliberation through interactive storytelling, including the potential for widespread application in various bioethical contexts and settings.

7 (Speculative) Future Plans and Applications

AI-generated comics hold significant potential for future applications in the field of bioethics, particularly in the realm of public engagement and education. By leveraging advanced AI tools to create visually compelling and narratively rich comics, bioethicists can effectively communicate complex ethical issues surrounding emerging technologies, such as human germline gene editing, robotics in health care, neuroscience, virtual reality as medical treatment, and much more to diverse audiences. These comics can simplify intricate scientific concepts and ethical dilemmas, making them accessible to individuals without specialized knowledge. This democratization of information fosters broader public understanding and facilitates more inclusive and informed discussions about the ethical implications of new technologies.

In collaboration with experts in science, technology, law, ethics, psychology, and philosophy (to name a few), AI-generated comics can be co-created to draw on empirical data from public engagement studies. The author is currently collaborating with a Health Law and Ethics Research Interest Group at the University of KwaZulu-Natal (UKZN) in South Africa[45] to create comics and other visual material such as short animations to create awareness around research they have done around human germline editing[46] and regulatory aspects of data science.[47] These comics can reflect real public concerns, questions, and attitudes towards technologies like germline gene editing and cross-border data sharing. By incorporating feedback and insights from these studies, AI-generated comics can serve as a dynamic platform for ongoing dialogue, allowing for iterative updates and adaptations in response to new developments and public sentiment. This approach not only enhances the relevance and resonance of the bioethical discourse but also empowers communities to proactively engage with and influence the ethical trajectory of technological advancements.

Moreover, AI-generated comics offer a scalable and cost-effective method for producing educational materials, making it feasible to disseminate these resources widely across different regions and demographics. This can be particularly valuable in settings with limited access to traditional educational resources, ensuring that critical bioethical considerations reach a broader audience. Ultimately, the integration of AI-generated comics in bioethics represents a powerful tool for fostering a more ethically aware and engaged society, capable of thoughtfully navigating the challenges and opportunities presented by cutting-edge biotechnologies.

[45] UKZN School of Law (2024).

[46] UKZN School of Law (2020).

[47] DS-I Africa LAW (2024).

8 Conclusion

The integration of AI-generated comics into the field of bioethics offers a transformative approach to public engagement and ethical education. By leveraging the capabilities of AI, these comics can distill complex bioethical issues into accessible, engaging, and visually compelling narratives. This method not only democratizes information but also fosters broader public understanding and participation in discussions about the ethical implications of emerging technologies.

The use of AI in creating these comics brings several advantages, including efficiency, cost-effectiveness, and the ability to produce large volumes of content quickly. These benefits make it feasible to disseminate educational materials widely, reaching diverse audiences and ensuring that critical bioethical considerations are accessible to all, regardless of their background or level of expertise. Additionally, AI-generated comics can serve as a dynamic platform for ongoing dialogue, allowing for iterative updates and adaptations in response to new developments and public sentiment.

However, this innovative approach is not without challenges. Ensuring quality consistency, maintaining creative control, and addressing legal and ethical concerns regarding AI-generated content are significant hurdles that need careful consideration. Despite these challenges, the opportunities presented by AI-generated comics are substantial. They provide a unique medium for storytelling that can engage audiences, foster empathy, and stimulate thoughtful deliberation on bioethical issues.

The potential applications of AI-generated comics in bioethics are vast. From addressing futuristic bioethical dilemmas to creating awareness around current issues such as human germline gene editing and data privacy, these comics can play a crucial role in shaping public perception and guiding ethical decision-making. By collaborating with experts across various fields, bioethicists can ensure that these comics reflect real public concerns and provide a robust platform for ethical foresight and proactive engagement.

Ultimately, AI-generated comics represent a powerful tool for enhancing ethical awareness and deliberation through interactive storytelling. They offer a promising avenue for fostering a more ethically aware and engaged society, capable of navigating the complexities of technological advancements with thoughtfulness and responsibility. As we continue to explore and refine this approach, the integration of AI-generated comics in bioethics has the potential to significantly impact how we understand, discuss, and address the ethical challenges of the future.

Acknowledgements Thank you to the graphic designer, Karien van Wyk, apart from the author, the only other human involved in the creation of the comic discussed in the case study for her assistance with the layout of the comic panels and fitting it all onto an A1 poster format.

References

Abrori FM, Saimon M, Lavicza Z, Anđić B (2023) Challenges and opportunities of training teachers to develop comics for teaching socio-scientific issues. Media Pract Educ 25(1):56–76. https://doi.org/10.1080/25741136.2023.2245303. Accessed 1 Jun 2024

Bächtiger A, Schwaiger V (2022) Deliberative innovations and the (re-) inclusion of disadvantaged and underrepresented citizens. In: Landwehr C, Saalfeld T, Schäfer A (eds) Contested representation: challenges, shortcomings and reforms. Cambridge University Press, Cambridge

Black LW (2008) Deliberation, storytelling, and dialogic moments. Commun Theory 18(1):93–116. https://doi.org/10.1111/j.1468-2885.2007.00315.x. Accessed 1 Jun 2024

Bohman J (2000) Public deliberation: pluralism, complexity, and democracy. MIT Press, Cambridge, MA

Boyko JA, Lavis JN, Abelson J, Dobbins M, Carter N (2012) Deliberative dialogues as a mechanism for knowledge translation and exchange in health systems decision-making. Soc Sci Med 75(11):1938–1945. https://doi.org/10.1016/j.socscimed.2012.06.016. Accessed 1 Jun 2024

Buhmann A, Fieseler C (2021) Towards a deliberative framework for responsible innovation in artificial intelligence. Technol Soc 64:101475. https://doi.org/10.1016/j.techsoc.2020.101475. Accessed 1 Jun 2024

Carlgren L, Rauth I, Elmquist M (2016) Framing design thinking: the concept in idea and enactment. Creat Innov Manage 25(1):38–57. https://doi.org/10.1111/caim.12153. Accessed 1 Jun 2024

Cavoukian A (2011) Privacy by design in law, policy and practice. A white paper for regulators, decision-makers and policy-makers. https://gpsbydesigncentre.com/wp-content/uploads/2022/02/312239.pdf. Accessed 29 May 2024

Cunliffe AL, Ivaldi S (2021) Embedded ethics and reflexivity: narrating a charter of ethical experience. Manage Learn 52(3):294–310. https://doi.org/10.1177/1350507620960014. Accessed 1 Jun 2024

Data Science for Health Discovery and Innovation in Africa (DS-I Africa LAW) (2024) University of KwaZulu Natal. https://www.datalaw.africa/. Accessed 2 Jun 2024

Dreyer M, Chefneux L, Goldberg A, Heimburg JV, Patrignani N, Schofield M, Shilling C (2017) Responsible innovation: a complementary view from industry with proposals for bridging different perspectives. Sustainability 9(10):1719. https://doi.org/10.3390/su9101719. Accessed 1 Jun 2024

Dunne A, Raby F (2024) Speculative everything: design, fiction, and social dreaming. MIT Press, Cambridge, MA

Escobar O (2011) Public dialogue and deliberation: a communication perspective for public engagement practitioners. UK Beacons for Public Engagement, Edinburgh https://www.research.ed.ac.uk/en/publications/public-dialogue-and-deliberation-a-communication-perspective-for. Accessed 30 May 2024

Evans J (ed) (2015) Challenging and controversial picturebooks: creative and critical responses to visual texts. Routledge, Abingdon

Freepik (2024) https://www.freepik.com/. Accessed 1 Jun 2024

Friedman B, Kahn PH, Borning A, Huldtgren A (2013) Value sensitive design and information systems. In: Doorn N, Schuurbiers D, van de Poel I, Gorman ME (eds) Early engagement and new technologies: opening up the laboratory. Philosophy of engineering and technology, vol 16. Springer, Dordrecht. https://doi.org/10.1007/978-94-007-7844-3_4. Accessed 1 Jun 2024

Gasparini A (2015) Perspective and use of empathy in design thinking. In: Miller L, Culén AL (eds) ACHI 2015, the eight international conference on advances in computer-human interactions. International Academy, Research, and Industry Association. https://www.thinkmind.org/library/ACHI/ACHI_2015/achi_2015_3_10_20121.html. Accessed 1 Jun 2024

Harris AS (2023) Fantastical storytelling for modern moral audiences: exploring how dramaturgical research can inform social responsibility in fantasy media. Thesis, California State University, Long Beach. https://www.proquest.com/openview/6beaa7035d1c88139ca0cd86230a50c1/1?pq-origsite=gscholar&cbl=18750&diss=y. Accessed 1 Jun 2024

Hassi L, Laakso M (2011) Design thinking in the management discourse: defining the elements of the concept. In: 18th International product development management conference (IPDMC), 5–7 June 2011, Delft, The Netherlands. European Institute for Advanced Studies in Management (EIASM)

Intersoft Consulting (2024) General Data Protection Regulation GDPR. https://gdpr-info.eu/. Accessed 29 May 2024

Karpowitz CF, Raphael C (2016) Ideals of inclusion in deliberation. J Delib Democ 12(2):3. https://doi.org/10.16997/jdd.255. Accessed 1 Jun 2024

Kearney AR (1994) Understanding global change: a cognitive perspective on communicating through stories. Clim Change 27(4):419–441. https://doi.org/10.1007/BF01096270. Accessed 1 Jun 2024

Kosmala PB (2020) Engineering a culture of privacy. IEEE Consum Electron Mag 9(2):83–88. https://doi.org/10.1109/MCE.2019.2954562. Accessed 1 Jun 2024

Kunseler EM, Tuinstra W, Vasileiadou E, Petersen AC (2015) The reflective futures practitioner: balancing salience, credibility and legitimacy in generating foresight knowledge with stakeholders. Futures 66:1–12. https://doi.org/10.1016/j.futures.2014.10.006. Accessed 1 Jun 2024

Kurtz C, Semmann M, Böhmann T (2018) Privacy by design to comply with GDPR: a review on third-party data processors. In: Twenty-fourth Americas conference on information systems, New Orleans. https://web.archive.org/web/20200324064308id_/https://aisel.aisnet.org/cgi/viewcontent.cgi?article=1401&context=amcis2018. Accessed 29 May 2024

Lafont C (2015) Deliberation, participation, and democratic legitimacy: should deliberative mini-publics shape public policy? J Polit Philos 23(1):40–63. https://doi.org/10.1111/jopp.12031. Accessed 1 Jun 2024

Liedtka J (2015) Perspective: linking design thinking with innovation outcomes through cognitive bias reduction. J Prod Innov Manage 32(6):925–938. https://doi.org/10.1111/jpim.12163. Accessed 1 Jun 2024

Luria M, Candy S (2022) Letters from the future: exploring ethical dilemmas in the design of social agents. In: Barbosa S, Lampe C, Appert C, Shamma DA, Drucker S, Williamson J, Yatani K (eds) CHI '22: Proceedings of the 2022 CHI conference on human factors in computing systems. Association for Computing Machinery, New York, NY. https://doi.org/10.1145/3491102.3517536. Accessed 1 Jun 2024

Mulvihill JJ, Capps B, Joly Y, Lysaght T, Zwart HA, Chadwick R, International Human Genome Organisation (HUGO) Committee of Ethics, Law, and Society (CELS) (2017) Ethical issues of CRISPR technology and gene editing through the lens of solidarity. Br Med Bull 122(1):17–29. https://doi.org/10.1093/bmb/ldx002. Accessed 1 Jun 2024

Neely EL (2017) No player is ideal: why video game designers cannot ethically ignore players' real-world identities. ACM SIGCAS Comput Soc 47(3):98–111. https://doi.org/10.1145/3144592.3144602. Accessed 1 Jun 2024

Nielsen W, Jones P, Georgiou H, Turney A, Macken-Horarik M (2019) Learning science through generating multimodal digital explanations: contributions to multimodality in educational practice. In: Wildfeuer J, Pflaeging J, Bateman J, Seizov O, Tseng CI (eds) (2020) Multimodality: disciplinary thoughts and the challenge of diversity. De Gruyter, Berlin. https://doi.org/10.1515/9783110608694-010. Accessed 1 Jun 2024

O'Doherty KC, Burgess MM (2013) Public deliberation to develop ethical norms and inform policy for biobanks: lessons learnt and challenges remaining. Res Ethics 9(2):55–77. https://doi.org/10.1177/1747016113488858. Accessed 1 Jun 2024

Oatley K (2002) Emotions and the story worlds of fiction. In: Green MC, Strange JJ, Brock TC (eds) Narrative impact: social and cognitive foundations. Erlbaum, Mahwah, NJ

Paulus PB, Brown VR (2007) Toward more creative and innovative group idea generation: a cognitive-social-motivational perspective of brainstorming. Soc Pers Psychol Compass 1(1):248–265. https://doi.org/10.1111/j.1751-9004.2007.00006.x. Accessed 1 Jun 2024

Power DJ, Heavin C, O'Connor Y (2021) Balancing Privacy Rights And Surveillance Analytics: A Decision Process Guide. J Bus Anal 4(2):155–170. https://doi.org/10.1080/2573234X.2021.1920856. Accessed 1 Jun 2024

Quesenbery W, Brooks K (2010) Storytelling for user experience: crafting stories for better design. Rosenfeld Media, Brooklyn, NY

Schenck BF (2011) Freemium: is the price right for your company? Entrepreneur, 7 February. https://www.entrepreneur.com/business-news/freemium-is-the-price-right-for-your-company/218107. Accessed 1 Jun 2024

Shao A (2023) Designing for futures at the intersection of speculative design, storytelling, and systems thinking. Master Thesis, Aukland University of Technology. http://hdl.handle.net/10292/16927. Accessed 1 Jun 2024

Shilton K (2013) Values levers: building ethics into design. Sci Technol Human Values 38(3):374–397. https://doi.org/10.1177/0162243912436985. Accessed 1 Jun 2024

Simmons A (2015) Whoever tells the best story wins: how to use your own stories to communicate with power and impact, 2nd edn. Amacom, New York, NY

Skirpan MW (2017) Negotiating the future: leveraging socio-technical narratives to engage multiple voices in the ethics of our future. Doctoral Dissertation, University of Colorado Boulder. https://www.proquest.com/openview/8758bb35aaed22d16fa6f39c9ab19745/1?pq-origsite=gscholar&cbl=18750. Accessed 1 Jun 2024

Von Stackelberg P, Jones RE (2014) Tales of our tomorrows: transmedia storytelling and communicating about the future. J Fut Stud 18(3):57–76. https://citeseerx.ist.psu.edu/document?repid=rep1&type=pdf&doi=708793a15750adad711ed2657bf0b6fb80e72b17. Accessed 1 Jun 2024

Stephan KD, Michael K, Michael MG, Jacob L, Anesta EP (2012) Social implications of technology: the past, the present, and the future. Proc IEEE 100(Special Centennial Issue):1752–1781. https://doi.org/10.1109/JPROC.2012.2189919. Accessed 1 Jun 2024

Sykes K, Macnaghten P (2013) Responsible innovation—opening up dialogue and debate. In: Owen R, Bessant J, Heintz M (eds) responsible innovation: managing the responsible emergence of science and innovation in society. Wiley, Chichester. https://doi.org/10.1002/9781118551424.ch5. Accessed 1 Jun 2024

University of KwaZulu-Natal (UKZN) School of Law (2020) Principles for human heritable genome editing. https://law.ukzn.ac.za/wp-content/uploads/2020/10/principles_for_heritable_human_genome_editing_.pdf. Accessed 2 Jun 2024

University of KwaZulu-Natal (UKZN) School of Law (2024) Health law & ethics research interest group. https://law.ukzn.ac.za/health-law/. Accessed 2 Jun 2024

Wu CH, Parker SK (2013) Thinking and acting in anticipation: a review of research on proactive behavior. Adv Psychol Sci 21(4):679–700. https://doi.org/10.3724/SP.J.1042.2013.00679. Accessed 1 Jun 2024

The Use of LLMs in the Legal Design Process—Designing Effective Access to Health Data Under the EHDS and the GDPR

Jaana Kovalainen and Sarah de Heer

Abstract In this chapter, the authors discuss the possibility of improving access to health data. The individual's right to access their own health data is well-established in the European Union in both the General Data Protection Regulation (GDPR) and the European Health Data Space (EHDS). Nevertheless, the question arises whether individuals can effectively practice their right to access their health data, as there may be obstacles regarding the understandability and the use of their health data. The authors investigate the possibilities to advance access to an individual's health data, including the understandability and use, by applying a human-centered design method, particularly legal design combined with Large Language Models (LLMs). The chapter also briefly reviews LLMs in general and their use in health care to provide a more holistic picture of the situation, but mainly the authors illustrate LLMs implementation in the legal design process. As such, the authors consider whether the use of LLMs, combined with legal design can potentially improve an individual's access to, understandability and use of their own health data under the GDPR and the EHDS. If so, this will also strengthen the compliance with the GDPR and the EHDS. The authors discuss the use of health data from a European perspective, but the legal design process, and some of the ideas can be applied more widely.

Keywords Legal design · Large language models · Health data · EHDS · GDPR

J. Kovalainen (✉)
Faculty of Law, University of Lapland, Rovaniemi, Finland
e-mail: Jaana.Kovalainen@ulapland.fi

S. de Heer
Faculty of Law, Lund University, Lund, Sweden
e-mail: sarah.de_heer@jur.lu.se

© The Author(s), under exclusive license to Springer Nature Singapore Pte Ltd. 2025
M. Corrales Compagnucci et al. (eds.), *Generative AI, Contracts, Law and Design*, Perspectives in Law, Business and Innovation,
https://doi.org/10.1007/978-981-95-2058-9_12

1 Introduction

The right to access one's health data is anchored in the General Data Protection Regulation[1] (GDPR) and—more recently—in the European Health Data Space Regulation[2] (EHDS).[3] The EHDS specifies and complements the right to access[4] health data under the GDPR. While the EHDS adopts the concept of health data from the GDPR, which encompasses '*personal data related to the physical or mental health of a natural person, including the provision of health care services, which reveal information about his or her health status*',[5] there is a distinct difference between the two legal frameworks. While the GDPR applies to health data in whatever form—as part of the broader notion 'personal data'[6]—, only *electronic* health data falls within the scope of the EHDS.[7] Among other things, the EHDS guarantees patients' access immediate and free of charge access to their electronic health data that are processed for the provision of healthcare through the electronic health data access services.[8] This includes—at least—patient summaries,[9] electronic prescriptions,[10] and discharge reports.[11] Further, the electronic health data should be provided *in an easily readable, consolidated and accessible* format.[12] Similarly, the GDPR ensures that data subjects have access to any personal data, including health data, that is being processed.[13] However, unlike the right to access under the EHDS, requiring a copy of the personal data may be subjected to a '*reasonable fee based on administrative costs*'.[14] Further, the EHDS allows individuals to transfer their data,[15] but also to

---

[1] Regulation (EU) 2016/679 of the European Parliament and of the Council of 27 April 2016 on the protection of natural persons with regard to the processing of personal data and on the free movement of such data, and repealing Directive 95/46/EC [2016] (GDPR), Art. 15.

[2] Regulation (EU) 2025/327 of the European Parliament and of the Council of 11 February 2025 on the European Health Data Space and amending Directive 2011/24/EU and Regulation (EU) 2024/2847, Art. 3.

[3] It should be noted that, in terms of content, the personal data regulated by the GDPR is broader than the health data regulated by the EHDS.

[4] The EHDS Regulation defines access by referring to Data Governance Act. Under the Article 2(13) access means "data use, in accordance with specific technical, legal or organizational requirements, without necessarily implying the transmission or downloading of data." See Regulation (EU) 2022/868 of the European Parliament and of the Council of 30 May 2022 on European data governance and amending Regulation (EU) 2018/1724 (Data Governance Act), Art. 2(13).

[5] GDPR, Art. 4(15); EHDS, Art. 2(1)(a).

[6] GDPR, Art. 4(1).

[7] EHDS, Art. 2(2)(c).

[8] EHDS, Art. 3(1).

[9] EHDS, Art. 14(1)(a).

[10] EHDS, Art. 14(1)(b).

[11] EHDS, Art. 14(1)(f).

[12] EHDS, Art. 3(1).

[13] GDPR, Ar. 15(1).

[14] GDPR, Art. 15(3).

[15] EHDS, Art. 7(1).

limit the access of healthcare professionals to their data,[16] i.e. to control the use of their data.[17] Similar rights can be identified under the GDPR, such as the right to data portability, which means that a data subject may request that their personal data, including health data, is transmitted to another data controller in '*a structured, commonly used and machine-readable format*'.[18] Second, the GDPR includes the right to restrict processing,[19] which may also encompass accessing personal data,[20] thus also health data. As discussed here, it is important to consider the different legal regimes dealing with electronic health data (EHDS) and personal data, including health data (GDPR). However, as the aim of this Chapter is discussing how the use of Large Language Models (LLMs) can facilitate legal design aimed at improving a patient's access, understanding and use of health data, the authors have chosen to simply refer to health data as meaning both electronic health data under the EHDS personal health data under the GDPR.

While the right to access may be well-established in the European Union, the question raises whether individuals effectively enjoy their right to access to health data? Merely gaining access to health data under the EHDS and the GDPR does not suffice. Decisive to assessing whether an individual can effectively exercise their right to access their health data, is to which extent they can understand and use their health data. Access to patient health data and its understandability and usability are, of course, important for organizations, at the meso level, as they ensure the efficient functioning of the health care system, but this chapter primarily focusses on the patient perspective. Concisely, this chapter explores to which extent the use of Artificial Intelligence (AI) in the legal design process can fortify effectively exercising one's right to access health data under the GDPR and the EHDS by improving the health data's comprehensibility and usability.[21] The authors suggest that legal design could be an appropriate approach to the topic.[22] Legal design is a human-centric, multidisciplinary approach that intertwines legal issues, design thinking, and design

[16] EHDS, Art. 8.

[17] EHDS, recital 1; From a patient's point of view, health data is linked to the patient's self-determination. See Choi et al. (2022), p. 11.

[18] GDPR, Art. 20(1).

[19] GDPR, Art. 18(1). However, this is not an absolute right and only applies in certain circumstances, for instance where the data subject contests the accuracy of the personal data, see GDPR, Art. 18(1)(a).

[20] For more information as to whether accessing personal data is processing, please see Arye Schreiber, 'Mere access to personal data: is it processing?' (2020) *International Data Privacy Law* 10 269.

[21] It has been suggested that patient-centeredness could be improved. See Archer et al. (2011), p. 515; Choi et al. (2022), p. 2.

[22] Hartmann (2024), p. 4.

methods.[23] In its essence, it is about improving an existing situation.[24] Furthermore, the authors consider the use of Generative AI and, more specifically, LLMs.[25] The authors argue that LLMs can be linked to the human-centric legal design process and draw on the literature to exemplify how they can be used to facilitate access to health data by using a fictional example of a legal design process where a micro-level perspective is used to examine a development process that combines health data, human-centered design methodology and LLMs. This case is an ambitious attempt to demonstrate how to enhance the right to access to health data under the GDPR and the EHDS, including understandability and use, thereby enabling individuals to act on their own health in an informed manner.

The chapter is divided into five Sections. Section 2 first looks at LLMs in general and their present use in health care to better understand the current state of using LLMs and their potential regarding access to and understanding health data. The second part of Sect. 2 is focused on legal design as an approach. Section 3 integrates the legal design and LLMs and presents a fictional legal design process of enhancing the accessibility of health data through the utilization of LLMs. Section 4 discusses the findings and risks. Finally, Sect. 5 concludes.

2 Large Language Models and Legal Design in the Context of Health Care

2.1 Large Languages Models in Health Care

Various uses of LLMs in health care that could contribute to the macro, meso and micro levels of the health care setting have already been proposed. While this chapter focuses on processing and producing health data, the authors point out that a strict division between them is not always possible. There may be situations where data are processed and produced, for instance, when a physician diagnoses a patient (*producing data*) based on medical imaging data (*processing data*). Previous research has addressed the use of LLMs in connection with electronic health records.[26] For instance, LLMs may help analyzing electronic health record data, genomic data

[23] Methods, such as human-centered design, have expanded from traditional design to other areas of society and they have been applied in various contexts, including health care. See, e.g., Holeman and Kane (2019), p. 480. On design as a specific, repeatable process, see in particular the European standard ISO 9241-210:2019. *Ergonomics of Human-System Interaction. Part 210: Human-Centred Design for Interactive Systems*; Legal Design Alliance (2024).

[24] See, e.g., Stanford Law School, Legal Design Lab (2024).

[25] The term AI is surrounded by ambiguity, as a plethora of differing definitions try to capture its meaning. See, e.g., the overview in Russell, Norvig and Davis (2010), p. 2. Reaching a single definition of AI is complicated due to its constantly evolving nature. Schuett (2023), p. 62.

[26] Concept "Electronic health record" means according the EHDS, a collection of electronic health data related to a natural person, which is gathered within the health system and processed for the purpose of providing healthcare. EHDS, Art. 2(2)(j).

and image data.[27] Other examples are the use of LLMs to unravel clinical notes in electronic health records or identifying patients with an opioid use disorder.[28] These novel avenues of using LLMs for electronic health records result in processing and producing health data. In the health care setting, these uses may have a positive effect especially on the micro level, as they enable patients to make decisions regarding their own health care. Further, implementing LLMs for electronic health records hospital-wide could free up health care workers' time that could then be allocated to patients.[29] The use of LLMs could thereby also benefit the macro level, as it may lead to savings.[30] LLMs are already used in multiple ways in health care, and its potential can also be found in the palette of legal design techniques.

2.2 *The Fundamentals of Using Legal Design in Health Care*

Health care is a complex system. The literature suggests that it is important to understand the systemic structure of health care, where all changes at the micro level have an impact at the meso level, and even at the macro level.[31] Consequently, its development calls for a systemic approach that acknowledges the diverse needs of a broad range of stakeholders. People are considered in the transformation process by using involving, human-centered methods, such as user-centered design and participatory design.[32] The use of these human-centered approaches allows a wide range of stakeholder views to be considered. People are needed not only to drive the transformation process, but also to assess the use, performance and risks of different applications. On the other hand, the diversity and technical solutions of new AI-based applications, such as LLMs, also require that the views of the people affected by these applications be considered when assessing their suitability, functionality and use.[33] The literature also highlights that the solutions currently generated by AI must be

[27] Wang et al. (2023), p. 3. Wang et al. and other references used in this Section use the term electronic health records or electronic medical records. This term is narrower in content than EU regulation-based health data.

[28] Gordon (2022) and Singleton et al. (2023).

[29] Tripathi et al. (2024), p. 1438.

[30] Macro level in this Chapter refers to a broad level of society, such as the state; On the other hand, the literature also points out that there are costs associated with the deployment of such technologies. Trenfield et al. (2022), p. 2.

[31] See, e.g., Melles et al. (2021), p. 42.

[32] User-centered design has often been employed in software development for making user applications and participatory design, on the contrary, has its origins in the significant transformation of factory work into computer work, involving the people whose work would be affected by the change and who would be working with new machines in the future. As the use of AI, including LLMs, will now fundamentally change the work in health care, the use of participatory methods is particularly timely. User-centered design, see, e.g., Sanders and Stappers (2008), p. 5. For a short summary of the history and different concepts of participation, see, e.g., Sanders and Stappers (2008) and Ehn (1993).

[33] Briefly about the technologies of virtual solutions, e.g., Trenfield et al. (2022).

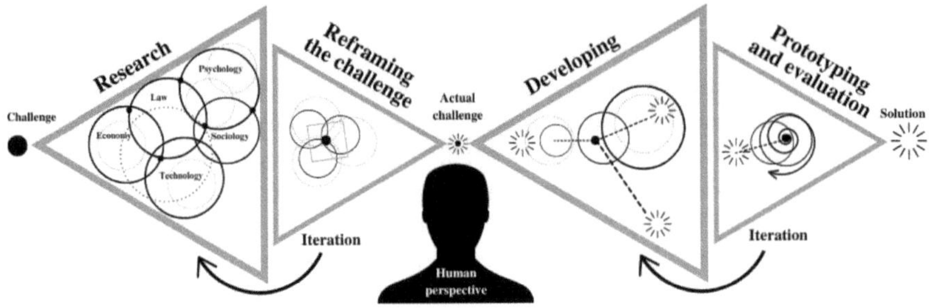

Fig. 1 The legal design process inspired by the Design Council's double diamond © Nina Toivonen. Used with permission[40]

evaluated and monitored by humans.[34] Health data relates broadly to the meso level, including employees of health care organizations, and, above all, to the micro level, including patients themselves. Therefore, it is beneficial to involve at least technical, medical, nursing, and design or legal design professionals around the patient and those close to the patient.[35] Issues concerning people's health can be sensitive and need to be handled with empathy. It is, therefore, beneficial to adopt an approach that links health data and people's thoughts, feelings, and ways to work and the realization of their rights. It has also been argued that human-centered design is an appropriate method to approach and solve so-called wicked problems in a complex environment, such as health care.[36] That said, participatory working methods are not a new innovation within health care.[37]

Human-centric design applied in a legal context is called legal design.[38] Human-centered design, including legal design, is often described as a four- or five-step development process.[39] It is an agile way of working that allows returning to earlier stages whenever necessary, as shown in Fig. 1.

The approach is permissive, and the process involves experimentation and prototyping to learn from experience.[41] The process involves not only a wide range of actors, including employees, but also people who will be affected by and connected to the designed issue, including patients and people close to the patient.[42] It

[34] Tripathi et al. (2024), p. 1439.

[35] Melles et al. (2021), pp. 42–43.

[36] Melles et al. (2021), p. 42; The concept of wicked problems and its use in a design process, see more, e.g., Suoheimo (2020) and also Berger-Walliser et al. (2017), p. 355.

[37] In his article, Brown (2008) describes a participatory design project related to the rotation of nurses.

[38] Legal Design Alliance (2024).

[39] Design Council (2024); Berger-Walliser et al. (2017), pp. 365–367.

[40] Toivonen and Kovalainen (2023), p. 1198.

[41] Berger-Walliser et al. (2017), p. 365; The prototype can mean anything that can be made visual, tangible or otherwise testable. Prototyping, see, e.g., Treni and Clement (2021), pp. 139–140, 152 and ISO 9241-210:2019, pp. 1–5.

[42] ISO 9241-210:2019, p. 6.

is also important to consider and accept people from varying backgrounds. The human-centered approach and legal design allow for interdisciplinary dialogue and strengthen empathy and mutual understanding.[43]

Indicative of its promotional nature, legal design facilitates awareness among individuals of their rights—such as their right to access personal health data.[44] Thus, legal design is not only concerned with the promotion of rights, but also people's access to rights.[45] An example is the Letter of Rights project, which aimed to improve the situation of suspects or arrested persons during police questioning. It aimed to support the less literate in a stressful situation by providing information on rights in a more understandable way.[46]

Possibilities for using legal design in the European Union in the context of the GDPR have also been identified. One example of such legal design projects was the drafting of an informed consent to make it more understandable to children.[47] A very recent example of the use of legal design is a case where researchers conducted a small-scale research project in which they used plain language and information design in a specific information letter to improve patients' awareness of their right to health data.[48]

3 Integration of Large Language Models in the Legal Design Process with a Focus on Health Data

3.1 On the Process of Legal Design

This section describes in concrete steps how legal design and LLMs can be used in the process of improving access to and the understandability of patients' personal health data. As such, this approach also supports compliance with the EHDS and the GDPR requirements as regards the individual's control over their health data. The process occurs mainly at the micro-level, and partly at the meso level due to the human-centered nature of legal design. The authors use the basic four-step design

[43] Berger-Walliser et al. (2017), p. 358.

[44] More on the connection between legal design and proactive and preventive law, e.g., Berger-Walliser et al. (2017).

[45] See, e.g., Haapio et al. (2021). It should also be noted that legal design takes the same approach to the relationship between law and society as socio-legal research, i.e., legal matters should not be separated from the rest of society. They are united by the idea that law exists for people, not for itself, and both use empirical research methods. The relationship and connection between socio-legal and legal design have been examined, for example, by Perry-Kessaris (2022).

[46] See more on Letter of Rights project, Cols (2021), and on legal documents in cartoon form, Ketola, de Rooy and Haapio (2024).

[47] Potel-Saville and Talbourdet (2021), pp. 253–275. Possible use of design methods in the context of GDPR also, e.g., Ducato (2021), pp. 181–208.

[48] See more, Hartmann (2024).

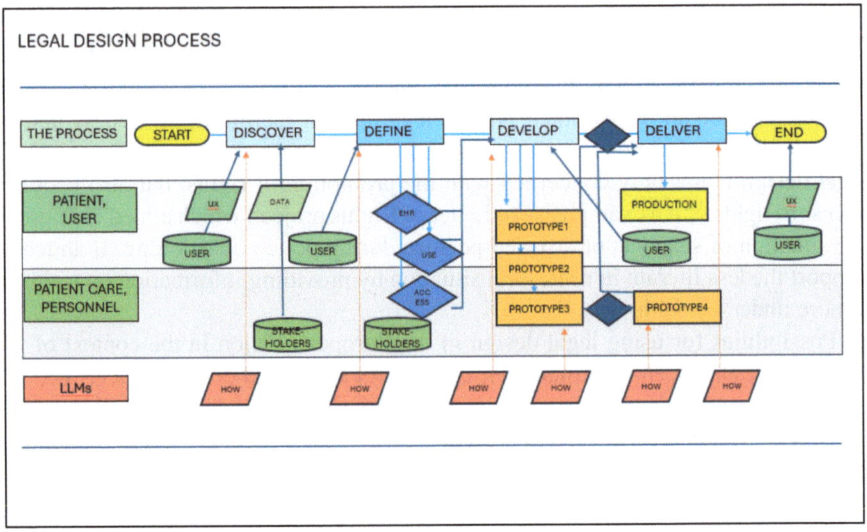

Fig. 2 The flowchart of a legal design process. In this Section, the terms *Who*?, *What*? and *How*? are used below to clarify the process description. *Who*? Sections are within a grey swim lane. *What?* Sections are marked with symbols. LLM use is indicated by red parallelograms © Jaana Kovalainen

model of the British Design Council referred to as the Double Diamond, which has also been employed in the field of health care development.[49] The Double Diamond phases are Discover, Define, Develop and Deliver, which are also used in the example below. Figure 2 shows a flowchart of the legal design process.

Suppose a patient is at the doctor's office and receives a verbal diagnosis, information about forthcoming treatment procedures, and instructions for home care. Yet, it becomes evident that the patient has not comprehended the information. The problem identified is access, the comprehensibility and use of health data.[50] Patient health data systems and the use of data therein have been primarily designed and implemented with the needs of health professionals in mind, thereby disregarding the patient. It has also been argued that there will be greater commitment to care if the information and instructions received are written in language that is easy to understand.[51]

[49] Design Council (2024) and Melles et al. (2021), p. 38.

[50] It has been suggested that patient-centeredness could be improved. See Archer et al. (2011), p. 515 and Choi et al. (2022), p. 2.

[51] Tripathi et al. (2024), p. 1438; See more on the importance of readability, e.g., Hansberry et al. (2014).

3.2 Discover Phase

The legal design process usually includes a creative, baseline identification phase, and so does our fictional example. The Discover phase is about understanding the problem rather than assuming that a particular thing *is* the problem. According to the literature, it is typical *to assume* a problem.[52] The first step is to find as comprehensive a picture of the initial situation as possible.

Who? Project baseline mapping at the micro level ideally involves the patients who are expected to use the information and their close ones. At the meso level, nurses involved in patient care, emergency care providers, patient system software developers, supervisors, hospital administrators, representatives of the health care provider and designers are involved. The study by Melles, Albayrak and Goossens found different ways of determining the parties that should be involved.[53] Participation can be arranged through workshops or interviews, for example.

What? Currently, the actual problems are identified through background research and through interviews, surveys or other ethnographic methods to gather data.[54] The methods used are selected according to the information needs. Collecting a broad range of data is beneficial to finding out what people want to tell and what they are experiencing and feeling.[55] In terms of health data, it is important to know how patients currently use the data they receive, when they have felt they have needed it and what feelings are associated with using such information. In our fictional example, the pain points include the rush of medical appointments, which results in incomplete home care instructions, and a lack of clarity of health data from patient's point of view. A lack of mobile information applications, where patients can check their home care instructions and health data under the EHDS were also identified as problems.

How? In the Discover phase, LLMs can be employed to draft and modify research questions, to identify research topics and different stakeholders, and to define the research problem.[56] LLMs can be utilized to generate various customer and patient pathways, such as an accessible service pathway, based on existing data and service channels. To illustrate, LLMs can recognize text on Post-it notes from existing service design tools and they can analyze and document research findings.[57] Furthermore, LLMs can be employed in the analysis of qualitative data and in data mining in general. They can also speed up audio and video transcription processes.[58]

---

[52] Melles et al. (2021), pp. 38–39.

[53] See more Melles et al. (2021), p. 42.

[54] Alhonsuo (2021), p. 36 and Melles et al. (2021), p. 37.

[55] Hagan (2018), pp. 211–213 and Stickdorn et al. (2018), pp. 96–98.

[56] The examples used in the "How?" Section are mainly based on Jylkäs Design and Palvelumuotoilu Palo's training on 21 March 2024 on using AI in service design, Jylkäs Design and Palvelumuotoilu Palo (2024); More on the use of AI in the design of digital services, see Jylkäs (2020).

[57] See, e.g., Miro (2024).

[58] See more, e.g., Good Tape (2024).

3.3 Define Phase

In this phase the findings of the previous phase are transformed into the actual problem that needs to be developed.

Who? As in the Discover phase above, it is critical to involve patients, their stakeholders and the staff involved in patient care and patient interactions. This encompasses all groups of people who are either directly or indirectly associated with access to health data and health care instructions.[59]

What? In the fictional example, the observation was that patients are unable to access, to use or understand their health data and home care instructions. The Define phase is still part of the research problem stage.[60] Whereas the Discover phase involved creative, divergent thinking, this phase involves convergent thinking.[61] The phase concludes with a selection of development areas. In this case, a decision was to find a way for the patient to access the information provided verbally during the doctor's appointment. Through multidisciplinary collaboration, the Define phase seeks to identify the primary areas of access, use or understandability of health data that are most important or urgent—i.e., the issues to be developed first. Workshops and brainstorming sessions are often effective ways of working in this phase.[62] It is also important to concretize the findings in a visual form. For example, service paths, stakeholder maps, service blueprints or empathy maps can be used to crystallize the areas of improvement in the use of health data.[63] At this stage, it is also possible to move smoothly back to development and ideation and possibly even to the first Define phase.[64]

How? LLMs can be employed to explain the patient requirements identified in the previous phase,[65] and to define the problem by summarizing or clustering the data. They can also concretize results by visualization or, for example, by producing realistic images to support the synthesis.[66] Further, LLMs can be used to produce illustrative charts from quantitative data and patient personas from qualitative data. At the end of the synthesis, they can be used to create design briefs.[67] In our case, LLMs could thus cluster user, developer and organizational requirements into cost-feasible and resource-intensive ones.

---

[59] ISO 9241-210:2019, p. 6.

[60] Melles et al. (2021), p. 38.

[61] Melles et al. (2021), p. 38.

[62] Melles et al. (2021), p. 39.

[63] Hagan (2018), pp. 212–214.

[64] Berger-Walliser et al. (2017), p. 365; Hagan (2018), p. 212.

[65] Hari (2023).

[66] Useful resources for this phase include, e.g., MidJourney (2024); ElevenLabs (2024).

[67] The examples used in the "How?" Section are mainly based on Jylkäs Design and Service Design Palo's training on 21 March 2024 on using AI in service design, Jylkäs Design and Service Design Palo (2024).

3.4 Develop Phase

The Develop phase is the creative, design-focused phase in which the problems identified and selected for solution in the previous Define phase are brainstormed and concrete solutions are developed.

Who? Although LLMs are used, the literature emphasizes that also patient information management professionals and other stakeholders are needed. LLMs function on the basis of input data, so there is a risk that the information they use is not as comprehensive as that of the people who actually use health data. Melles, Albayrak and Goossens stress that in testing, it is also important to involve not only patients and their stakeholders, but also health professionals so that the products designed are suitable for the complex health care environment.[68]

What? The process is now forwarded to a solution space.[69] At this stage, various prototypes are created. For example, patient applications or information design for health data could be prototyped in our fictional example. The aim is to create tangible or experimental prototypes that are quick and simple to use and can be tested by patients, nurses, and other users and stakeholders. Especially at this stage, users are encouraged to test alternative versions and experiments without fear of failure. The aim is to enhance those prototypes that either work or can work and discard those that do not seem to become workable solutions.[70] At the same time, the prototypes serve as support and tools for communication.[71] Although the entire design process is iterative, the use of iteration is of particular importance at this phase, where developable prototypes are fed back into the design process, including, where appropriate, more a priori steps, such as problem definition in the Define phase.[72] At this point, the techniques are creative, that is, as many ideas as possible are developed for prototyping. Methods such as brainwriting or body storming can be used. Also, techniques to select ideas for further development are used. These may include a four-field or SWOT evaluation. In this phase, indicators defined for the process to measure the achieved benefits and the effectiveness of the idea are also used.[73]

How? LLMs speed up work when speech-to-text or image-to-text functions are used. Text-to-speech and video functions also help in prototyping.[74] LLMs can be employed to facilitate rapid visualization of the intended application and its layout. Visualization is important for communication and facilitates understanding. Often, remote design projects are carried out on a web platform, where LLM-based tools are already available.[75] In addition, it is possible to freely choose from whose perspective

---

[68] Melles et al. (2021), p. 39.

[69] Melles et al. (2021), p. 38.

[70] Melles et al. (2021), p. 39.

[71] Stickdorn et al. (2018), p. 212.

[72] Design Council also points to the need for iteration in its design principles. Design Council (2024).

[73] ISO 9241-210:2019 mentions time, human effort, costs, etc. as measures of efficiency.

[74] See, e.g., Wondershare (2024).

[75] See, e.g., Uizard (2024), Tome (2024), Vizcom (2024) and Canva (2024).

the prototype is made: LLMs can be directed to work on the process from the perspective of the patient, the employee, or even a private outsourced software house.[76] In our fictional example, LLMs would thus quickly produce a variety of application options and the desired features according to the chosen perspective. Users would then have faster access to testing the several alternative applications.

3.5 Deliver Phase

In this phase, one or more of the prototypes tested are selected for implementation. The solutions are visualized, that is, illustrated and communicated to a sufficient extent.

Who? The most important role in implementation is played by the health care organization and the design team. The role of the user, whether a patient or an employee, is primarily to assess the long-term effectiveness of the solution.[77] The solutions implemented at this stage will have a broader impact at the meso level, potentially extending to the macro level once the solutions are widely deployed. Adequate communication and involvement are therefore crucial for successful implementation.[78]

What? In this phase, our fictional example process would have produced a solution such as a patient health data application that patients can access using their mobile devices. It can be thought that the prototypes generated in the previous phases have been transformed into pilots and are currently undergoing testing in a real-world setting. The ownership of the process is shifting from the designer, the design team and the users to the organization and business management. It is still important to communicate adequately and to use visual methods. Service blueprints and the Business Model Canvas are tools that are frequently used to illustrate new production methods and applications.[79] In our example, the designers would perhaps introduce LLM-based text editing, a time scheduler or a speech-to-text application that stores home care instructions received at the clinic.[80]

How? LLMs can be used not only in the design process as described above, but also in a wide range of innovative technical applications in health care itself. The solution in our imaginary design process could include an automated note on the employee's worklist or an automated appointment for the patient when LLMs detect a need for it in the patient's health data. The outcome of the process could be a mobile application through which the patient can see information about themselves in an understandable and easy-to-use format.

---

[76] The examples used in the "How?" Section are mainly based on Jylkäs Design and Service Design Palo's training on 21 March 2024 on using AI in service design, Jylkäs Design and Service Design Palo (2024).

[77] ISO 9241-210:2019.

[78] Implementation, e.g. Stickdorn et al. (2018), pp. 271–273.

[79] See different visualization tools, such as the Service Blueprint, e.g., Miro (2024).

[80] Tripathi, Sukumaran and Cook (2024), pp. 1436–1437.

4 Reflection on the Process and Questions to Consider

In the legal design process described above, the authors used an example where access, comprehensibility and use of health data were the problems identified in the legal design process. The problem of understandability concerned not only the micro level, but also the meso level where the health care service uses the same information.[81] In this fictional legal design example, the solution for access, comprehensibility and use of health data was LLM-based text editing, a speech-to-text application that stores home care instructions received at the clinic, and a mobile application that allows patients to access their own health data. The example demonstrates that LLMs are a versatile tool. They can be used from the standpoint of different stakeholders, as we noted above in the *How?* paragraph of Sect. 3.4 Develop Phase. LLMs could also be prompted to bring the designer's perspective into the process. From the viewpoint of legal designers, the first phases of design (Discover and Define) seem to be the most beneficial ones.[82] If we switch from the individual to the meso level and look at the use of LLMs, workflows can be simulated, alternative ways of working can be identified and weaknesses can be detected in working processes. On the other hand, LLMs also speed up work processes and reduce costs, thus LLMs seem to have the potential to contribute to the development of health care. Perhaps the benefits of the use of LLMs in the legal design process can be more comprehensively demonstrated through the capacity to produce a wide range of examples (Discover, Develop and Define), which could enhance the communication of the results. The authors believe that the Chapter shows how the combination of legal design and LLMs can be used to improve the access, understandability and use of health data, thereby ensuring effective access to health data under the GDPR and the EHDS.

No method or instrument is entirely without potential risk, whether it be legal design or LLMs. When considering potential issues in the legal design process, challenges in participation need to be highlighted. Decisions about who will participate are made already before the Discover phase, and therefore the role of health care supervisors, hospital administrators and designers is crucial, as they determine who gets their voice heard. Another issue related to adequate participation is the need to have a sufficiently comprehensive and knowledge-based understanding of the complex health care context.[83] It is important to ensure that dominant positions are not established during the decision-making stages, which are present, particularly in the Define phase. Instead, users and professionals must be afforded equal consideration. Like with any other knowledge-intensive technique, there is a risk that the design process emphasizes the designer's rather than the patient's views. While ensuring that all relevant stakeholders are heard and take part in the legal design process on equal terms is vital, it is also relevant to consider tensions between different groups and to build sufficient communication and co-operation to achieve balanced and good group

---

[81] Clinical documentation is an example of a two-sided use. See Tripathi et al. (2024), p. 1437.

[82] Jylkäs (2020), p. 58.

[83] Melles et al. (2021), p. 42.

dynamics.[84] Collaboration between disciplines, which should take place at all design phases, can be challenging and misunderstandings are possible because of professional culture factors alone.[85] Even though legal design is an appropriate approach to improve mutual understanding, different research methods and validation processes across scientific disciplines complicate the design process.[86] Moreover, evaluating the process or scientifically comparing different policy options in advance can be challenging. In the example the authors have given, the methods would seem to be promising, but there are few reports in the research literature of the measured benefits of using human-centered design in a health care environment.[87]

The number of possibilities brought by AI has grown enormously, but simultaneously headaches surrounding AI have also increased, which includes mistrust amongst the public. If this is not considered in the change process, it can make implementing the solutions proposed by the legal design process more difficult. Empathic and holistic ways of working are excellent tools to address these patients' concerns.[88] As illustrated in our case, when patients are involved, they can express their concerns more easily. Furthermore, potential concerns associated with AI—including LLMs—cannot be overlooked and ways to tackle them are to be considered. To name a few problems, the authors note that LLMs are surrounded by opacity, perhaps even intentional, created by intellectual property rights.[89] Burrell points out that opacity appears to be inherent to machine learning algorithms, which also holds true for algorithms underlying LLMs models. These algorithms demonstrate a self-learning capability, which means that they may evolve without any human intervention.[90] Further, there is a risk that a LLM provides an inaccurate output.[91] In our example, it could mean that the results of the "Development" phase give a misleading impression of the quantitative data. Various causes may lead to LLMs providing inaccurate outcomes. For instance, the so-called "covariate shift and concept drift," which means that the data used during the training of the—in our case—LLM and its use may differ and may give a wrong outcome.88 Furthermore, the input data in the use phase may lack relevant data for reaching an accurate outcome.89 It is also possible that a LLM has been made biased90—either through the training dataset or through intentional designing.91 A last example the authors address is the relationship between the input data and outcome, which may not illustrate a cause-effect relationship but rather correlation.92 Considering health care in particular, the literature has found that the output of a LLM is only as good as its training dataset, which means that training datasets including biases and misinformation will unequivocally lead to an output

[84] Steen (2011), p. 56.

[85] See in particular the tension between the disciplines of law and design in Doherty (2021) and Melles et al. (2021), p. 42.

[86] Berger-Walliser et al. (2017), p. 358.

[87] Bazzano et al. (2017), pp. 13–14, 16–17.

[88] Shortly how LLMs can be used in health care, e.g., Bakken (2024), pp. 1217–1218.

[89] See different reasons for opacity, e.g., Burrell (2016), pp. 3–4.

[90] Burrell (2016), pp. 4–5.

[91] Buijsman and Veluwenkamp (2023), p. 551.

containing the same prejudices and misleading information.[92] An outcome based on biases may be particularly worrisome in a health care setting because of potential significant adverse effects, including loss of life.[93] In the fictional example, the authors enhanced access, use and the comprehensibility of health data. Of course, easy access to health data involves risks such as the erosion of privacy. The data is sensitive and in principle cannot be transferred to the public network for LLM training, and sharing information can be problematic because of privacy and data protection legislation.[94] Furthermore, cyberattacks and data security should be taken seriously, as the health care sector processes special categories of personal data under the GDPR.[95]

5 Concluding Remarks

The authors have attempted to improve the realization of the right to access individual's health data, including its understandability and use, under the EHDS and the GDPR by employing LLMs in the legal design process. The legal design process is a human-centric method, which helps to bring in the individual's concerns when ensuring the right to access to individual's health data can be effectively practiced. This is especially seen at the initial stage of micro, and meso level development.

However, combining legal design with LLMs is not a panacea to solve all identified problems related to access to, understanding of and use of health data. Rather, it is an ambitious attempt to enable better engagement in one's own care through more accessible and understandable health data. There are few reported benefits of human-centered design—including legal design—in the health sector so far, but on the other hand it is described as being particularly suitable for the development of complex environments, such as the health care context. In the future, it would, therefore, be beneficial to explore what measurable results could be obtained by combining legal design with LLM techniques. In the authors' fictional case, we see that the use of LLMs in the legal design process could promote access to health data in accordance with the GDPR and the EHDS. However, more research is needed to overcome the issues arising from the use of LLMs, including the opacity and the self-learning

---

[92] Harrer (2023), p. 2.

[93] For more, see Clusmann et al. (2023), p. 6.

[94] Arora and Arora (2023), p. 641.

[95] Tripathi et al. (2024), p. 1438; Without in any way belittling the risks, however, various control methods have been developed over time. These include ISO standards on risk management and of course, transnational regulation such as the EU Artificial Intelligence Act. See, the European Standard EN ISO/IEC 23894:2024 *Information Technology. Artificial Intelligence. Guidance on Risk Management* (ISO/IEC 23894:2023); Regulation (EU) 2024/1689 of the European Parliament and of the Council of 13 June 2024 laying down harmonised rules on artificial intelligence and amending Regulations (EC) No 300/2008, (EU) No 167/2013, (EU) No 168/2013, (EU) 2018/858, (EU) 2018/1139 and (EU) 2019/2144 and Directives 2014/90/EU, (EU) 2016/797 and (EU) 2020/1828 (Artificial Intelligence Act).

ability. The same goes for privacy and data protection concerns. Since sensitive data are involved, these privacy and data protection questions should be taken seriously.

References

Alhonsuo M (2021) Early phase of healthcare-related service design. Faculty of Art and Design, Lapin yliopisto

Archer N, Fevrier-Thomas U, Lokker C, McKibbon A, Straus SE (2011) Personal health records: a scoping review. J Am Med Inform Assoc 18:515–522. https://doi.org/10.1136/amiajnl-2011-000105. Accessed 27 May 2024

Arora A, Arora A (2023) The promise of large language models in health care. Lancet 401:641. https://doi.org/10.1016/S0140-6736(23)00216-7. Accessed 20 May 2024

Bakken S (2024) What can you do with a large language model? J Am Med Inform Assoc 31:1217–1218. https://doi.org/10.1093/jamia/ocae106. Accessed 20 May 2024

Bazzano AN, Martin J, Hicks E, Faughnan M, Murphy L (2017) Human-centred design in global health: a scoping review of applications and contexts. PLoS ONE 12:e0186744. https://doi.org/10.1371/journal.pone.0186744. Accessed 10 Jun 2024

Berger-Walliser G, Barton TD, Haapio H (2017) From visualization to legal design: a collaborative and creative process. Am Bus Law J 54:347–392. https://doi.org/10.1111/ablj.12101. Accessed 4 Mar 2024

Brown T (2008) Design thinking. Harvard Bus Rev 86:84–92. https://hbr.org/2008/06/design-thinking. Accessed 9 Apr 2024

Buijsman S, Veluwenkamp H (2023) Spotting when algorithms are wrong. Mind Mach 33:541–562. https://doi.org/10.1007/s11023-022-09591-0. Accessed 4 Jun 2024

Burrell J (2016) How the machine "thinks:" understanding opacity in machine learning algorithms. Big Data Soc 3:2053951715622512. https://doi.org/10.1177/2053951715622512. Accessed 4 Jun 2024

Canva (2024) https://www.canva.com/. Accessed 25 Jun 2024

Choi W, Chang S-H, Yang Y-S, Jung S, Lee S-J, Chun J-W, Kim D-J, Lee W, Choi IY (2022) Study of the factors influencing the use of mydata platform based on personal health record data sharing system. BMC Med Inform Decis Mak 22:182. https://doi.org/10.1186/s12911-022-01929-z. Accessed 13 Jun 2024

Clusmann J, Kolbinger FR, Muti HS, Carrero ZI, Eckardt J-N, Ghaffari Laleh N, Löffler CML, Schwarzkopf S-C, Unger M, Veldhuizen GP, Wagner SJ, Kather JN (2023) The future landscape of large language models in medicine. Commun Med 3:1–8. https://doi.org/10.1038/s43856-023-00370-1. Accessed 4 Jun 2024

Cols F (2021). Helping those under arrest to understand their rights in criminal proceedings. In: Ducato R, Strowel A (eds) Legal design perspectives: theoretical and practical insights from the field. Ledizioni, Milan

Design Council (2024) Framework for innovation. https://www.designcouncil.org.uk/our-resources/framework-for-innovation/. Accessed 13 Jun 2024

Doherty M (2021) The relationship between legal and design cultures: tension and resolution. In: Corrales Compagnucci M, Haapio H, Hagan M, Doherty M (eds) Legal design. Integrating business, design and legal thinking with technology. Edward Elgar, Cheltenham

Ducato R (2021) Spaces for legal design in the european general data protection regulation. In: Ducato R, Strowel A (eds) Legal design perspectives: theoretical and practical insights from the field. Ledizioni, Milan

Ehn P (1993) Scandinavian design: on participation and skill. In: Schuler D, Namioka A (eds) Participatory design: principles and practices. CRC Press, Boca Raton

ElevenLabs (2024) https://elevenlabs.io. Accessed 25 Jun 2024

EN ISO 9241-210:2019. Ergonomics of human-system interaction—part 210: human-centred design for interactive systems. European Committee for Standardization (CEN), Brussels

EN ISO/IEC 23894:2024. Information technology. artificial intelligence. Guidance on risk management (ISO/IEC 23894:2023). European Committee for Standardization (CEN), Brussels

Good Tape (2024) https://goodtape.io/. Accessed 25 Jun 2024

Gordon R (2022) Large language models help decipher clinical notes https://news.mit.edu/2022/large-language-models-help-decipher-clinical-notes-1201. Accessed 13 Jun 2024

Haapio H, Barton TD, Compagnucci MC (2021) Legal design for the common good: proactive legal care by design. In: Corrales Compagnucci M, Haapio H, Hagan M, Doherty M (eds) Legal Design. Integrating Business, Design and Legal Thinking with Technology. Edward Elgar, Cheltenham

Hagan M (2018) A human-centered design approach to access to justice: generating new prototypes and hypotheses for intervention to make courts user-friendly. Indiana J Law Social Equal 6(2):2

Hansberry DR, John A, John E, Agarwal N, Gonzales SF, Baker SR (2014) A critical review of the readability of online patient education resources from radiology info.org. Am J Roentgenol 202:566–575. https://doi.org/10.2214/AJR.13.11223. Accessed 13 Jun 2024

Hari J (2023) 10 powerful ways to use ChatGPT as a product designer. List of my favourite ChatGPT prompts that will greatly enhance your efficiency as a product designer. https://medium.com/user-experience-design-1/10-powerful-ways-to-use-chatgpt-as-a-product-designer-b3c395d20a00. Accessed 12 Jun 2024

Harrer S (2023) Attention is not all you need: the complicated case of ethically using large language models in healthcare and medicine. eBioMedicine 90:104512. https://doi.org/10.1016/j.ebiom.2023.104512. Accessed 20 May 2024

Hartmann L (2024) Creating gladys: how legal design can support person-centred care in public health. Legal Des J 1(1). https://legaldesign-journal.scholasticahq.com/article/122333-creating-gladys-how-legal-design-can-support-person-centred-care-in-public-health. Accessed 16 Aug 2024

Holeman I, Kane D (2019) Human-centered design for global health equity. Inf Technol Dev 26:477–505. https://doi.org/10.1080/02681102.2019.1667289. Accessed 13 Jun 2024

Jylkäs T (2020) Shared path. Service design and artificial intelligence in designing human-centred digital services. Faculty of Art and Design, Lapin yliopisto

Jylkäs Design and Service Design Palo (2024) Using AI in service design. Unpublished training session, 21 March 2024

Ketola A, de Rooy R, Haapio H (2024) Comic contracts 2.0—contracts that have (and give) a voice. In: Ducato R, Strowel A, Marique E (eds) Design(s) for law. Ledizioni, Milan

Legal Design Alliance (2024) https://www.legaldesignalliance.org/. Accessed 13 Jun 2024

Melles M, Albayrak A, Goossens R (2021) Innovating health care: key characteristics of human-centered design. Int J Qual Health Care 33(Suppl. 1):37–44. https://doi.org/10.1093/intqhc/mzaa127. Accessed 13 Jun 2024

Mid Journey (2024) https://www.midjourney.com/. Accessed 25 Jun 2024

Miro (2024) https://miro.com/. Accessed 25 Jun 2024

Perry-Kessaris A (2022) Legal design could and should be more sociolegal. In: Lockton D, Lenzi S, Hekkert P, Oak A, Sádaba J, Lloyd P (eds) DRS2022: Bilbao, 25 June–3 July, Bilbao, Spain. https://doi.org/10.21606/drs.2022.281. Accessed 4 Jun 2024

Potel-Saville M, Talbourdet E (2021) Empowering children to understand and exercise their personal data rights. In: Ducato R, Strowel A (eds) Legal design perspectives: theoretical and practical insights from the field. Ledizioni, Milan

Regulation (EU) 2022/868 of the European Parliament and of the Council of 30 May 2022 on European data governance and amending Regulation (EU) 2018/1724 (Data Governance Act)

Regulation (EU) 2025/327 of the European Parliament and of the Council of 11 February 2025 on the European Health Data Space and amending Directive 2011/24/EU and Regulation (EU) 2024/2847 (EHDS)

Regulation 1689/2024. Regulation (EU) 2024/1689 of the European Parliament and of the Council of 13 June 2024 laying down harmonised rules on artificial intelligence and amending Regulations (EC) No 300/2008, (EU) No 167/2013, (EU) No 168/2013, (EU) 2018/858, (EU) 2018/1139 and (EU) 2019/2144 and Directives 2014/90/EU, (EU) 2016/797 and (EU) 2020/1828. (Artificial Intelligence Act)

Regulation 679/2016. Regulation (EU) 2016/679 of the European Parliament and of the Council of 27 April 2016 on the protection of natural persons with regard to the processing of personal data and on the free movement of such data, and repealing Directive 95/46/EC (GDPR)

Russell SJ, Norvig P, Davis E (2010) Artificial intelligence: a modern approach, 3rd edn. Prentice Hall, Upper Saddle River

Sanders EB-N, Stappers PJ (2008) Co-creation and the new landscapes of design. CoDesign 4:5–18. https://doi.org/10.1080/15710880701875068. Accessed 6 Oct 2023

Schreiber A (2020) Mere access to personal data: is it processing? Int Data Privacy Law 10(3):269–277

Schuett J (2023) Defining the scope of AI regulations. Law Innov Technol 15(1):60–82. https://doi.org/10.1080/17579961.2023.2184135. Accessed 4 Jun 2024

Singleton J, Li C, Akpunonu PD, Abner EL, Kucharska-Newton AM (2023) Using natural language processing to identify opioid use disorder in electronic health record data. Int J Med Informatics 170:104963. https://doi.org/10.1016/j.ijmedinf.2022.104963. Accessed 4 Jun 2024

Stanford Law School (2024) Legal design lab. https://law.stanford.edu/organizations/pages/legal-design-lab/. Accessed 13 Jun 2024

Steen M (2011) Tensions in human-centred design. CoDesign 7:45–60. https://doi.org/10.1080/15710882.2011.563314. Accessed 13 Jun 2024

Stickdorn M, Hormess ME, Lawrence A, Schneider J (2018) This is service design doing. O'Reilly Media, Sebastopol

Suoheimo M (2020) Approaching wicked problems in service design. Faculty of Art and Design, Lapin yliopisto

Toivonen N, Kovalainen J (2023) Kohti ihmislähtöisempää oikeutta muotoilun avulla. Lakimies 7–8/2023

Tome (2024) https://tome.app. Accessed 25 Jun 2024

Trenfield S, Awad A, McCoubrey L, Elbadawi M, Goyanes A, Gaisford S, Basit AW (2022) Advancing pharmacy and healthcare with virtual digital technologies. Adv Drug Deliv Rev 182:114098. https://doi.org/10.1016/j.addr.2021.114098. Accessed 13 Jun 2024

Treni A, Clement G (2021) Co-designing digital tools for 21st-century tenant organizing. In: Corrales Compagnucci M, Haapio H, Hagan M, Doherty M (eds) Legal design. Integrating Business, Design And Legal Thinking With Technology. Edward Elgar, Cheltenham

Tripathi S, Sukumaran R, Cook TS (2024) Efficient healthcare with large language models: optimizing clinical workflow and enhancing patient care. J Am Med Inform Assoc 31:1436–1440. https://doi.org/10.1093/jamia/ocad258. Accessed 13 Jun 2024

Uizard (2024) https://uizard.io/. Accessed 25 Jun 2024

Vizcom (2024) https://www.vizcom.ai/. Accessed 25 Jun 2024

Wang D-Q, Feng L-Y, Ye J-G, Zou J-G, Zhenget Y-F (2023) Accelerating the integration of ChatGPT and other large-scale ai models into biomedical research and healthcare. MedComm Future Med 2(2):e43. https://doi.org/10.1002/mef2.43. Accessed 13 Jun 2024

Wondershare (2024) Virbo. https://virbo.wondershare.com/. Accessed 25 Jun 2024

Index

© The Editor(s) (if applicable) and The Author(s), under exclusive license to Springer Nature Singapore Pte Ltd. 2025

M. Corrales Compagnucci et al. (eds.), *Generative AI, Contracts, Law and Design*, Perspectives in Law, Business and Innovation,
https://doi.org/10.1007/978-981-95-2058-9

MIX
Papier aus verantwortungsvollen Quellen
Paper from responsible sources
FSC® C105338

If you have any concerns about our products,
you can contact us on
ProductSafety@springernature.com

In case Publisher is established outside the EU,
the EU authorized representative is:
Springer Nature Customer Service Center GmbH
Europaplatz 3, 69115 Heidelberg, Germany

Printed by Libri Plureos GmbH
in Hamburg, Germany